T0355024

INTERNATIONAL HUMAN RIGHTS LAW ENFORCEMENT:
THE INCONGRUOUS VOICES THAT PREVAIL

How Acts of States Precipitate Gross Violations of Human Rights
and Threaten International Peace and Security by Religious
Nationalism, Ethnic Nationalism and Secular Governments

MACDONALD I J MOPHO

Order this book online at www.trafford.com
or email orders@trafford.com

Most Trafford titles are also available at major online book retailers.

Print information available on the last page.

ISBN: 978-1-6987-1519-3 (sc)
ISBN: 978-1-6987-1520-9 (e)

Library of Congress Control Number: 2023914955

Because of the dynamic nature of the Internet, any web addresses or links contained in
this book may have changed since publication and may no longer be valid. The views
expressed in this work are solely those of the author and do not necessarily reflect the
views of the publisher, and the publisher hereby disclaims any responsibility for them.

Any people depicted in stock imagery provided by Getty Images are models, and such images are
being used for illustrative purposes only.
Certain stock imagery © Getty Images.

Trafford rev. 01/10/2025

 www.trafford.com

North America & international
toll-free: 844-688-6899 (USA & Canada)
fax: 812 355 4082

Do not stand idly by when your neighbor's life is threatened.

- Leviticus 19:16b. [NLT]

Speak up for those who cannot speak for themselves; ensure justice for those being crushed.

- Proverbs 31:8 [NLT]

Those who work without knowledge damage more than they can fix, and those who walk quickly on the wrong path distance themselves from their goal.

- Arab Proverb

PREFACE TO THIS EDITION

My sense of disillusionment with the decisions of the Courts in various cases on religious freedoms such as Eweida and Others v. The United Kingdom [2013] ECHR 37 and the seemingly disregard for human rights protection of religious freedom led to my research and writing of this book. However, the research led me into finding that Christianity historically influenced law and human rights development and this comes out in Part 1 of the book. In fact, in some parts of the world such as the United States, it was Christianity that led to the promotion of the mass education to enable people to read the Holy Bible and know God for themselves and avoid being deceived by satan. This was what led to the passing of the law that known as the "Old Deluder Satan Act (1647). Although this is the Second Edition, I have not revised the contents of the chapters of the First Edition of this book so much in detail besides some minor emendations of obvious editorial errors and some rearrangements.

What has fundamentally driven me to work on this Second Edition within a year of the publication of the First Edition in 2023 is the fact that I did not cover the issues that had to do with the Armenia-Azerbaijan conflict, the Israel-Palestine conflict and also the rather often forgotten perennial inhuman degradation of the indigenous and Torres Strait Islanders (Aboriginal) peoples of Australia which is now discussed. Equally important in this Second Edition are the discussions of the various cases at the International Court of Justice, such as The Gambia v. Myanmar, South Africa v Israel and Ukraine v Russian Federation.

This Second Edition has three new chapters bringing the total chapters in this book to 21.

In effect, the discussion in this book reveals the discordant voices of States that argue for human rights protection and enforcement but act in gross violation of them as well as threatening international peace and security. It also discusses issues about the effectiveness of the United Nations General Assembly and the United Nations Security Council in implementing the UN Charter towards maintaining international peace and order.

I hope that the human rights law practitioner, teacher, researcher, activist, diplomat, policy maker, government official, international civil servant, political scientist, theologian, historian, and student will get something out of reading this book in the same way that I got something enriching out of researching and writing it.

MacDonald I J Mopho
London UK
21February 2024

TABLE OF CONTENTS

TABLE OF CASES

South Africa v. Israel (Application of the Convention on the Prevention and Punishment of the Crime of Genocide in the Gaza Strip), ICJ, Document Number 192-20231229-PRE-01-00-EN

Stedman v United Kingdom [1997] 23 EHRR 168 ECHR.

The Gambia v. Myanmar (Application of the Convention on the Prevention and Punishment of the Crime of Genocide), ICJ, Document Number 178-20220722-SUM -01-00-EN

Ukraine v Russian Federation: 32 States intervening in the case Concerning Allegations of Genocide under the Convention on the Prevention and Punishment of the Crime of Genocide, ICJ. CR 2023/14

X v Switzerland (Application No 7865/77) Decision of 27 February 1979

Yeo-Bum Yoon v Republic of Korea and Myung – Jin Choi v Republic of Korea, Communications nos. 1321/2004 and 1322/2004, UN doc. CCPR/C/88/D/1321-1322/2004, 23 January 2007.

TABLE OF INTERNATIONAL AND REGIONAL HUMAN RIGHTS INSTRUMENTS

United Nations Charter (1945)

Universal Declaration of Human Rights (1948)

Convention on the Prevention and Punishment of the Crime of Genocide (1948)

European Convention for the Protection of Human Rights and Fundamental Freedoms (1950)

International Covenant on Civil and Political Rights (1966)

American Convention on Human Rights (1969)

International Convention on the Elimination of All Forms of Racial Discrimination (1969)

Convention on the Elimination of All Forms of Discrimination Against Women (1979)

African Charter on Human and Peoples' Rights (1981)Convention on the Rights of the Child (1989)

INTRODUCTION

Humanity is already in the third decade of the twenty-first century. However, with all the technological advancement, human behaviour and reaction to events especially through governments have not always been directed towards peaceful resolutions of disputes but towards the use and display of force to silence the weaker parties or states. Respect for human rights and international peace and security is not demonstrably foremost in some acts of states, especially the Superpower nation-states.

Both the secular states which are more widely assumed to be more democratic such as the United States, Russia, and states practising religious nationalism such as the Islamic Republic of Iran have failed to show restraint in their actions, where it should be manifestly obvious that their actions would lead to gross violations of human rights and threaten international peace and security. Hence, the following question and answer given by Mark Juergensmeyer, are worthy of reflection:

Will the confrontation between religious and secular nationalism harden into a new cold war? That depends, in part, on how religious nationalism behaves, and in part on how it is perceived.[1] Undoubtedly, however, the United Nations ...will have to continue to be vigilant about the possibility of abuses of human rights and irresponsible international behaviour.[2]

Conflicts and civil unrests leading to human rights violations, crimes against humanity and in certain extreme cases genocide in human societies have their foundations and roots in inequalities, unfair

---

[1]   Juergensmeyer, M., The New Cold War? Religious Nationalism Confronts the Secular State © 1993 University of California Press. p. 193

[2]   Ibid. p,195

treatments, and in some cases outright injustices which sometimes might have gone on for over a long period of time and provoked reactions that get totally out of control. Unfortunately, religion with all its promises of peace and goodness, has also played a significant role through some of its bad leaders and their poisonous religious and nationalistic approaches in creating some of the deadliest human conflicts that the world has ever known. Because of the Christian influence in the early development of modern law and human rights through the Roman Empire, it is imperative to give some account of how religious nationalism developed from Christianity and flowed to other religions such as Islam, Hinduism and Buddhism, to create the opposing twin faces of peace to their adherents and threats to non-adherents.

This book begins with several chapters dealing with how Roman law and Christianity have more or less defined the legal and justice systems around the world. It discusses the historical account of how Christianity and Roman law fused into one in the sixth century and religious nationalism emerged out of it and became a threat towards the destruction of human existence with the European thirty years [1618 – 1648) of religious war. It then discusses the emergence of individual freedoms and human rights as enshrined in modern human rights laws and the increasing tendency of states to violate the same human rights they have bound themselves to protect and enforce. Then it shows how humanity still faces the threat of self-destruction today.

At the individual level, it discusses the violations of the right to freedom of religion and belief. A number of cases to buttress the arguments are cited. For example, Lillian Ladele v London Borough of Islington [2009] EWCA Civ 1357, which was one of the four cases that was considered by the European Court of Human Rights in Eweida and Others v. The United Kingdom [2013] ECHR 37.

It argues for respect for the right to freedom of thought, conscience, and religion, noting that religions such as Christianity still have worldwide adherents now put at 2.3 billion people according to the Pew Research Center study of 2017[3].

---

[3] The Study puts Christianity as the world's largest religion with a population of 2.3 billion people followed by Islam with 1.8 billion people and Hinduism with professing practitioners at 1.1 billion: https://www.pewresearch.org/fact-tank/2017/04/05/christians-remain-worlds-largest-religious-group-but-they-are-declining-in-europe/

As will be seen in the discussion that follows, the violations of individual right to freedom of conscience, thoughts and religion, which occur in virtually every state that is a state party to the international human rights treaties leaves a lot to be desired. But the most threatening cases are instances of violations of human rights and crimes against humanity in states led by religious nationalists.

In countries where religious nationalists are in power such as in Afghanistan, where the Taliban regained power from August 2021, the violations of human rights cut across various human rights treaties such as the International Covenant on Civil and Political Rights, ICCPR (1966) and the Convention on the Rights of the Child, CRC, (1989).

The following articles for example are manifestly violated in Afghanistan since August 2021:

> No one shall be subjected to torture or to cruel, inhuman or degrading treatment or punishment."

> > - Article 7, ICCPR (1966).

> States Parties recognize the rights of the child to education, and with a view to achieving this right progressively and on the basis of equal opportunity, they shall, in particular:

> (a) Make primary education compulsory and available free for all;

> (b) Encourage the development of different forms of education, including general and vocational, make them available and accessible to every child, and take appropriate measures such as the introduction of free education and offering financial assistance in case of need;

> (c) Make higher education accessible to all on the basis of capacity by every appropriate means;

> > - Article 28 (1) (a) (b) (c), CRC (1989).

States Parties agree that the education of the child shall be directed to:

(a) The development of the child's personality, talents and mental and physical abilities to their fullest potential;

(b) The development of respect for human rights and fundamental freedoms, and for the principles enshrined in the Charter of the United Nations;

(c) The development of respect for the child's parents, his or her own cultural identity, language and values, for the national values of the country in which the child is living, the country from which he or she may originate, and for civilizations different from his or her own;

(d) The preparation of the child for responsible life in a free society, in the spirit of understanding, peace, tolerance, equality of sexes, and friendship among all peoples, ethnic, national and religious groups and persons on indigenous origin;

- Article 29, CRC (1989)

Afghanistan is a typical example of what can happen in a religious nationalistic state because the rights of individuals are not often given prominence. It is clear that since August 2021 the Taliban are subjecting the women and children (girls) of Afghanistan to degrading and inhuman treatment in gross violation of Article 7 of the International Covenant on Civil and Political Rights (1966) and articles 28 and 29 of the Convention on the Rights of the Child. There is no indication that there will be an imminent change in the way the women and the girls of Afghanistan are being treated with respect to their right to freedom of movement within Afghanistan and the right to pursue secondary and higher education.

A delegation of UN Women led by the United Nations Deputy Secretary-General, Ms Amina Mohammed, to Afghanistan in January 2023 to entreat the Taliban leaders to stop the abuse of women's rights[4] did not

---

[4]   "Afghanistan: Top UN delegation tells Taliban to end confinement, deprivation, abuse of women's rights." 21 January 2023. See UN Women - https://www.unwomen.org/en/news-stories/news/2023/01/afghanistan-top-un-delegation-tells-taliban-to-end-confinement-deprivation-abuse-of-womens-rights

receive any assurances or guarantees that the Taliban would change their degrading treatment of women and girls.

However, the most notorious violators of human rights and perpetrators of crimes against humanity are the powerful states and in fact, the ultimate superpowers. With North Korea officially known as the Democratic People's Republic of Korea, DPRK, following as the discussion in chapter 19.6 show, the flagrant disregard for human rights in gross violation of international human rights law that are in force, which the DPRK government appears to pride itself in showing contempt for, is a matter that warrants international sanction.

The Russian Federation's invasion of Ukraine which is also discussed was something done in flagrant disregard for the international law principles on state sovereignty and in breach of the United Nations Charter. It is a case of a superpower showing disregard for gross violations of human rights and boldly threatening the rest of the international community to dare to resist it. However, as also discussed, the United States' invasion of Iraq, under President George W. Bush, in 2003, and the gross violations of human rights and crimes against humanity that resulted from it, show that they were more interested in displaying their might than in respecting human rights. The same thing can be said of the United States invasion of Libya under President Barack Obama in 2011 that has left that once prosperous country in ruins with hundreds of thousands of its citizens killed and millions displaced in the conflict that followed the US-NATO invasion to kill Muammar Gaddafi, the then head of State.

State restraint is advocated in this book as a means of preventing human rights violations and threat to international peace and security. Where State restraint fails, the United Nations Security Council and the United Nations General Assembly must adopt a robust application of Articles 42-46 of the United Nations Charter in the context of both guaranteeing the protection and enforcement of human rights and the maintaining of international peace and order.

In order to enhance a better understanding of the challenging subject matter of this book, I have divided the book into five parts. In the first part, I discuss the historical overview of law and religious freedom beginning with its development in the Christian religion and how subsequently, Christian influence in the Roman Empire and subsequently, British Empire, during the latter's global colonisation drive influenced the world until the twentieth century.

In the second part, I set out to discuss the development of human rights and the legal foundation of it globally. In the third part, I discussed the challenge of state protection and enforcement of individual right to religious freedom. In the fourth part, I present the discussion on religious nationalism and its hindrance to the individual enjoyment of religious freedom where it is not violating anyone else's right.

I also discuss the incongruous voices of states towards keeping their commitments to protect human rights in the pursuits of their interests. I discuss the inability of the United Nations to maintain peace and security in places of long-term conflict such as Armenia-Azerbaijan, Israel-Palestine conflict, and the rather degrading and inhuman treatment of indigenous (Aboriginal) peoples of Australia, who for centuries have not been considered as citizens to be included in the Constitution of Australia, and therefore deprived of their human rights. Most interestingly, the emerging trend of states trying to hold states accountable for acts of genocide or seeking to prevent genocide under The Convention for the Prevention and Punishment of the Crimes of Genocide (1948) as the on-going cases of The Gambia v. Myanmar, 2019, and South Africa v Israel, 2023, at the International Court of Justice, show.

Finally, in the fifth part, I conclude with arguments to prevent the incongruous voices that prevail with recommendations towards better protection of human rights and maintenance of international security.

PART I

HISTORICAL OVERVIEW OF THE DEVELOPMENT OF LAW

1

THE UNIVERSAL INFLUENCE AND EFFECT OF ROMAN LAW AND JUSTICE

"I pointed out to them that Roman law does not convict people without a trial. They must be given an opportunity to confront their accusers and defend themselves." – Acts 25:16.

1.1 Historical Development of Law

To understand the right to Christian religious freedom under international human rights law, it is important to understand the origin and development of law in its present universal form; and subsequently, international human rights law. While there is no doubt that every community of people in every part of the world must have had laws that regulated their private and public lives, given to them either by divine prescription or voluntary agreement of the members of the community, the truth today is that the form of laws that have been in universal usage for over the last two thousand and five hundred years, that is, before Christianity even came into existence as a religion, is Roman law.

How did Roman law become universal law? Well, Paul Sieghart in his book, The Lawful Rights of Mankind gives a transparently understandable account:

"In establishing a monopoly of force to take the place of self-help and outlawry, and developing a single set of laws to hold sway throughout his domain, our Prince has taken on a great deal. He has become the maker of laws in the place of the gods, their interpreter in the place of the priests, and their enforcer in the place of the collective community. In short, he has become the fountain-head of all law and all justice. That is precisely what happened in the Roman Empire. And it happened in many other principalities too: as late as 1655, King Louis XIV of France was still able to assert, quite correctly under the political system then still in place in his domain, 'L'Etat, C'est moi' – I am the State."[5]

Sieghart went on to state that because Princes do not live alone and because Roman emperors emerged from the army they had to initiate policies acceptable to their allies in order to secure their positions and avoid possible overthrow.[6] Against that backdrop comes this historic account of Roman law.

Initially, the Romans practiced an unwritten legal and justice system premised upon religious and secular norms.

The law and justice system was guarded by pontifices or priests who resolved conflicts and decided cases based on what they thought were right or just. Legal historians argue that Roman law gained recognition from ancient times such as the period from the eighth to fourth century BCE. The legal system which emerged out of the time was known as ius civile or civil law.[7] The system had litigants and defendants who invoked causes of actions and responses that involved taking religious oaths.

However, the turning point of Roman law is believed to have come about with the organised body of laws known as the Twelve Tables which was written and published in the fifth century BC. In her account of

---

5   Sieghart, Paul, The Lawful Rights of Mankind. An Introduction to the International Legal Code of Human Rights © 1985 Oxford University. First Issued as an Oxford University Press Paperback 1986. P. 18

6   Ibid. pp.18-19.

7   Herzog, Tamar, A Short History of European Law The Last Two And Half Millennia © 2018 Harvard University. Pp.14-16 discusses this period of the history of Roman law in appreciative depth and details.

European legal history in the last two and half millennia, Tamar Herzog discusses the Twelve Tables as setting out:

> "the obligation of litigants to appear in court, sanctioning them if they did not. The Tables also spell out procedural rules, regulate forms of legal transactions, and list other basic norms of communal life, enumerating elements of family law and the management of property (contracts, torts, inheritance, loans, real estate, theft, and so forth)."[8]

It was the publication of the Twelve Tables that revealed what was otherwise a mystery in Roman law where people previously thought the law was a secret between the community and its gods that were understood only by the pontifices. The Twelve Tables took the law out of the control and dictates of the religious experts. It introduced "a political sphere of action controlled by lawmakers who published the law rather than religious experts who guarded it."[9]

However, the full effect of the Twelve Tables is said to have taken time to manifest.

It is stated that it was around the fourth century that public officers known as praetors started replacing the pontifices.[10]

While praetors followed the procedures previously set out by the pontifices in resolving conflicts, the development of adjudication processes following the Twelve Tables led to two distinct processes of attending a case:

(1) Preliminary hearing to determine the merits of case which was done by the praetors who incidentally also decided thereafter who will be (apud iudicem) the trial judge in the case; and,
(2) The judicial trial of the case before a (iudex) a presiding judge.[11]

---

[8]   Ibid. page 16.

[9]   Ibid.

[10]   Ibid.

[11]   Ibid. p.17.

While praetors were public officers appointed then to serve for a period of one year, a presiding judge (iudex) was usually chosen from a number of private individuals by the praetors to resolve the issues of dispute between the parties.[12] Although at this stage, nothing was stated about the competence of the individual chosen by praetor to be the presiding judge, the justice system of Roman still gave powers to the judge (iudex) to make decisions that could not be appealed.[13] The implication of this is that in spite of the noble intentions of Roman law to grant remedies to those who have suffered wrongs, the system was all the long from the time pontifices decided cases to the time of the implementation of the Twelve Tables that led to the appointment of praetors and iudex, the juridical system did not preclude miscarriages of justice either because a pontifice did not receive divine wisdom to deliver a just decision in a matter or a praetor excluded a case at the time of preliminary hearing from progressing to a trial judge or a presiding judge (iudex) simply erred in the judgment he delivered. This is the historic account of the juridical process:

> "By granting or refusing to grant access to the courts, by indicating which circumstances deserved a remedy and which did not, and by allowing defendants to invoke certain defences but not others, praetors intervened in the legal order by creating or denying what today we would identify as rights. Their intervention was so important and so massive that the norms they created by granting or refusing to grant remedies were identified as forming a new source of law, which parallel the old ius civile and was later designated as ius honorarium, literally, the law that was made while their exercised office (honos). The importance of ius honorarium as a legal source allowing historians to characterise Roman law as a "law of remedies."[14]

But the above account does not tell people today how parties who refused access to the courts felt. It leaves people today to assume that the praetors were right and just when they denied a person the right to access justice or that people at the time who felt they had been denied justice accepted to simply put up with it because they had no recourse to any remedy.

---

[12]   Ibid. pp. 17-18

[13]   Ibid. p.18.

[14]   Ibid. pp.19-20.

While the ius honorarium produced by praetors prescribed remedies to wrongs suffered by victims and defined casuistic law, there was still opening for unjust decisions or conclusions to be made.

However, the introduction of investigation and litigation was a major procedural change in the juridical system of Roman law that brought some improvement. The process ended the dual functions of a praetor and a iudex and is traced to the time of Emperor Augustus Caesar (27 BC – 14AD)[15] The introduction of investigation and litigation also led to the selection of new officers to serve as judges[16] But the process also had the emperors as well as Roman governors in the provinces also hearing cases and acting as judges.[17]

The historic development of Roman law shows that from the time when praetors were still involved in the resolution of disputes, Roman intellectuals known as jurists (iuris consultus or jurisprudentes) were engaged in guiding "the praetors and the parties"[18] by creatively interpreting the juridical formulas.

It was Roman jurists that defined the legal perimeters of social relations or contracts and also formulated the concept of legal presumption (praesumptio iuris) which allows the assumption:

> "that certain things were true without having to prove their existence. Reversing the burden of proof by placing it, not on the person who wished to demonstrate the presumptions, as is usually the case, but on the person who wanted to refute them, presumptions allowed jurists to infer, from what they knew, what was not known or could not be proved. A typical presumption from this period involved the conclusion that all property possessed by a married woman was given to her by her husband...Other presumptions included the idea that cancellations of a deed testified to the extinction of the debt, or for resolving

---

[15]   Ibid. p.20.

[16]   Ibid.

[17]   Ibid.

[18]   Ibid. p.21.

questions of inheritance, that various individuals who died in a shipwreck all died at exactly the same time."[19]

As in all walks of life, some jurists were more renowned than others. And while initially the idea of jurists who were private individuals giving opinions which determined the outcome of cases was not well appreciated by the Roman people at the time, their relevance gained recognition even from the time of Emperor Augustus who is known to have listed jurists in order of preference based on their individual reputation. More notable perhaps is the fact by the time of Emperor Constantine in the fourth century AD, outstanding works of jurists were cited in the Roman courts and when the imperial authorities realised that they cannot control the contributions of jurists to the legal system, the imperial authorities succumbed to employing jurists of high reputes, and even allowed to be members of their council. Effectively, jurists became imperial officers and made decisions that were binding because they were considered to be orders of the emperors.[20]

1.2 Juridical Development

The formal development of juridical training is traced to the second century AD when places of legal training were established by some prominent jurists who trained interested students and awarded certificates to them. However, it is said that by the fourth century AD, the emperors took over control of the training schools.[21]

> "In 425 CE, Theodosius II (r. 408 – 450 CE) declared illegal the teachings of law outside these state-sanctioned institutions."[22]

Insofar as legislation was concerned, it is stated that this was developed in various ways right from the time of the praetors.

---

[19]   Ibid. page 22.

[20]   Ibid. pp.23-24.

[21]   Ibid. p.25

[22]   Ibid.

There were assemblies of plebeians who made laws as well as Senate which consisted of the leading influential among Roman citizens. But the laws that were made mostly covered public law issues such as crime, testamentary succession and family law matters.[23] However, the process was not void of interference as some emperors influenced it by legislating massively. [24]

Added to that was the fact that some emperors perhaps in a bid to have their way as opposed to actually serving the interest of justice "disguised themselves as judges and jurists" and "rendered judgments." [25]

1.3 Ius Gentium and Citizenship Across the Roman Empire

The discussion on Roman law above has covered the ius civile which includes ius commune and the ius honorarium. But this body of laws applied only to Roman citizens within their respective communities in Rome. Any group of non-Romans that were resident in Rome had their own ius commune.[26] However, to address any conflict that arises from the dealings between people from different communities or between Roman citizens and foreigners a special governor for foreigners (praetor peregrinus)[27] was appointed to attend such matters. And it was from such that the principle of ius gentium metamorphosed. Ius gentium which became known as the Law of Nations, Peoples, Gentiles and Tribes[28] had universal legal principles and rules which were applicable to people of any community or nation.

But unlike ius civile which were laws made by the Roman Assemblies of Plebeians or Senate, the rules and laws of ius gentium were developed by praetors peregrinus in the course of their decision making in resolving matters. While on the one hand this would raise issues of excessive

---

[23] Ibid.

[24] Ibid.

[25] Ibid. p.26

[26] Ibid.

[27] Ibid

[28] Ibid. p.26. Some historical account of ius gentium otherwise jus gentium is given by Antonio Padoa-Schioppa in in his book, A History of Law in Europe From the Early Middle Ages to the Twentieth Century. Translated by Caterina Fitzgerald © 2017 Cambridge University Press Pp. 157-158.

liberty for the praetor peregrinus to arbitrarily decide cases, the manifest evident of what transpired is that decisions were made with due regards to "obligations to have good faith (bona fides) in contracts."[29]

Tamar Herzog stated that:

> "eventually ius gentium was said to represent human reason and the nature of things. As a result of this understanding, on occasions Romans considered it also as embodying a natural law (ius natural). They suggested that it was so reasonable and compelling that nature, rather than human convention, was responsible for its creation."[30]

Herzog's remark above echoes similar remarks made by other writers such as Clive Parry and Paul Sieghart who respectively stated thus:

> "The ius gentium of the Romans – that amalgam of the laws of all the peoples of the empire...constituted an actually operative common system of law providing a basis ready made for international law."[31] "the jus gentium – that is, those laws which the Romans found to be common to the legal systems of different subject peoples – commanded high respect as reflecting some universal values."[32]

In course of the development of ius gentium was another historic development in the Roman Empire dating back 'from the fourth to the first century BCE'[33] which in Herzog's account says:

> "Roman citizenship was extended to most individuals living in the Italian peninsula and Gaul (present-day France). In 212 CE, Emperor Caracalla granted it to all free residents of the empire. As a result of this extension, Roman law was

---

[29]   Ibid. Herzog, pp. 26-27.

[30]   Ibid. p.27.

[31]   Parry, Clive, 'The Function of law in the international community' in M. Sorensen (ed.), Manual of Public International Law. London: Macmillan, 1968. P.17.

[32]   Sieghart, Paul, The Lawful Rights of Mankind ©1986 Oxford University Press. p.22

[33]   Herzog, A Short History of European Law p.27

no longer the exclusive system of the citizens of the city, but instead the common stock of all imperial subjects."[34]

By the act of making foreigners Roman citizens, Roman law equally became applicable to them. Although it is stated that Roman law became influenced by Iberia and Visigoths laws as a result of the extension of Roman citizenship to foreigners in the Empire. The further implication of it was that rules and practice of the law became loosed in interpretation and application from one place to another. And while Roman jurists were aware of this they overlooked it and went on to address what should be customary law.[35]

However, when it could have been assumed that the universalization of Roman law and the extension of citizenship would have given stability to the Roman Empire, one of the Roman emperors thought differently.

Emperor Diocletian in AD 285 in an effort to contain the crisis that he had been faced with decided to divide the Roman Empire into two parts[36] which became the Eastern and Western parts of the Roman Empire. However, his intention of simply building two capitals and appointing two rulers to effectively administer the two parts invariably led to the emergence of two empires. The Eastern and Western Roman Empires.

According to Antonio Padoa-Schioppa in his book – A History of Law in Europe at page 3:

> "In the last centuries of the ancient world – the centuries between the age of Constantine (313-334) and the age of Justinian (527-565) – Roman law experienced a series of profound changes, which were to have an influence on the entire successive cycle of legal history in Europe. The vast territory of the late Empire included the area of the whole Mediterranean basin extending as far as the Rhine, the Danube and Southern England. It was divided into 114 administrative provinces, equally split between the Eastern

---

[34] Ibid.

[35] Ibid. For a more detailed discussion on this see Herzog's discussion on it from pp 27-30.

[36] Ibid. p.30.

and Western Empires, the first with a capital to begin with Rome then in Milan and Trier; the second with a capital in Constantinople."[37]

1.4 Evaluation and Summary

From the above discussion, it would be correct to state that at the heart of the spirit of the Roman juridical system is the noble objective to remedy wrongs and do justice to those who have suffered damage or are victims of harmful acts perpetrated by others. However, the legal system from its conception at the time when pontifices acted as mediators between God and man and it was assumed that they resolved disputes between parties in dispute with the spirit of God to the time of the appointment of praetors and subsequently, judges, the juridical system for most part had no mechanism to detect any act of injustice done to those who have sort justice for any alleged wrong done them. Injustice could have taken places at every stage of the development of Roman law because pontifices could have decided cases based on their human bias without the spirit of God and that could have occasionally resulted in injustice for which there was no redress for the victim concerned. This situation was neither remedied nor prevented with the appointment of praetors who even when judges were appointed still unilaterally decided which cases would go to the judges and which would not and there was no formula to eliminate their possible bias in the process. People were just expected to accept their decisions as valid juridical decisions. Perhaps more worrying was the finality of the decisions of early judges whose judgments could not be appealed. The system in its development to the point of having jurists certainly improved in ensuring that justice was mostly done but it did not ensure that injustice is not done if a judge or jurist chooses to make a bad judgment. The incidents of possible cases of injustices been meted out to parties in disputes that went to court could most likely have occurred at the times when some emperor disguised themselves as judges and went on to pronounce judgments in the courts.

The Roman juridical system was structured in such a way that justice could be seen to have been done even when justice might not have been

---

[37]   Padoa-Schioppa, Antonio, A History of Law in Europe From the Early Middle Ages to the Twentieth Century © 2007 Cambridge University Press 2018.p.3

done. This was, and indeed still is, an unfilled serious residual lacuna embedded in the development and application of the juridical system universally. Equally adversarial to justice was and still is the fact that the system as universally applied can sometimes be open to political interference and influence; and also to excessive delays by judges in deciding the final outcome of cases.

The Jewish Authorities v. Apostle Paul

A typical example of this is in the facts of the case of Paul v. the Jewish authorities from which the opening quote to this chapter was taken from Acts 25:16, which in every way is demonstrative of these truths. While the persecutions that Christians went through from the first century through the third century will be discussed in the subsequent chapters, suffice it to say that the person under trial in the case here was a mid-first century AD famous Christian leader and apostle called Saul of Tarsus but became more well known as Paul, who was kept in custody over trumped up charges. According to the account in the Holy Bible:

> "some Jews from the province of Asia saw Paul in the Temple and roused a mob against him. They grabbed him, yelling, "Men of Israel, help us! This is the man who preaches against our people everywhere and tells everybody to disobey the Jewish laws. He speaks against the Temple – and even defiles this holy place by bringing in Gentiles." (For earlier that day they had seen him in the city with Trophimus, a Gentile from Ephesus, and they assumed Paul had taken him into the Temple.) The whole city was rocked by these accusations, and a great riot followed. Paul was grabbed and dragged out of the Temple, and immediately the gates were closed behind him. As they were trying to kill him, word reached the commander of the Roman regiment that all Jerusalem was in an uproar. He immediately called out soldiers and officers and ran down among the crowd. When the mob saw the commander and the troops coming, they stopped beating Paul. Then the commander arrested him and ordered him bound with two chains. He asked the crowd who he was and what he had done. Some shouted one thing and some another. Since he couldn't find out the truth in

all the uproar and confusion, he ordered that Paul be taken to the fortress. As Paul reached the stairs, the mob grew so violent the soldiers had to lift him to their shoulders to protect him. And the crowd followed behind, shouting, "Kill him, kill him!"[38]

While it was evidently the case that Paul was grievously assaulted and might have been killed but for the intervention of the commander and his officers and soldiers, he still persuaded the commander to let him to address the very people that wanted to kill him and the commander obliged him. Paul addressed them as: "Brothers and esteemed fathers" (Acts 22:1), and he went on to tell them that he was a Jew who was educated in Jerusalem under a famous Jewish religious law teacher called Gamaliel. He explained his depth of knowledge of the Jewish laws and customs, as a student who was taught by Gamaliel. Paul confessed how he himself persecuted Christians until he had a supernatural encounter on his way to Damascus with letters to the Jewish people there to enable him to bring the Christians in chains from there to Jerusalem for punishment and this happened on to him:

> "As I was on the road, approaching Damascus about noon, a very bright light from heaven suddenly shone down around me. I fell to the ground and heard a voice saying to me, Saul, Saul, why are you persecuting me?" "Who are you, Lord?' I asked. "And the voice replied, 'I am Jesus of Nazareth, the one you are persecuting?' The people with me saw the light but didn't understand the voice speaking to me. "I asked, 'What should I do, Lord?' "And the Lord told me, 'Get up and go into Damascus, and there you will be told everything you are to do.' "I was blinded by intense light and had to be led by hand to Damascus by my companions. A man named Ananias lived there. He was a godly man, deeply devoted to the law, and well regarded by all the Jews of Damascus. He came and stood beside me and said, 'Brother Saul, regain your sight.' And that very moment I could see him! "Then he told me, 'The God of our ancestors has chosen you to know his will and to see the Righteous One and hear him speak. For you are to be his witness, telling everyone what you have seen and

---

[38]   Holy Bible, Acts 21:26-36 (New Living Translation).

heard. What are you waiting for? Get up and be baptized. Have your sins washed away by calling on the name of the Lord.'...But the Lord said to me, 'Go, for I will send you far away to the Gentiles!" The crowd listened until Paul said that word. Then they all began to shout, "Away with such a fellow! He isn't fit to live!"[39]

They were to pounce on Paul but for the commander who intervened to take Paul inside away from the aggressive crowd. However, the commander ordered that Paul should be 'lashed with whips', in other words, be tortured until he confesses his crime. But when Paul was "tied down" for lashing, he protested that he was a Roman citizen and it was not legal for him to be whipped without first being tried. Paul was released from been lashed upon the commander hearing that he was a Roman citizen. The commander then decided to order the Jewish leaders and members of their high council to appear before him and explain to him what the trouble was about. (Acts 22:24-30)

As they appeared before the commander Paul also appeared before them. However, in yet another attempt to explain his innocence to the leading priests and the Jewish high council he met another violent opposition. And yet again, the commander had to ask soldiers to take Paul away to safety from the aggressive members of the high council. (Acts 23:1-10). But some of the hoodlums among the Jews swore an oath to the effect of not eating or drinking until they had killed Paul. The plot to kill Paul got into the ears of Paul's nephew who swiftly communicated it to Paul and the commander. The commander promptly reacted by sending several hundreds of soldiers to escort Paul with a letter from Jerusalem to the (praetor peregrinus) Governor Felix in Caesarea. The commander clearly outlined the case in the letter he sent with Paul to Governor Felix, thus:

> "From Claudius Lysias, to his Excellency, Governor Felix: Greetings!
>
> "This man was seized by some Jews, and they were about to kill him when he arrived with the troops. When I learned that he was a Roman citizen, I removed him to safety. Then I took him to their high council to learn the basis of the

---

[39]   Ibid. Acts 22:6-16, 21-22.

accusations against him. I soon discovered the charge was something regarding their religious law – certainly nothing worthy of imprisonment or death. But when I was informed of a plot to kill him, I immediately sent him on to you. I have told his accusers to bring their charges before you."[40]

The commander had stated the facts of the case as clearly and accurately as it were in his letter to Governor Felix, but would the Governor acquit Paul of the trumped-up charges that the Jewish high council brought against him, since Roman law is the law of remedies that should correct wrongs done to Roman citizens? A number of factors outside the evidence and facts of the case as the discussion below will show dictated the approach Governor Felix who was the judge in the case took, without due regards to justice been done to Paul.

When the troop that took Paul to Caesarea handed Paul to Governor Felix with the letter from the Commander, Felix went on to establish from Paul that he was from the province of Cilicia, and he assured him that he would hear the case himself when his accusers arrived (Acts 23:31-35). Some days later, the high priest and the Jewish elders with their lawyer Tertullus arrived. Governor called the case; Tertullus went on to make his submission on behalf of the Jewish authorities. He started by flattering the Governor and to make him to see Paul also as a threat to the province and to his administration as the governor. Here was Tertullus's submission:

> "You have provided a long period of peace for us Jews and with foresight have enacted reforms for us. For all of this, Your Excellency, we are grateful to you. But I don't want to bore you, so please give me your attention for only a moment. We have found this man to be a troublemaker who is constantly stirring up riots among the Jews all over the world. He is a ringleader of the cult known as the Nazarenes. Furthermore, he was trying to desecrate the Temple when we arrested him. You can find out the truth of our accusations by examining him yourself." Then the

---

[40]   Ibid. Acts 23:26-30.

other Jews chimed in, declaring that everything Tertullus said was true."[41]

As it is with the case with every trial, as the prosecuting lawyer (Tertullus) finished his submission, the judge (Governor Felix) called Paul to make his defence submission and he presented his defence thus:

> "I know, sir, that you have been a judge of Jewish affairs for many years, so I gladly present my defense before you. You can quickly discover that I arrived in Jerusalem no more than twelve days ago to worship at the Temple. My accusers never found me arguing with anyone in the Temple, nor stirring up a riot in any synagogue or on the streets of the city. These men cannot prove the things they accuse me of doing.

> "But I admit that I follow the Way, which they call a cult. I worship the God of our ancestors, and I firmly believe the Jewish law and everything written in the prophets. I have the same hope in God that these men have, that he will raise both the righteous and unrighteous. Because of this, I always try to maintain a clear conscience before God and all people. After several years away, I returned to Jerusalem with money to aid my people and to offer sacrifices to God. My accusers saw me in the Temple as I was completing a purification ceremony. There was no crowd around me and no rioting. But some Jews from the province of Asia were there – and they ought to be here to bring charges if they have anything against me! Ask these men here what crime the Jewish council found me guilty of, except for the one time I shouted out, 'I am on trial before you today because I believe in the resurrection of the dead! At that point Felix, who was quite familiar with the Way, adjourned the hearing and said, "Wait until Lysias, the garrison commander arrives. Then I will decide the case."[42]

One of the problems of the Roman juridical and justice system is the opening in the system that enables the judge to adjourn hearings or reserve judgment just when he would be expected to deliver judgment.

---

[41]   Ibid. Acts 24:2-9.

[42]   Ibid. Acts 24:10-22.

Sometimes a judge may do this when there are no good grounds but for reasons simply known to him and for his benefit. Governor Felix knew Lysias the commander who rescued Paul and also wrote a letter stating the facts of the case to him, was a useful witness and as governor, he had the power to order for his presence as a witness, but he never did so. He proceeded to hear the prosecution submission and then Paul's defence but he adjourned the case just when Paul might have thought that he would be acquitted. However, what eventually happened was that Lysias never came because Governor Felix never sent for him in the first place. In his capacity as (praetor peregrinus) judge, Governor Felix actually had other thoughts and expectations that had nothing to do with justice insofar as the facts of the case were concerned because this was what happened:

> "A few days later Felix came back with his wife, Drusilla, who was Jewish. Sending for Paul, they listened as he told them about faith in Christ Jesus. As he reasoned with them about righteousness and self-control and the coming day of Judgment, Felix became frightened. "Go away for now," he replied. "When it is more convenient, I'll call for you again." He also hoped that Paul would bribe him, so he sent for him quite often and talked with him. After two years went by in this way, Felix was succeeded by Porcius Festus. And because Felix wanted to gain favor with the Jewish people, he left Paul in prison.[43]

Since Paul did not bribe Governor Felix as he expected and since it was more important to the Governor to please the Jewish people who wanted to kill Paul for no just reason than to release the innocent man, the Governor played politics with the case and left Paul in prison for two years on the false allegations that were made against him on grounds of his beliefs in Jesus Christ of Nazareth. But Paul's ordeal did not end with the two years' imprisonment he suffered under Governor Felix. The Governor who succeeded Felix just as well allowed the political influence and interference from the Jewish authorities to prevail over him from rendering justice to Paul. This is what we are told:

---

[43]   Ibid. Acts 24:24-27 [Holy Bible, New Living Translation © 1996, 2004, 2007 by Tyndale House Foundation].

"Three days after Festus arrived in Caesarea to take over his new responsibilities, he left for Jerusalem, where the leading priests and other Jewish leaders met with him and made their accusations against Paul. They asked Festus as a favor to transfer Paul to Jerusalem (planning to ambush and kill him on the way). But Festus replied that Paul was at Caesarea and he himself would be returning there soon. So he said, "Those of you in authority can return with me. If Paul has done anything wrong, you can make your accusations." About eight or ten days later Festus returned to Caesarea, and on the following day he took his seat in court and ordered that Paul be brought in. When Paul arrived, the Jewish leaders from Jerusalem gathered around and made many serious accusations they couldn't prove. Paul denied the charges. "I am not guilty of any crime against the Jewish laws or the Temple or the Roman government," he said. Then Festus, wanting to please the Jews, asked him, "Are you willing to go to Jerusalem and stand trial before me there?" But Paul replied, "No! This is the official Roman court, so I ought to be tried here. You know very well I am not guilty of harming the Jews. If I have done something worthy of death, I don't refuse to die. But if I am innocent, no one has a right to turn me over to these men to kill me. I appeal to Caesar!" Festus conferred with his advisers and then replied, "Very well! You have appealed to Caesar, and to Caesar you will go."[44]

A number of people today think of a prisoner of conscience (POC) as a concept that originated in the twentieth century with reference to people that were imprisoned for their beliefs, but as this case of the Jewish authority against Paul shows, Paul was actually a prisoner of conscience, so there have been prisoners of conscience for well over two thousand year. Governor Festus could have released Paul if he wanted to do justice to the case but he was succumbing to political influence and interference of the Jewish leaders to keep Paul in prison. Governor Festus appeared to pleased let Paul out of his court by granting his appeal to Caesar when he has not even concluded his trial and passed a verdict on the matter. To Paul, going to Caesar will take him away from the easy reach of Jewish authorities who were plotting to kill and to Governor Festus perhaps he

---

[44]   Ibid. Acts 25:1-12 [NLT].

would have the pleasure of not ruling against the Jewish authorities and releasing Paul, so sending him to Caesar as he had appealed was a fair ending to a case that threatened his political relationship with the Jews that he would govern. What is fundamental in this is that Roman law and justice can sometimes be manipulated by the judges and nothing untoward can be perceived to have occurred.

The full account of the political interference and influence that the Jewish leaders brought to bear upon Governor Festus with pressure for him to condemn Paul to death at all costs, irrespective of the fact that no offence warranting such condemnation was committed by Paul was told by the Governor to a visiting King as follows:

> "...King Agrippa arrived with his sister, Bernice, to pay their respects to Festus. During their stay of several days, Festus discussed Paul's case with the king. "There is a prisoner here," he told him, "whose case was left for me by Felix. When I was in Jerusalem, the leading priests and Jewish elders pressed charges against him and asked me to condemn him. I pointed out to them that Roman law does not convict people without a trial. They must be given an opportunity to confront their accusers and defend themselves. When his accusers came here for the trial, I didn't delay. I called the case the very next day and ordered Paul brought in.
>
> But the accusations made against him weren't any of the crimes I expected. Instead, it was something about their religion and a dead man named Jesus, who Paul insists is alive. I was at a loss to know how to investigate these things, so I asked him whether he would be willing to stand trial on these charges in Jerusalem. But Paul appealed to have his case decided by the emperor. So I ordered that he be held in custody until I could arrange to send him to Caesar."
>
> "I'd like to hear the man myself," Agrippa said. And Festus replied, "You will – tomorrow!" So the next day Agrippa and Bernice arrived at the auditorium with great pomp, accompanied by military officers and prominent men of

the city. Festus ordered that Paul be brought in. Then Festus said, "King Agrippa and all who are here, this is the man whose death is demanded by all the Jews, both here and in Jerusalem. But in my opinion he has done nothing deserving death. However, since he appealed his case to the emperor, I have decided to send him to Rome. But what shall I write the emperor? For there is no clear charge against him. So I have brought him before all of you, and especially you, King Agrippa, so that after we examine him, I might have something to write. For it makes no sense to send a prisoner to the emperor without specifying the charges against him!"[45]

Injustice is one of the things that arouses human curiosity because people want to understand the mitigating reasons for any unfair treatment given to their fellow human being or to find grounds to condemn injustice. Upon hearing Governor Festus' explanation that Paul had not done anything that should warrant his death as the Jewish leaders demanded, King Agrippa told Governor Festus that he would like to hear Paul himself. While Governor Festus was not hesitant in obliging King Agrippa's request, he lamented his own dilemma in the case. As a Governor, he was also the supreme judge of the province and yet he was going to send Paul to the emperor when he had not found legal basis for the case and therefore has not passed verdict? What will he write to the emperor as the facts of the case? He wondered! Governor Festus realised that he was about to ridicule himself by merely sending Paul to the emperor because he has appealed to Caesar. It was not just a matter of the fact that Paul had not been properly charged but also the fact that he had not been properly tried. Appeal becomes necessary in law only when a judge has erred in law by how he had decided a case, but here was a case in which the charges are not clear and no ruling was made by the provincial judge; and yet an appeal and the appellant would be sent to the emperor. But in the politics of personal interest and preservation, the ancient definitions of justice propounded by Thrasymachus in Plato, The Republic, where he stated that "justice or right is simply what is

---

45   Ibid. Acts 25:13-27 [NLT].

in the interests of the stronger party"[46] was certainly having bearing in the experience that Paul was going through. In fact, to the extent that Governor Festus is inclined to do the bidding of the Jewish leaders, it might perhaps be the case that the less quoted definition of justice by Simonides in Plato, The Republic, was probably what was finding expression in the trial of Paul. Simonides in his own definition of justice had stated that: "justice is to benefit one's friends and harm one's enemies."[47] The Jewish leaders have been both the stronger party and the ones whose friendship Governor Festus would prefer to have than to do justice to Paul. It turned out that Paul's ordeal was a means by which the Governor and King would forge good relationship. King Agrippa not wanting to hear Paul himself in order to do him justice but just to satisfy his curiosity as to who Paul was and why the Jewish leaders wanted to kill him? This is what happened next:

> "Then Agrippa said to Paul, "You may speak in your defense."

> So Paul, gesturing with his hand, started his defense: "I am fortunate, King Agrippa, that you are the one hearing my defense today against all these accusations made by the Jewish leaders, for I know you are an expert on all Jewish customs and controversies. Now please listen to me patiently! As the Jewish leaders are well aware, I was given a thorough Jewish training from my earliest childhood among my own people and in Jerusalem. If they would admit it, they know that I have been a member of the Pharisees, the strictest sect of our religion. Now I am on trial because of my hope in the fulfilment of God's promise made to our ancestors. In fact, that is why the twelve tribes of Israel zealously worship God night and day, and they share the same hope I have. Yet, Your Majesty, they accuse me for having this hope!

---

[46]   Plato, The Republic, With an introduction by Melissa Lane © 2007, Penguin Classics. P.18. To this day, the decisions of the Courts at both the national and international courts tend to favour the stronger party who often can afford the best lawyers or the State Government whose actions is often justified at international courts as necessary or inevitable, even as the cases that will be discussed in subsequent chapters of this book will show.

[47]   Ibid. page 9

Why does it seem incredible to any of you to believe that God can raise the dead?

"I used to believe that I ought to do everything I could to oppose the very name of Jesus of Nazareth. Indeed, I did just that in Jerusalem. Authorized by the leading priests, I caused many believers there to be sent to prison. And I cast my vote against them when they were condemned to death. Many times I had had them punished in the synagogues to get them to curse Jesus. I was so violently opposed to them that I even chased them down in foreign cities. One day I was on such a mission to Damascus, armed with the authority and commission of the leading priests. About noon, Your Majesty, as I was on the road, a light from heaven brighter than the sun shone down on me and my companions. We all fell down, and I heard a voice saying to me in Aramaic, 'Saul, Saul, Why are you persecuting me? It is useless for you to fight against my will.

"Who are you, lord?' I asked.

"And the Lord replied, 'I am Jesus, the one you are persecuting. Now get to your feet! For I have appeared to you to appoint you as my servant and witness. You are to tell the world what you have seen and what I will show you in the future. And I will rescue you from both your own people and the Gentiles. Yes, I am sending you to the Gentiles to open their eyes, so they may turn from darkness to light and from the power of satan to God. Then they will receive forgiveness for their sins and be given a place among God's people, who are set apart by faith in me.'

"And so, King Agrippa, I obeyed that vision from heaven. I preached first to those in Damascus, then in Jerusalem and throughout all Judea, and to the Gentiles, that all must repent of their sins and turn to God – and prove they have changed by the good things they do. Some Jews arrested me in the Temple for preaching this, and they tried to kill me. But God has protected me right up to this present time so I can testify to everyone, from the least to the greatest. I teach nothing except what the prophets and Moses said would happen – that the Messiah would suffer and be the first to rise from the dead, and in this way announce God's light to Jews and Gentiles alike."

Suddenly, Festus shouted, "Paul, you are insane. Too much study has made you crazy!"

But Paul replied, "I am not insane, Most Excellent Festus. What I am saying is the sober truth. And King Agrippa knows about these things. I speak boldly, for I am sure these events are all familiar to him, for they were not done in a corner! King Agrippa, do you believe the prophets?" I know you do – "Agrippa interrupted him. "Do you think you can persuade me to become a Christian so quickly?" Paul replied, "Whether quickly or not, I pray to God that both you and everyone here in this audience might become the same as I am, except for these chains."

Then the king, the governor, Bernice, and all the others stood and left. As they went out, they talked it over and agreed, "This man hasn't done anything to deserve death or imprisonment."

And Agrippa said to Festus, "He could have been set free if he hadn't appealed to Caesar."[48]

The purpose of a judge sitting to hear a suspect in any trial is to adjudge a case but strangely, after King Agrippa heard Paul's defence submission, he stood up with Governor Festus and left without ruling on all what he had heard. King Agrippa said to Governor Festus outside the court that:

"He could have been set free if he hadn't appealed to Caesar?"[49]

Before King Agrippa asked Paul to speak in his defence, Governor Festus had said he didn't know what to write as the grounds for sending Paul's appeal to the emperor and had hoped that after Agrippa had heard Paul, he would know what to write but now all that Agrippa could say was that "Paul could have been set free if he had not appealed to Caesar." Both King Agrippa and Governor Festus were deviating from their

---

[48]   Acts 26:1-30.

[49]   Ibid. 26:32

responsibilities and justifying their decision to do what was right and just on the juridical technicality that since Paul had appealed to the emperor he had to go to the emperor. It did not matter to the King and the Governor that passing a case that had no legal merit under Roman law as Governor Festus himself observed would be an unnecessary increase in the court cases and workload that would be waiting for the emperor's attention and decision. It did not matter that Paul was unduly made to suffer the fate of a prisoner for offences he did not commit. But these sorts of cases where the accused has not committed any offence and it has been established that there were no prima facie grounds to arrest and detain the accused are still clogging the criminal justice system of many nations even today. The actual people that should have been arrested and tried were those had assaulted Paul and would have killed him but for the intervention of the Commander. But those men were walking free, because they did what was of interest to the Jewish priests and leaders even though their actions were acts of crime.

Paul the victim was under trial and could not be set free by two judges: Governor Festus and King Agrippa that were already satisfied that he had not committed any crime or done anything that deserved death or even imprisonment. Once a legal system is obliquely embedded with unintended schemes of injustice in the pursuit of justice as the case of Paul shows, the innocent can be made to suffer the consequences meant for the guilty and it may not be apparent that injustice has taken place. Paul and other prisoners under the custody of a Roman officer named Julius were put in a ship sailing to Rome where he has appealed to the emperor to hear his case. Nothing is said about what Governor Festus wrote about Paul's case to the emperor but Paul was on his way to know his fate in the matter.

Paul and his co-prisoners and travellers to Italy had a rough sail because of the intense battering of gale-force winds on their ship. At a point they all feared for their lives until Paul assured everyone in the ship to:

> "take courage! None of you will lose your lives, even though the ship will go down. For last night an angel of the God to whom I belong and whom I serve stood beside me, and he said,

'Don't be afraid, Paul, for you will surely stand trial before Caesar! What's more, God in his goodness has granted safety to everyone sailing with you.' So take courage! For I believe God. It will be just as he said. But we will be shipwrecked on an Island."[50]

Just as Paul said to all those sailing with him, they had a shipwreck but everyone escaped to safety. (Acts 27:27-28:11). Paul and those who were sailing with him spent almost four months including the 3 months they spent in Malta following their shipwreck before they eventually got to Rome. Here then is what was said of Paul as they arrived in Rome:

> "When we arrived in Rome, Paul was permitted to have his own private lodging, though he was guarded by a soldier. Three days after Paul's arrival, he called together the local Jewish leaders. He said to them, "Brothers, I was arrested in Jerusalem and handed over to the Roman government, even though I had done nothing against our people or the customers of our ancestors. The Romans tried me and wanted to release me, because they found no cause for the death sentence. But when the Jewish leaders protested the decision, I felt it necessary to appeal to Caesar, even though I had no desire to press charges against my own people, I asked you to come here today so we could get acquainted and so I could explain to you that I am bound with this chain because I believe that the hope of Israel – the Messiah – has already come." They replied, "We have had no letters from Judea or reports against you from anyone who has come here...........For the next two years, Paul lived in Rome at his own expense. He welcomed all who visited him, boldly proclaiming the Kingdom of God and teaching about the Lord Jesus Christ. And no one tried to stop him."[51]

Mindful of the two years Governor Felix kept Paul in custody, hoping he would give him bribe to free him (Acts 24:27) and the period of time Paul was under trial under Governor Festus and the two years he was said to have spent in Rome (Acts 28:30) where the case from the account in the Bible appeared to have been adjourned *sine die*, it is clear that

---

[50]   Ibid. Acts 27:22-26

[51]   Acts 28:16-21 and 30-31.

about five years out of Paul's life was wasted in a case that should not have proceeded to trial if the noble goal of Roman law of doing remedies to the party that had been wronged was manifestly achievable in every case of a wrong done to an innocent person. But clearly, the political interference and influence dictated the outcome of some politically and religiously motivated cases as the case of Paul shows. Some respected theologians in their Bible commentaries have pointed out that the details of Paul's suffering and trial as accounted for in Acts chapters twenty-one through twenty-eight was done to acquaint a judge called Theophilus about Paul's innocence in the whole matter.[52] And that the trial of Paul "most likely" failed and he was released.[53] Against the backdrop of these historic accounts of Roman law and its universal influence and effect, its use in the persecution of Christians from the onset came also the Christian influence and effect after about three centuries of horrendous persecutions, as the discussions in the subsequent chapters will show.

---

[52] David Pawson takes this view in his book UNLOCKING THE BIBLE OMNIBUS © David Pawson 2003 Harper Collins Publishers where in the conclusion on Acts he remarked about the writer of Acts that "his overall goal of briefing Theophilus so that his friend Paul might be declared innocent at his trial." P.885.

[53] Conrad Gempf, commentary on the book of Acts in New Bible Commentary, Consulting Editors D.A. Carson, R.T. France, J.A. Motyer & G.J. Wenham © Universities and Colleges Christian Fellowship, Leicester, England, 1953, 1954, 1970, 1994. P.1107.

2

HOW CHRISTIANITY BECAME A WORLD RELIGION AND DEFINED THE UNIVERSAL LEGAL SYSTEM

"He will judge the world with justice and rule the nations with fairness." – Psalm 9:8 [NLT].

"Constantine is best known as the Roman emperor who converted to Christianity and in so doing made it possible for Christianity to become a world religion."[54]

The whole of human race was freed from the oppression of tyrants. We especially, who had fixed our hopes upon the Christ of God, had gladness unspeakable.[55]

---

[54]   Potter, David, Constantine The Emperor © 2013 Oxford University Press. p.1.

[55]   This is recorded by Eusebius in his account of Church History as what the jubilant Christians said when Emperor Constantine then ruler of the Roman Empire met Licinius then ruler of the Balkan provinces and they both issued the Edict of Milan in AD 313 that gave Christians freedom of worship. See Constantine in 131 Christians Everyone Should Know © 2000 Christianity Today, Inc. p.307. See also Milan, Edict of, in the Oxford Dictionary of the Christian Church Edited by F.L. Cross and E.A. Livingstone © 1974 reprinted with corrections 1977 Oxford University Press. p.915.

2.1 Rulers, Priests and the Persecutions of Christians

The persecutions that Christians have suffered from the stories in the Holy Bible and Church historical sources of information[56] reveal that rulers such as kings and emperors and sadly even religious leaders such as popes and priests wanted true Christians, those who were committed to living the way Jesus Christ has commanded his followers to do, to be annihilated.

Religious leaders by their spiritual position of authority often have a lot of influence and control over the people under their religious denominations, groups, traditions and beliefs. Even today we know that the pope of the Catholic Church has a tremendous influence over the one billion members of the Catholic Church[57] and the same can be said of other religious leaders. The effect of religious leaders on their members means that individual members of religious organisations sometimes do not really act on their own convictions but rather under the influence and dictates of their religious leaders, in some cases they do so even if such may be contrary to the laws of God and also the laws of the land. That was demonstrably clear in the prosecution and trial of Paul as was discussed in chapter one where the judges said he had not committed any crime worthy of condemnation and even imprisonment, but yet the Jewish leaders still wanted him condemned. But the case of Paul was not an isolated case of Christian persecution from the first century and to some extent and degree to this day.

However, what might have been the worst form of persecution and brutality against Christians in the first century was what the Roman Emperor Nero did. In one account:

---

[56]   A good account of Christians who were persecuted especially the disciples of Jesus Christ who became known as apostles and some outstanding early Christian believers between the first and sixth centuries are mentioned and discussed in The Oxford Dictionary of the Christian Church Edited by F.L. Cross, Second Edition revised by F.L. Cross and E.A. Livingstone © Oxford University Press 1958, 1974 Reprinted 1977 with (corrections.); a number of other faithful Christian believers who did not yield their faith at the face of persecution and threat of death by tyrants and oppressors right up to the twentieth century are mentioned and discussed in 131 Christians Everyone Should Know Editors Mark Galli and Ted Olsen © 2000 Christianity Today, Inc.

[57]   BBC News in March 2013 stated that there are over 1.2 billion Roman Catholics in the world. See http://www.bbc.co.uk/news/world-21443313

"On 19 July AD64 a fire began in the city of Rome which lasted three days, devastating much of the city. It engulfed the centre of Rome, destroying temples and houses. The citizens looked for a scapegoat, and found one in the Emperor Nero. They knew he had ambitions to pull down old buildings and put up new magnificent structures, so they assumed he was behind it. Nero in turn, shifted the blame onto the Christians, and so began a serious persecution of the church. They faced awful times. They were tortured, sewn into the skin of wild beasts and made to crawl round the amphitheatres on all four, while they were set upon by lions and other wild animals. They were hunted by dogs and some of them were crucified."[58]

It is dangerous for anyone to be above the law and unaccountable to some other persons because such liberty can easily lead the person who has it, especially, if he is vested with power and authority, to lose his human feelings and sense of connection with other human beings, and proceed to destroy his fellow human beings without a sense of remorse. This can be seen not only from the above conduct of Nero but also in further acts of brutality and inhumane acts to the extent that he found it pleasurable to tie his fellow human beings who professed the Christian faith and burnt them in his palace garden just to provide lighting for his party guests.[59]

Such was the persecutions because for a greater part of the first three hundred years of this Common Era (CE) – Anno Domini (AD), Christians were misunderstood for what they stood for and everything was done to stop Christianity, by acts of persecutions and brutalities. At a time during the Roman Empire, religious oppression of Christians and denial of religious freedom was so severe, some of the emperors even considered Christianity as a political party and saw it as a threat to its power and authority, and therefore sought to eradicate its existence. In the historical account of one of the great martyrs of the Christian faith,

---

[58] See Pawson, David. Unlocking the Bible Omnibus, (Collins, An imprint of HarperCollinsPublishers, 2003) pp.1165-1166

[59] Ibid. "Nero's palace garden...He had some Christians coated with tar and bitumen, tied them to posts around the garden and set them on fire. They were burned alive to provide lighting for his party."

Polycarp[60] AD69-155, the Bishop of Smyrna[61], when he was arrested for the offence of being a Christian, the Roman proconsul who was in charge of deciding what punishment should be meted out to him, took pity at him and wanted to free him from persecution and death, and so asked him to proclaim, "Caesar is Lord." If only Polycarp would make that declaration and offer some incense to Caesar's statue[62] then he would be free, but Polycarp refused to deny his Lord and Master Jesus Christ. He affirmed his position of faith in Jesus Christ by saying:

> "Eighty-six years I have served Christ, and He never did me wrong. How can I blaspheme my king who saved me?"[63]

For that honest confession of his religious beliefs and refusal to compromise his faith by proclaiming Caesar is Lord in place of Jesus Christ, Polycarp "was burned alive at the stake."[64] That was the extent to which the emperors of the Roman Empire went to strip Christians of the freedom to hold and practice their belief in God.

The persecution of Christians in the Roman Empire went on for well over the first three hundred years. In 312 under Emperor Maximinus Daia, Christians were still persecuted and killed for no reason other than their religious beliefs. In Alexandria in present day Egypt, "Bishop Peter was arrested and executed."[65] In Ankara in Turkey, "seven virgins"[66] who were "leaders of a Christian community, were arrested and drowned"[67] and a man who felt it was not right for the virgins to have been killed in that way and verbally attacked the governor of the province at the time for the cruelty was "publicly incinerated" for criticising the governor.

---

60   Polycarp, was said to be the leading Christian figure in Roman Asia between c.69 – c. 155 . He is said to have been burnt to death on 23 February 155. See Polycarp inside The Oxford Dictionary of the Christian Church early quoted at page 1107.

61   Smyrna is now known as Izmir Turkey.

62   See history of Polycarp Martyrdom. http://www.polycarp.net/

63   Ibid.

64   Ibid

65   Potter, David, Constantine The Emperor © Oxford University Press 2013. P.147.

66   Ibid.

67   Ibid.

Although, prior to Christianity the Romans were religious and worshipped many gods such as Jupiter, Mercury, Dionysus, Heracles and female gods such as Diana, Venus [68], they were not generally moral and compassionate, therefore people found Christianity as a more compassionate way of life for the oppressed and downtrodden. But this made the Christians abhorrent to the Roman authorities and consequently led to the persecution of Christians. Nevertheless, it did not halt the rapid growth of Christianity by the third century. At the time, women were encouraged to abort their babies if they were girls and those that were born were murdered. Infanticide as a way of getting rid of girls was practiced and legally justified.[69] Christianity treated such actions as evil and was opposed to it in spite of the fact that it attracted the brutality of the Roman authorities. As Stephenson further stated in his account:

> "Christianity offered a new vision, where both abortion and infanticide were forbidden, and virginity before marriage was prescribed......One must add that the rate of reproduction among pagans was very low: men favoured birth control (including anal and less commonly, oral sex), indulged in homosexual sex, took concubines and patronized both male and female prostitutes, who in turn favoured various methods of birth control and abortion when necessary. All of these practices were forbidden to Christians...Roman men who converted to Christianity were obliged to have vaginal intercourse with their wives, and if pregnancy results, were obliged to have a child and raise it, regardless of its sex."[70]

Hence, Christianity was attractive to most people especially to women and their daughters who were the most victims of Roman rule of killing the girl child and aborting pregnancies that would produce baby girls at delivery. It is stated that the Christian faith grew exponentially even from the third century.[71] Christianity began to appeal to those in high positions of power and authority and one of the most important figures

---

[68] Stephenson, Paul, Constantine Unconquered Emperor, Christian Victor © 2009. Pp.24-25. "The Roman was generally free to worship any and all deities according to his or her own conscience.... With Jupiter's closest peers being his traditional companions, notably Mercury..."

[69] Ibid. p.40

[70] Ibid.

[71] Ibid. p.38

that got converted to Christianity was Constantine. He became known in the history of the Roman Empire as Emperor Constantine the Great, the unconquered Christian emperor.

2.2 The Significance of the Conversion of Emperor Constantine

> "For kingship belongs to the LORD, and he rules over the nations."[72]

While the persecution of Christians lasted from the first century into the fourth century and the advancement of the Christian faith did not abate inter alia for the reasons stated above, the Christians neither had freedom nor licence to hold and practice their beliefs. What then subsequently happened after all the persecutions between the various Roman Emperors from the reigns of Nero from AD 54 to Emperor Galerius 311 was the sudden realisation of Emperor Constantine that the gods that the other emperors relied on was not as reliable and dependable as the Christian God. In Potter's account of Emperor Constantine he stated thus:

> "Constantine knew that emperors needed the aid of the gods to succeed, but who would his god be? He also knew that no god was more at odds with the ideology of Diocletian and Galerius than the god of the Christians."[73]

The divisions in the Roman Empire with the number of divisional emperors ruling in both the Western and Eastern empires was no longer viable so the unification of the empire becomes a necessary task, the battles that would lead to the elimination of some emperors and bring about unification stared each of the divisional emperors in the face. Constantine faced such a challenge as he had to go to battle against an army that was greater in number than his army. Like other Roman emperors he needed the support of a god but not the gods that other emperors before him had pledged allegiance to. The Christian God was what appealed to Constantine. In a similar account, Stephenson stated:

---

[72]   See Psalms 22:28 (English Standard Version of the Holy Bible).

[73]   Potter, David, Constantine The Emperor, p.135.

"Constantine identified aspects of Christianity that correlated best with his own expectations of a religion. In particular, he saw the god of the Christians as the bringer of victory, the 'greatest god' (in Latin, the summus deus) who had hitherto been misidentified as Zeus or Jupiter or as the Sun. Constantine's militant interpretation of Christianity was founded on the Roman understanding of the interactions between faith and power."[74]

Faced with a defining moment in the civil war that would determine who would eventually emerge as sole emperor of the western axis of the Roman Empire at the battle of Milvian Bridge in October 312 against Emperor Maxentius, Constantine looked up to the God of the Christians that have appealed to him for help and guidance to victory. The moment of his divine guidance and instruction for victory by the God of the Christians that he had put his faith in came with a vision in which he saw a sign in the sky with the inscription "in this sign, conquer."[75]

Constantine complied with the divine instruction he received in his dream and went to the battle with the heavenly sign inscribed on the shields of his soldiers and defeated the overwhelming number of Maxentius army and marched triumphantly into Rome.[76] This defining moment of victory appears to have sealed any iota of doubt Constantine had left about the God of the Christians being real and able to bring victory to those who have faith and trust in him. So he went on as Emperor to take measures to free Christians including slaves from whatever hardships they suffered under previous emperors and tyrants of the Roman Empire.

2.3 Emperor Constantine and The Liberation of Slaves

Some of the letters that are in the Holy Bible especially those of the apostle Paul to the Churches and some Christian leaders show that there was recognition of the cultural setting of the first century in which the

---

[74]   Stephenson, Paul, Unconquered Emperor, Christian Victor. P.13.

[75]   Ibid. pp.135; see also Potter, Constantine The Emperor as already quoted, pp.142-143; also see MacDonald I.J.Mopho, Beyond the Crown © 2010 Holy Fire Publishers. Pp.43-44.

[76]   Ibid.

Christian church started. There was then the tradition of master and servant or master and slave relationships. The idea that some would be more materially well off than others and that those materially and financially well off would employ the less well off as servants or slaves was a matter that the Christian faith and religion recognised and addressed in various places in the Holy Scriptures notably in the New Testament of the Holy Bible where for instance in Ephesians 6:5-9 it is stated:

> "Slaves, obey your earthly masters with deep respect and fear. Serve them sincerely as you would serve Christ. Try to please them all the time, not just when they are watching you. As slaves of Christ, do the will of God with all your heart. Work with enthusiasm, as though you were working for the Lord rather than for people. Remember that the Lord will reward each one of us for the good we do, whether we are slaves or free. Masters, treat your slaves in the same way. Don't threaten them; remember, you both have the same Master in heaven, and he has no favorites." [New Living Translation © 1996, 2004, 2007 by Tyndale House Foundation.]

What the Christian faith and religion did not permit was the degradation and inhumane treatment of a person who was a slave. The Holy Bible was actually written and printed at a time that Europeans were practicing slavery among themselves. Eusebius Hieronymus Sophronius otherwise known as Jerome is known to have translated the Bible into Latin between 382 and 405.[77] However the first printed Holy Bible was not done until 1456 when it was produced in Gutenberg.[78] And at a time, Africans actually enslaved the rest of the world. We know for a fact from the historical account in the Holy Bible that the Israelites for example were slaves in Egypt in Africa for several hundreds of years. We read thus in Exodus 2:23 and Exodus 12:40:

> "Years passed, and the king of Egypt died. But the Israelites continued to groan under the burden of slavery. They cried to out for help, and their cry rose to God."

---

[77] See 131 Christians Everyone Should Know pp. 337-339

[78] Ibid. See table of outline of Henry VIII where it begins with 1456 Gutenberg produces first printed Bible. P.329.

And,

> "The people of Israel had lived in Egypt for 430 years."

While Constantine was in Rome as a victor and as the indisputable ruler of the western axis of the Roman Empire, he ordered the restitution of property confiscated from the Christian church.[79] This was a signal of licence to Christians that they could serve their God free from the fear of persecution and loss of their properties. And he went on further to do something quite outstanding. In 314 Constantine took action towards emancipating slaves by writing to one of his urban prefects Volusianus, requesting that those who had been enslaved "under the tyrant"[80] should be freed. However, Christianity had been stigmatised in the Roman Empire to the extent that people generally held the view that a good Roman was someone who was not a good Christian.[81] The idea became what the psychologists today would regard as social proof[82] and so even without persecution, people felt dissuaded from becoming Christians as they wanted to remain good Romans. But this was to change with Constantine as emperor who had experienced the manifest divine power of the God of the Christians by his victory in battle.

Constantine's faith in the Christian God was quite firm as he is credited with authoring these actual words which is part of the Nicene creed read in Church prayers regularly especially during sacraments or Eucharist:

> "We believe in One God, the Father Almighty, maker of Heaven and Earth."[83]

The precedent Constantine set to free people from slavery in the hands of tyrants continued for several hundred years so much so that by the time of Pope Gregory the Great (504 – 604), the compassion for humanity had pervaded the heart of Gregory and he intervened in freeing English slaves

---

[79]   Ibid. Potter, David, p.145.

[80]   Ibid. p.172

[81]   Ibid. p.146.

[82]   Cialdini, Robert B., Influence, The Psychology of Persuasion © 2007 Collins Business An Imprint of HarperCollinsPublishers. "The greater the number of people who find any idea correct, the more the idea will be correct." P. 128

83
See Potter, David as already quoted. P. 2.

that were for sale in a Roman marketplace in the sixth century. He did not only free the English people from being sold as slaves in Rome when he became Pope, he sent "St Augustine and later about 40 missionaries to go and evangelise and convert England.

It is rather a sad irony that the British that had a history of being sold in a Roman market as slaves when they became "free and converted as Christians" ended up a thousand years later having a British empire had no moral restraint in indulging in the worst form of human slave trade with extreme barbaric and degrading acts in which they first used Indians but found Africans more fit and suitable for slave labour for a span of over 300 years. Besides the slave trade which was employed to meet up the demand of labour during the agricultural revolution of the 15th through the 19tth century prior to the industrialisation revolution, the height of the unchristian and ungodly act of the British slave trade was the alteration of the Holy Bible which amounted to the desecration of Holy Scripture in a bid to mislead the slaves in believing that it was the will of God for them to be perpetual slaves by the publishing of The Slaves Bible in 1808[84] even after the British Parliament House of Commons had passed the Slave Trade Abolition Act 1807.

2.4 The 313 Edict of Milan and Subsequent Fusion of Church and State

Events have a way of conspiring to change the course of things in history in ways that point to the fact that man is neither in charge nor really in control of the course of human affairs. After several hundred years of persecutions and unsuccessful efforts to stop Christianity was a divine reversal through a chain of events that could not have been physically orchestrated by the Christians but by God himself through the hands of repentant pagans who derided Christianity.

While Constantine took control of the Western part of the Roman Empire by his defeat of Maxentius, there remained the Eastern part of the Roman Empire to conquer. However, one of the emperors of the Eastern axis of the Roman Empire, Licinius became Constantine's brother-in-law and was apparently influenced by Constantine at their meeting in

---

[84]   Mills, David Charles, Unholy The Slaves Bible © 2009. Introduction p.xi.

Milan to embrace Christianity. In the process they reached an agreement that gave legal recognition to Christians as well as other religions and it has been what is referred to as the Edict of Milan. But there are some controversies surrounding it as a number of historians argue that no such edict took place. For instance, it is stated in The Oxford Dictionary of the Christian Church © 1974 Oxford University Press at p.915:

> "Milan, Edict of. Early in 313 the Emps. *Constantine and Licinius met at Milan and agreed to recognize the legal personality of the Christian Churches and to tolerate all religions equally. Their policy marked the triumph of Christianity over *persecution, but did not 'establish' the Church. The document commonly known as the 'Edict of Milan' (it is not an edict and was not issued at Milan) is to be found in divergent forms in *Lactantius (De Mortibus Persecutorum, xlviii) and *Eusibius (Hist. Eccl., x.5).

The argument that there was no such document as the Edict of Milan is collaborated by David Potter in his book, Constantine The Emperor © 2013 Oxford University Press at p.149 where he stated:

> "What is most significant is that the document, once wrongly known as the Edict of Milan (there was never any such thing) and attributed to Constantine, is the product of a pagan emperor who had decided that Constantine's approach to the "Christian question" was correct. Although the "Edict of Milan" is really a letter of Licinius to the governors of the eastern provinces, it still represents a sea change in the direction of imperial policy. Christianity is no longer to be shunted aside as "un-Roman" or the practice of eccentrics."

However, in contrast to the above, the account of Paul Stephenson in his book, Constantine Unconquered Emperor, Christian Victor © 2009 Quercus, p. 158 shows what is a joint agreement between emperors Constantine and Licinius in Milan which is said to be the 313 Edict of Milan and it reads in part, thus:

> "When I, Constantine Augustus, and I, Licinius Augustus, happily met at Milan and had under consideration all

matters which concerned the public good and security, we thought that among all the other things that would profit men generally that which merited our first and chief attention was reverence for the divinity. Our purpose is to grant both to the Christians and to all others the freedom to follow whichever religion they might wish; whereby whatsoever divinity dwells in heaven may be appeased and made propitious towards all who have been set under our power."

Whatever that transpired between emperors Constantine and Licinius during their meeting at Milan in 313 certainly resulted to a greater good and resulted in freedom of worship for Christians which they never had before in the entire Roman Empire. In fact besides Christians having liberty to worship the Christian God was a connection that resulted in the fusion of Church and State.

In his own account, Antonio Padoa-Schioppa in his book, A History of Law in Europe From the Early Middle Ages to the Twentieth Century, Translated by Caterina Fitzgerald © 2017 Cambridge University Press at p.17, states:

"The Christian religion, after two centuries in which its followers were ferociously persecuted and the Church was considered an illicit organisation, within the span of less than a century went from being tolerated, to being recognised by Constantine in the year 313 with the Edict of Milan, and then granted privileges, particularly that of exemption from taxes. In the year 380 Theodosius declared the Catholic religion to be the only religion recognised and admitted within the Empire......The connection created between the Church and the Empire in the fourth century explains how particular and intricate connections were established in the administration of justice. Constantine allowed litigants to choose (in a joint agreement) to be judged by the bishop rather than the lay judge and governor of the province."

2.5 Evaluation and Summary

In essence, freedom of worship was not only granted to Christians with Constantine's victory in 312, but the entire Roman Empire and society was revamped to bear a Christian appearance. Tamara Herzog in her book, A Short History of European Law © 2018 Harvard University Press sums it up quite succinctly at p.34 where she remarked:

> "In 312 Constantine recognized Christianity as one of the permissible religions, and in 383 Theodosius I declared Christianity the official religion of the empire. The combining of Christianity with the Roman Empire produced an earthquake. It shook some of the basic foundations of Roman law, and once the seismic activity was over, what emerged was a new system. This system no longer linked law with citizenship. Nor did law become territorial…In theory, it united all Christians, regardless of their origin or location…both Christianity and Roman law were introduced across Europe."

Constantine eventually emerged the sole emperor of the unified Roman Empire after going to battle against Licinius who was the sole emperor of the Eastern axis of the empire in 324.[85] While his conversion to Christianity led to Christianity becoming a world religion[86] it was actually Emperor Theodosius I who "in 383 declared Christianity the official religion"[87] of the entire Roman Empire.[88] The discussion in How Christianity Became A World Religion the next chapter will address the harm and evil implication of forcefully converting people whose hearts and consciences have not been convicted to embrace the Christian message of salvation and faith into the Christian faith and religion.

---

[85]   Potter, David, Constantine the Emperor p.2

[86]   Ibid. p.1.

[87]   Herzog, Tamara, A Short History of European Law, pp.34.

[88]   Ibid.

3

EMPEROR JUSTINIAN I'S LAW OF FORCEFUL CONVERSION TO CHRISTIANITY AND ITS RELIGIOUS NATIONALISTIC EFFECTS

"....the great moral decisions of humanity are subordinated to decisions taken one after another by institutional agencies....Once the truth is denied to human beings, it is pure illusion to try to set them free. Truth and freedom either go together hand in hand or together they perish in misery."[89]

3.1 The Legalised Conversion of Pagans

From the time of Constantine's clear demonstration of his Christian conversion in AD312 and the Edict of Milan in AD313 in which Christians were granted freedom of worship to the freeing of slaves from tyrants in AD314, the Roman Empire under subsequent emperors for several hundreds of years had Christian emperors. But the climax of the Roman Empire's becoming an absolute Christian empire albeit by forceful conversion of pagans came with the reign of Justinian I who reigned for 37 years from 527 to 565. Herzog in her book: A Short

---

[89]   John Paul II, Encyclical Letter of John Paul II, Fides et Ratio, On the Relationship between Faith and Reason © 1998, Libreria Editrice Vaticana, Citta del Vaticano Published by Pauline Books and Media Boston. P.111

History of European Law already quoted at p.40 stated that under Justinian reign as emperor "pagans were forcefully converted."

Justinian took great strides in ensuring that the Roman Empire was an absolute Christian nation by making laws that forced pagans to convert to Christianity by denying them public jobs. He is known to have justified these actions by stating that:

> "It is right that those who do not worship God correctly should be deprived of worldly advantages too."[90]

In 529 Justinian I published a legal code which effectively ended the previous 1000 years of Roman law[91] by creating:

> "what became known as the Code of Justinian – the Corpus Juris Civilis – part of the authoritative statement of Roman law that was gradually accepted throughout Western Europe."[92]

In their account of English Law for instance, Frederic William Maitland and Francis C. Montague in their book: A Sketch of English Legal History Edited with Notes and Appendices by James F Colby © 1998, 2010 The Lawbook Exchange Ltd. at pp.3-4 stated thus:

> "The First English Code. About the year 600, Aethelbert, King of Kentings, by the counsel of his wise men, caused the laws of his people to be set down in writing. He had just received the Christian faith at the hands of Roman missionaries, and it was in the imitation of the Romans that he and his folk desired to have written laws. His reign overlaps the reign of Justinian, and perhaps he had heard how in the far east the Roman Emperor had been legislating on a magnificent scale. English law begins to speak just when Roman law has spoken what will, in a

---

[90] Galli, Mark and Olsen, Ted, 131 Christians Everyone Should Know © 2000 Christianity Today, Inc. p.313.

[91] Padoa – Schiopa, Antonio, A History of Law in Europe Translated by Caterina Fitzgerald Cambridge University Press © 2017.

[92] Ibid as in footnote 89 above.

certain sense, be its final words. On the Continent of Europe the same thing had been happening."

While Justinian I might have had good intentions in his legal actions to make all peoples under the Roman Empire Christians during his reign, his good intentions could not actually have produced godly results as people might have simply professed to be Christians outwardly for fear of execution or other unpleasant consequences without a heart that was changed and convicted by the Holy Spirit and faith in God.

3.2 The Biblical Example of Conversion

The examples in the Bible about Christian conversion from the time of Jesus Christ to the time of the apostles' ministries reveal that people made up their minds to become followers of Jesus Christ or Christians. They were not forced to do so:

Holy Bible, Mark 3:7-8; 13-15:

> "Jesus went out to the lake with his disciples, and a large crowd followed him. They came from all over Galilee, Judea, Jerusalem, Idumea, from east of the Jordan River, and even from as far north as Tyre and Sidon. The news about his miracles had spread far and wide, and vast numbers of people came to see him...Afterward Jesus went up on a mountain and called out those he wanted to go with him. And they came to him. Then he appointed twelve of them and called them his apostles. They were to accompany him, and he would send them out to preach,"

Clearly Jesus did not seek to force people to follow him as the above passage of scripture shows. The disciples or apostles as they were later known after the ascension of Jesus Christ to heaven (Luke 24:50-52) did not also force people to be converted to Christianity. They simply preached and those who heard and were convicted at heart to change their lifestyle simply confessed that they believed their message and would follow Jesus Christ.

Holy Bible, Acts 2:36-38; 41:

"So let everyone in Israel know for certain that God has made this Jesus, whom you crucified, to be both Lord and Messiah!" Peter's words pierced their hearts, and they said to him and to the other apostles, "Brothers, what should we do? Peter replied, "Each of you must repent of your sins and turn to God, and be baptized in the name of Jesus Christ for the forgiveness of your sins…Those who believed what Peter said were baptized and added to the Church that day – about 3,000 in all."

Conversion in Christianity from these examples from the Bible shows that it is a matter of irresistible conviction in the heart.

The case of Emperor Constantine also revealed a conviction from his heart backed by his vision of the sign in the sky for which he was instructed to inscribe on the shields of his soldiers for victory. Forceful conviction cannot convince the heart as those forced could only be consenting out of fear and not a desire to be converted. Hence what happened in the sixth century as discussed under Emperor Justinian quite certainly had led to some of the catalogues of heinous acts committed by some Christian leaders and people who professed Christianity throughout the last one thousand five years and counting without a spiritual regeneration that transformed the heart.

3.3 The Church and the Roman Empire

"Great was the turmoil and many the monstrous crimes committed in the name of Christ in the wake of the Reformation in Europe. Religious passions quickly passed into political conflict."[93]

The supernatural experience and conversion of Emperor Constantine 1 often referred to as Constantine the Great as discussed in chapter two, confirmed the truth of God's word in Psalm 22:28 of the Holy Bible, quoted in the opening of this chapter. God is the King of kings and ruler of the nations and every man or woman who is ruling any nation or kingdom on earth is simply holding fort for the duration of his life on

---

[93] See Peace At Augsburg https://www.christianity.com/church/church-history/timeline/1501-1600/peace-at-augsburg-11629989.html

earth, since man cannot live forever and God is eternal. The problem we have in the world today is that those who are leaders are trying to lead without depending on God for guidance and direction. We shall see this in the Church when divisions began to split the unity of the Church as some of the Church priests felt too important by the authority vested on them or by the authority they appropriated upon themselves to seek the guidance of God in their leaderships' roles or to give due diligence to what members of their congregation, being part of the body of Christ and bearers of the Holy Spirit of God were telling them.

While the spread of Christianity to the nations of the world cannot be accurately accounted for with specific dates because the disciples of Jesus Christ as far back as the first century AD sought to fulfil his command to preach the gospel to every nation on earth[94], it is sometimes possible in some cases to account for how the Christian faith came to some nations of the world with specific dates based on the missionary works of either the Catholic Church or the Protestant Christian Churches such as the Anglican Communion. The account of the first century missionary works of the disciples in the Holy Bible specifically in many cases mention the names and places where the apostles went to preach the gospel and those they converted to Christianity. For instance, we read that by angelic instruction, Philip, one of the disciples of Jesus Christ left Jerusalem and the territory of Israel through Gaza to meet a man from Ethiopia, who was of great standing because of his position under Queen Candace of Ethiopia. Philip preached Jesus Christ to him referred to as an Ethiopian eunuch and converted him to Christianity as well as baptising him.[95] We see in the account of Acts of the Apostles that Peter, the leading disciple of Jesus Christ by the witness of the Holy Spirit of God left where he was in Joppa for Caesarea to visit Cornelius, a non Jewish man otherwise known as a gentile and preached the gospel to Cornelius and members of his household and friends until they received salvation and became Christians.[96] Through the epistles of Paul, Peter, John etc. in the New Testament of the Holy Bible, we can read that

---

[94]   See Jesus' great commission to the disciples and indeed all who will believe his gospel in the Holy Bible, Matthew 28:18-20: http://biblehub.com/esv/matthew/28.htm

[95]   See the story of Philip and the Ethiopian Eunuch in the Holy Bible, Acts 8:26-39: http://biblehub.com/esv/acts/8.htm

[96]   See Cornelius vision, Peter's trance and his journey from Joppa to Caesarea all within the coastal line of Israel in the Holy Bible, Acts 10:1-48:
http://biblehub.com/esv/acts/10.htm

the disciples of Jesus Christ, especially, Peter, John and then Paul who became known as the apostles travelled widely in Europe especially across Italy, Greece, Cyprus and Turkey, and since words travel, there is no doubt that those they ministered to and converted went on to minister and convert others in different parts of the world, so indeed, the gospel had spread across the world before the legalisation of Christianity in the fourth century. So what the legalisation of Christianity did that was of benefit to the Christian Church in the world during the Roman Empire in the fourth century was the sponsorship of the missionary and Christian works with the resources and support of the State. Unlike before then when the disciples and believers struggled to travel and had to preach the gospel with trepidation, the legalisation of Christianity changed all that.

However, with an African in the person of Pope Miltiades crowned as the human spiritual leader of the world while Emperor Constantine the Great, reigned as a political ruler of the world, the first test of Pope Miltiades's spiritual authority and capability to dispense divine justice fairly as a Christian Spiritual leader came when divisions began to emerge in the Church. These divisions arose both as a result of theological and doctrinal differences among the priests and the Christian flocks. The differences eventually led to multiplicity of Christian denominations which caused disunity and aroused distrust and all forms of rivalries that were contrary to the teachings of love one another by Jesus Christ.

3.4 The Strain of Divisions in the Church

The prominence and dominance of the Church following the conversion of Constantine and the legalisation of Christianity as the religion of the Roman Empire was punctuated by disputes among the priests of the Catholic Church as well as the rank and file of the church because of what had happened during the great persecution under Emperor Diocletian from AD 303, which was almost ten years before the conversion of Emperor Constantine. According to The Oxford Dictionary of the Christian Church Edited by F.L. Cross and E.A. Livingstone © 1958, 1974 Oxford University Press p. 404 "It was in 303, that the Great Persecution broke out. Diocletian seems to have been instigated to it mainly through pressure from Galerius."

However, before the Diocletianic great persecution of Christians in 303, there had been several persecutions such as that which was perpetrated by Emperor Nero and then by Emperor Decius who carried out also persecutions of Christians in AD 250. On each occasion when Christians were subjected to persecutions, the option for freedom from persecution as was stated in the case of Bishop Polycarp of Smyrna was to deny the Christian Saviour Jesus Christ and renouncement of the Christian faith, followed by offering of sacrifices to the Roman gods. And on each occasion, some Christians took the option of renouncing their faith and escaping persecution. But those who would not bend to the oppressors who wanted them to renounce their Christian faith survived by divine protection or were martyred.

So the initial cracks leading to divisions in the Church were manifested when a Roman Priest of the Catholic Church known as Novatian opposed Pope Cornelius in AD 251 because he readmitted Christians who had renounced their faith and some who went further to perform ritual sacrifices to pagan gods under the persecution directed at them by Emperor Decius in AD 250. Novatian's opposition to Pope Cornelius made the pope to convene a synod in AD 251 which excommunicated him from the Catholic Church for heresy. But Novatian had a number of followers referred to as Novatianists, so he went on to form his own church until Emperor Valerian I martyred him. Besides his opposition to the acceptance of those who returned to the Christian faith after denying it, Novatian and his followers further opposed second marriages in the Church. They called themselves the purists while referring to the Catholic Church as corrupt.[97]

3.5 The Religious Stance of the Donatists and the Circumcellions

Whenever it is said that Novatian and his followers, the Novatianists, cracked the unity of the early church by their disagreements with Pope Cornelius, it is also said that Donatus Magnus and his followers, who became known as the Donatists split the church along with their associates, the Circumcellions. This was how the split between the

---

[97]   See Novatian in the Online Free Encyclopedia Britannica: http://www.britannica.com/ EBchecked/topic/421047/Novatian

Catholic Church and the Donatists came about. Following some edicts in AD 303 rescinding the legal rights of Christians and the demand for Christians to comply with traditional Roman religious practices as well as the later edicts targeted at the clergy with order for all inhabitants to sacrifice to the Roman gods, Christianity was banned because it was then against Roman law.[98] However, some Christians stood their grounds and remained committed to the Christian faith even in the face of the great persecution that followed. Among those who maintained their faith, in spite of the persecution, some were martyred while others simply survived the persecution without denying their faith. The Christians who stood their ground and did not renounce their faith in Christ, in the face of the great persecution by Emperor Diocletian included members of the African Church that were led by Donatus from which the name of the group Donatists originated.[99] When Emperor Diocletian abdicated his position as a Roman Emperor in AD 305, the persecution came to a natural end and the Christians who had stood their ground and did not renounce their faith felt a sense of triumph over the evil Emperor Diocletian and his persecutors.

Within the seven years that followed, Emperor Constantine the Great declared freedom for Christians in AD312 and subsequently proclaimed the Edict of Milan in AD 313 which granted both freedom of worship and legal protection to Christians throughout the Roman Empire as discussed earlier. At this point, some of the priests and Christians who had renounced their faith during the great persecution repented of their apostasy and returned back to the Church. This the Donatists found unacceptable.[100] While those who had not denied Christ in the face of the persecution frowned at the manner of admission of the backslidden priests and backslidden Christians, who they considered to have committed apostasy, their disappointment was exacerbated by the appointment of a priest called Caecilian[101], who was one of the priests who cooperated with the Roman persecutors, as their Bishop – Bishop of Carthage[102] in AD 311/312. The Donatists found the appointment

---

[98]   See footnote 55 above.

[99]   See Donatism in The Oxford Dictionary of the Christian Church Edited by F.L. Cross and E.A. Livingstone © 1957, 1974 Oxford University Press p.419

[100]   Ibid.

[101]   Ibid.

[102]   Carthage is now a suburb of Tunis in Tunisia

of Caecilian as the Bishop of Carthage unacceptable to them so they resisted Caecilian as Bishop over them. In his place they consecrated and recognised Majorinus[103] who was later succeeded by Donatus as Bishop of Carthage, because he was one of those, whom they knew as a faithful priest that had not cooperated with the Roman persecutors during the great persecution. Consequently, there were two Bishops of Carthage at the time. The one appointed by Pope Miltiades and the one appointed by the sect known as the Donatists. In AD 315, Bishop Majorinus died and Donatus Magnus the leader of the Donatists, who were named after him, was made Bishop of Carthage as a parallel bishop to the Pope Miltiades' appointee. Bishop Donatus Magnus maintained the hard line stance of not recognising the absorption of the priests who had committed apostasy during the great persecution.[104] So those who were in sympathy with these priests as well as those Christian believers with the same history had to build their own churches and run their own services different from those led by Donatus Magnus as Bishop.[105] As if the problem arising out of the Donatists split from the Church was not enough, another sect known as the Circumcellions[106] which were closely associated with the Donatists went about advocating cancellation of debts and condemning ownership of property and slavery. But the Circumcellions were feeding on those they were influencing to hold onto their beliefs. Furthermore, they provoked martyrdom upon themselves by assaulting Roman legionaries or armed travellers with wooden clubs who in turn reacted by killing them. Circumcellions who operated about one thousand seven hundred years ago usually shouted "Laudate Deum!" – Praise God! - when they were attacking Roman legionaries or armed travellers with clubs in order to provoke a reaction that led to death, which they assumed was martyrdom.[107] Today, in the twenty-first century, Laudate Deum! Praise the Lord (Praise God) is an expression that is proclaimed with joy and peace with no hint of violence in any Christian gathering. In fact, the expression attracts people's attention among Christians to hear a thing of joy, a good testimony. Christianity has become largely a religion of peace

---

[103] See History of the Early Church: http://earlychurch.com/donatists.php

[104] See a good scholarly article entitled - Early Christian History; Controversies: Donatism. http://www.earlychristianhistory.info/donatus.html

[105] Ibid.

[106] See Circumcellions in the Oxford Dictionary of the Christian Church Edited by F.L. Cross and E.A. Livingstone © 1957, 1974 Oxford University Press. p.294

[107] Ibid.

that abhors violence in line with the precepts of the Holy Bible. However, the same cannot be said of most of the other popular religions of the world. For example, the expression which Muslims hold in reverence such as "Allahu Akbar"[108] meaning "God is the greatest" that they utter during their prayers; and especially when "Muslim Hajj Pilgrims touch the Kaaba's wall and pray at the Grand Mosque in Mecca, Saudi Arabia"[109] is also heard from the lips of Islamic terrorists and extremists who utter it before they kill their innocent victims. They do that despite the Holy Quran instructing them to live in peace with their neighbours. This came out clearly in the reasoning and decision of the Supreme Court of the Islamic Republic of Pakistan which will be discussed in one of the subsequent chapters of this book. The point is violence can be traced and attributed to virtually every religion that has existed in human history. Buddhism which people associate with peace and non-violence was recently seen to be a violent religion when the Buddhists in Myanmar forced the Rohingya Muslims out of Myanmar.[110] What is noteworthy among the many issues which arose out of this sad incident is the overt expression of religious nationalism by some of the Buddhists majority in Myanmar.

One such expression was "To be Burmese is to Buddhist."[111] In other words, being born in Burma (Myanmar) does not confer citizenship except if the person was a Buddhist or becomes a Buddhist. These instances are evidence of the widely held view by religious scholars that religion can be used to promote violence or to promote peace.

With the forceful conversion of people whose hearts have not been touched by the Holy Spirit of the Christian faith as was the case in the Acts of the Apostles chapter 2:37-38 where it is stated thus:

> "Peter's words pierced their hearts, and they said to him
> and to the other apostles, "Brothers, what shall we do?"

---

[108] Beydoun, Khaled, "The perils of saying 'Allahu Akbar' in public, Global Opinion, The Washington Post, August 25, 2018.

[109] Ibid.

[110] BBC Asia: "Myanmar Rohingya: What you need to know about the crisis." See https://www.bbc.co.uk/news/world-asia-41566561

[111] Borchert, Thomas, Edited Theravada Buddhism in Colonial Contexts © 2020 Routledge 1st Edition, Chapter 2 With Juliane Schober "To be Burmese is to be Buddhist" "Formations of Buddhist Modernity in Colonial Burma 1. P.21.

Peter replied, "Each of you must repent of your sins and turn to God, and be baptized in the name of Jesus Christ for the forgiveness of your sins. Then you will receive the gift of the Holy Spirit"[112]

Men and women whose hearts were not in tune with the Christian God filled the church and substituted the leading of the Spirit of the God[113] of the Christians with human reasoning and in some cases outright wickedness, so controversies and divisions prevailed in the church. The Roman Empire also crumbled with the divisions and disagreements that tore the church apart.

But these issues were to be embedded in the Christian religion in such a way that seems to mark those who claim to be Christians by religious induction and those who are Christians by spiritual transformation and faith in the Word of God. However, the controversies and divisions appeared to have been the outcome of the freedom of worship which seemed to have taken people's focus away from God to theological views and doctrines that appeal to them or offend them.

3.6 Athanasius and the Theological Dispute with Arius

During the unfortunate era of the great persecution of Christians, especially, between the first century and early fourth century, the worst that happened to Christians who refused to renounce their faith by denying that Jesus Christ was their Lord and Saviour was martyrdom. While martyrdom was cruel and barbaric, those Christians who were faithful were not afraid of such death. They believed they were going to meet their creator and enjoy eternal life in heaven. They had already been admonished not to fear such suffering:

"Do not fear what you are about to suffer. Behold, the devil is about to throw some of you into prison, that you may be tested...Be faithful unto death, and I will give you the crown of life."[114]

---

[112] Holy Bible, Acts 2:37-38 (New Living Translation © 1957, 1974)

[113] The Holy Bible says Jesus Christ told his disciples that: "When the Spirit of truth comes, he will guide you into all truths..." John 16:13 (New Living Translation © 1996, 2004, 2007 by Tynedale House Foundation).

[114] See Holy Bible, Revelation 2:10: http://biblehub.com/esv/revelation/2.htm

However, with the freedom of religious worship granted to Christians by Constantine I in AD312 and the declaration of Christianity as the official religion of the Roman Empire in AD 383 by Theodosius I, came some priests and preachers who felt that they could use their new found freedom to score points against others and create a niche for their honour. One of such persons was a theologian called Arius.[115] He was involved in the leadership of one of the local churches in Alexandria in Egypt in Africa. But in AD 319, he started spreading a heresy about the divinity of Jesus Christ and was in conflict with Alexander, the Bishop of Alexandria in Egypt.[116] While the theological position that Arius took and preached was gradually becoming an acceptable view at the time, even at the top of the Catholic Church hierarchy, Athanasius[117], a well-respected theologian who was a deacon and secretary to Bishop Alexander of Alexandria in Egypt and later a Bishop of Alexandria as well took steps to correct Arius' heresy and the theological implications it bore. Athanasius stated that it was not just a matter of the Father and the Son, Jesus Christ being co-equal and co-eternal, but that it was indeed a matter of the Father, Son and Holy Spirit, being co-equal and co-eternal.[118] This truth later brought about Athanasius being highly regarded across the Catholic Church, the Orthodox Church, the Lutheran Church, the Anglican Communion etc. to the extent that Athanasius stands as the father of Canon[119] in the Christian faith. As neither darkness nor the deception of man can perpetually hinder the truth from being eventually known the truth that Athanasius taught to correct Arius's heresy eventually prevailed and the old Latin maxim found its bearings - vincit veritas – the truth always conquers.

However, the controversies continue and more of this shall be discussed in chapter four.

---

[115] Arius (c.250 – c.336), said to be an African of Libyan and known "as a champion of subordinationist teaching about the Person of Christ." See The Oxford Dictionary of the Christian Church Second Edition Edited by F.L. Cross and E.A Livingstone, Oxford University Press © 1958, 1974.p.87; See also Arianism at p.83.

[116] Ibid.

[117] Athanasius, St. (c.296-373) Bishop of Alexandria. His education, position and refusal to compromise with Arianism detailed under his name in the Oxford Dictionary of the Christian Church already quoted at p.101.

[118] Ibid.

[119] Ibid.

3.7 Evaluation and Summary

Critical to Justinian I's legalisation of Christianity in the Roman Empire as the sole religion to be professed by all is the fact that intentions and unintended consequences manifest in conflict when actions aimed at suppressing the will of others are thrust on people under duress. Justinian I started an act of religious nationalism in Christianity that turned out to be spiritually and morally Justinian's Law of Forceful Conversion detrimental to pure Christianity. Perhaps more harmful is the fact Islam went on start to replicate an act of religious nationalism from the seventh century in the form of jihad that in some cases had a far more detrimental effect than Emperor Justinian I's religious nationalistic act of legalising Christianity and consequently forcing people to convert. In chapter 5 the discussion about religious nationalism in Islam and its effect is explored.

4

THEOLOGICAL CONTROVERSIES: HERESY, CONFLICT AND THE FOUR REFORMERS

"we are aided by the grace of God, through Christ, not only to know, but to do what is right, in each single act, so that without grace we are unable to have, think, speak, or do anything pertaining to piety."[120] – Excerpt from The 214 African Bishops Letter in AD417 to Pope Zosimus on the excommunication of Pelagius and Celestius for the heresy of undermining Christ's work of divine grace and salvation.[121]

"Acquitting the guilty and condemning the innocent – the LORD detests them both."[122]

"For if we would judge ourselves, we should not be judged."[123]

---

[120] See White, James, Catholic Legends and How They get started: An Example April 11, 2000 https://www.aomin.org/aoblog/roman-catholicism/catholic-legends-get-started-example/; see also Council of 214 African Bishops: http://www.biblicalcatholic.com/apologetics/num17.htm

[121] Ibid

[122] See Holy Bible, Proverbs 17:15: http://biblehub.com/niv/proverbs/17.htm

[123] See Holy Bible, 1 Corinthians 11:31: http://biblehub.com/kjv/1_corinthians/11.htm

4.1 Heresy and Controversies

In the previous chapter the discussion showed how the Catholic Church survived three major heretical controversies generated by some influential preachers of the third and fourth centuries namely: Novatianism by Novatian; Donatism by Donatus Magnus; and Arianism by Arius. Whereas the heresies of the Novatians and the Donatists were dealt with and seemingly brought to an end by the respective Popes and the various synods that addressed the matter, the case of the Arian heresy however went on to lay a foundation for unjust verdicts against the innocent when Athanasius was exiled several times for his position against the Arianians.

The various conflicts arising from doctrinal and theological disputes that followed the Arian controversy were resolved by the Catholic Church with the lessons that should have been learned from the previous incidents of heretical doctrines, but what seemed to be an apparent politics of power and affiliations played out.[124]

4.2 Pelagius[125] and the Pelagian[126] Controversy

Another controversy that rocked the Catholic Church in the fourth and early fifth centuries was what was known as the Pelagian controversy. It got its name from a man called Pelagius[127]. By various accounts, Pelagius lived between AD 354 and AD 418. A number of accounts say he was from Britain. He went to Rome around AD 380 and was well known to have lived there, until Rome fell to Visigoth Alaric in AD

---

[124] See entries on Arianism and Arius as well as Athanasius in The Oxford Dictionary of the Christian Church already quoted at pp: 83, 87, 100, and 107.

[125] See entry on Pelagianism in the Oxford Dictionary of the Christian Church already quoted at pp. 1058-59. It is stated therein that Pelagius was a British "theologian and exegete who taught in Rome in the late 4ᵗʰ and early 5ᵗʰ cents."

[126] Ibid.

[127] In addition to what has been stated above these accounts of Pelagius by various writers does crystallise things further see "Pelagius" in the Free Encyclopedia Britannica: http://www.britannica.com/EBchecked/topic/449072/Pelagius; See "St. Augustine, Pelagianism, and the Holy See. "Rome has spoken; the case is closed" (Sermon 131:10): http://www.biblicalcatholic.com/apologetics/num16.htm; and see Dr James White's article "Catholic Legends And How They Get Started: An Example": https://www.aomin.org/aoblog/roman-catholicism/catholic-legends-get-started-example/

410.[128] He was an influential monk and theologian but was not a priest. In the course of his stay in Rome, Pelagius gained popularity and had adherents, to the extent that a lawyer who was called Celestius became his disciple. During the years he lived in Rome in the fifth century as a monk and theologian, he gained the good reputation of being a man of sanctity.[129] However, from being a good man who "achieved a virtuous repute for sanctity",[130] Pelagius went on to deny the cardinal Christian doctrines that underlies the faith. He denied that there was predestination and went on to teach that the original sin of Adam and his fall did not affect the will of man to choose between good and evil. Pelagius taught that people do not sin because they cannot resist sin but that they do so because they choose to sin. Pelagius viewed the doctrine of divine grace as a mere human excuse for sin. He rejected the idea of sin on grounds of human weakness occasioned by the imputed sin in man following the fall of Adam, in the Garden of Eden[131] as an act of "moral laxity."[132] Since it was not possible for man to be reconciled to God by man's own good works except through the accomplished work of Jesus Christ achieved by his death and resurrection, the teachings of Pelagius reduced the grace made available to Christians by Jesus Christ's death and resurrection which is the crux of the Christian faith to be of little or no effect. Jesus Christ himself made clear that he was the way to God the Father and therefore making it obvious that man cannot be reconciled to God any other way:

> "Jesus told him, "I am the way, the truth, and the life. No one can come to the Father except through me."[133]

Writing to the Ephesians and invariably to every believer in the Christian Faith, the apostle Paul went on to say:

---

[128] See the Editors write-up on "Pelagius" in the free Encyclopedia Britannica: http://www. britannica.com/EBchecked/topic/449072/Pelagius

[129] See "St. Augustine, Pelagianism, and the Holy See "Rome has spoken; the case is closed." (Sermon 131:10)": http://www.biblicalcatholic.com/apologetics/num16.htm

[130] Ibid.

[131] The story of the Garden of Eden and the fall of the first man and first woman - Adam and Eve – is in the Holy Bible, Genesis chapters 2 verse 8 through chapter 3:24. See http://biblehub.com/nasb/genesis/2.htm

[132] See Editors write-up on Pelagius http://www.britannica.com/EBchecked/topic/449072/Pelagius

[133] John 14:6, Holy Bible, New Living Translation.

"For by grace you have been saved through faith; and that not of yourselves, it is the gift of God; not as a result of works, so that no one may boast."[134]

It follows therefore that there is no place to lay claim that man by himself without the grace of God through Jesus Christ, can do good works and be saved by it in God's eyes. Isaiah a major prophet of the Old Testament in the Holy Bible realised the unrealistic prospects of man's good works in meeting God's standards and satisfying God and remarked thus:

"For all of us have become like one who is unclean, And all our righteous deeds are like a filthy garment; And all of us wither like a leaf. And our iniquities, like the wind, take us away."[135]

So the teaching which Pelagius propagated was proven to be heresy because it lacked Biblical basis. However, "when Rome was menaced by Goths, Pelagius and Celestius left Italy for Africa."[136]

4.3 St. Augustine, the African Bishops and the Condemnation of Pelagius, Celestius and Pelagianism

Between AD 410 and 411, Pelagius and his protégé Celestius stayed in Carthage (Tunis) in Tunisia and later went to Egypt. While in Africa they carried on teaching the doctrine of human 'perfectibility' and the denial of grace of God to the spiritual and theological irritation of the African Bishops of the fifth century which included one of the Fathers of the Church, Saint Augustine of Hippo. Pelagius and Celestius' teachings in Africa on human nature and man's freewill and their denial of the role of God's divine grace in our ability to do good and resist evil, was diametrically opposed to Saint Augustine's own teachings on divine grace. For in the "Confessions of Saint Augustine" and in his prayer for self discipline otherwise continence, he "beseeched God to grant whatever grace the divine will

---

[134]   See Holy Bible, Ephesians 2:8-9: http://biblehub.com/nasb/ephesians/2.htm

[135]   See Holy Bible, Isaiah 64:6: http://biblehub.com/nasb/isaiah/64.htm

[136]   See Pelagianism in The Oxford Dictionary of the Christian Church as already quoted at p.1058.

determined."[137] While Saint Augustine and other African Bishops who were abreast of the teachings of Pelagius and Celestius were disenchanted at the heresy they were spreading, Pelagius left Africa and went to Palestine where he continued to spread his heresy of the perfect nature of man and the freewill, and the human ability to do good or evil without the necessity of God's divine grace. But, while Pelagius was at liberty teaching his heretical doctrine, his disciple Celestius was accused of heresy by a deacon of Milan known as Paulinus in AD 411 and was duly condemned and excommunicated that year. He initially appealed against this to the Pope, the Bishop of Rome, but failed to successfully pursue the appeal as he rather opted to go to Ephesus in the hope of obtaining the priesthood there.[138] As for Pelagius, his liberty to spread this heresy which was being embraced by some in the Church at the time was brought to a halt albeit momentarily. How Pelagius and Pelagianism was dealt with by the Catholic Church was accounted for in a historically packed articled in defence of Catholicism entitled: "St. Augustine, Pelagianism, and the Holy See. "Rome has spoken; the case is closed." (Sermon 131:10).[139] It is stated that around AD 414, St Jerome, one of the Catholics Church Fathers of all time, "wrote a letter to Ctesiphon against Pelagius, promising a fuller treatise, which he commenced in July 415."[140] At the same time around AD 414, St. Augustine also "wrote a letter against the Sicilian Pelagians, and in 415 the treatise De natura et gratia (on nature and grace), addressed to Timasius and Jacobus, two young men of good family, who were much troubled by the book ascribed to Pelagius."[141] It is further stated in this said article which is historically in-depth that a Spanish priest by the name of Paulus Orosius, who was a disciple of St. Augustine, and was sent by him to St Jerome in Bethlehem for further learning, that at the behest of John the Bishop of Jerusalem, Orosius was given the opportunity to tell what he knew about Pelagius and the heresy linked with his teachings. Accordingly, Orosius related his knowledge and experience of the matter before Bishop John thus:

---

[137] See the write-up of the Editors of Encyclopedia Britannica on Pelagius and the discussion of the Confessions of Saint Augustine therein: http://www.britannica.com/EBchecked/topic/449072/Pelagius

[138] See "Pelagius and Celestius teach heresy" in St. Augustine, Pelagianism, and the Holy See, "Rome has spoken, the case is closed." At: http://www.biblicalcatholic.com/apologetics/num16.htm

[139] St. Augustine, Pelagianism, and the Holy See "Rome has spoken; the case is closed" (Sermon 131:10) see: http://www.biblicalcatholic.com/apologetics/num16.htm

[140] See Pelagians opposed by Augustine and Jerome, ibid.

[141] Ibid. Translation in bracket is mine.

"I was in retirement in Bethlehem, having been sent by my Father Augustine that I might learn the fear of God sitting at the feet of Jerome; from thence I came at your bidding to Jerusalem. I sat down with you in the assembly at the command of the Bishop John. Thereupon with one accord you demanded of my littleness to relate faithfully and simply whatever had been done to my knowledge in Africa as to this heresy sown by Pelagius and Celestius. I exposed shortly, as best I could, how Celestius, who was then intending to creep into the order of the priesthood, was at Carthage, before many bishops in judgement, exposed, heard, convicted, that he confessed, was excommunicated, fled from Africa; and how the blessed Augustine had most fully answered the book of Pelagius, at the request of the heretic's own disciples (viz. Timasius and Jacobus); and that I had in my hands a letter of the said bishop, which he had lately sent into Sicily, in which he mentions many of the heretic's views. You ordered me to read the letter, and I read it.

"Upon this John the bishop asked for Pelagius to be introduced. You gave him your consent, both for the reverence due to the bishop, and because the thing was itself good, for you thought he would be more rightly refuted in the bishop's presence. When Pelagius was admitted, you inquired of him unanimously whether he acknowledged that he had taught the doctrines which Bishop Augustine had confuted. He replied at once: 'And what is Augustine to me?' And when all cried out that a man who blasphemed against a bishop by whose mouth God had vouchsafed to heal the unity of Africa (viz. by the conversion of the Donatists) ought to be expelled not only from that assembly but from the whole Church, Bishop John thereupon told him to sit down, he a layman in the midst of the priests, he accused of manifest heresy in the midst of Catholics, and then said: 'I am Augustine, 'forsooth, that assuming his person he might the more easily pardon the wrongs which he took to himself, and so soothe the minds of his sorrowing audience. After making Pelagius acknowledge his doctrine, I continued:

"This is what the African Synod condemned in Celestius; this is what Bishop Augustine rejected in his writings as you heard; this is condemned by Pelagius in his own

writings by his present answer; this is condemned by
Jerome, whose words are awaited for by the whole west as
the dew upon the fleece...."[142]

Although Bishop John heard Orosius' oral presentation as a witness
and the evidence by way of the letter he brought from St Augustine,
which was collaborated by Jerome, he simply ordered Pelagius to sit
down and thereafter to be silent until the matter is decided. There was
no obvious rebuke from Bishop John to Pelagius save for the order that
he remain silence. He went on to order that the case-file be sent to
Bishop Innocent I, the Pope of Rome, to pass judgement on the case.
In a manner consistent with how the controversy of Arius which was
discussed in the previous chapter was handled by the Council of Rome,
and how Arianism was allowed to fester, Pelagianism was in a sense given
room to fester by Bishop John of Jerusalem, who overlooked the witness
statement presented to him by Orosius with the evidence from Augustine
and Jerome, respectively. Well, as it were, Bishop John did not decide
the case, so Pelagius and pelagianism remained a problem. Nevertheless,
the implication of Bishop John's deferred decision to Bishop Innocent I,
the Pope of Rome bore the potential to polarise the church then along
theological divisions with the possibility of leaving some outside the truth
and grace that Jesus Christ has made available to them by faith.

However, in no distant time from that incidence, two other bishops -
Heros of Arles and Lazarus of Aix - vexed by the heresy Pelagius was
spreading by his teaching, made a formal complaint against Pelagius
while in Palestine to Eulogius of Caesarea. And a synod of fourteen
bishops was convened to hear the case against Pelagius. But in a way that
seemed like an orchestrated act to spare Pelagius of condemnation, the
accusers were not present in December 415, to testify against Pelagius,
when the case was heard at Lydda (Diospolis). Furthermore, Pelagius
was presented with a written accusation in Latin to respond to and the
fourteen bishops who sat in the synod to decide the case spoke only
Greek and therefore depended on an interpreter to understand what was
being said and decide the case on that understanding. Pelagius seized the
opportunity orchestrated to acquit him by inexplicable circumstances
hinging on the illness of one of the accusers, for which the synod did not
postpone the trial, to not only deny the charge of heresy against him,

---

[142]   Ibid. See Pelagius tried at Jerusalem.

but went further to condemn it and lay blame at the feet of his protégé, Celestius.[143]

After his acquittal, Pelagius broke his silence to celebrate his position of right standing by writing a book "De libero arbitrio" – "In Defence of Freewill." While he was yet causing damage in the church with his heresy, Paulus Orosius who had returned to Africa with letters from Bishop Heros and Bishop Lazarus, made it known to the African Synod of sixty-eight bishops which met at Carthage in June 416[144] that Pelagius was still at liberty to do harm to the Church with his heresy.

Accordingly, the African Bishops after their deliberations at Carthage wrote a Synodal letter to Bishop Innocent I, Pope of Rome as thus:

> "We had come according to custom to the Church of Carthage, and a synod was held for various affairs, when our fellow - priest Orosius presented us with letters from our holy brothers and fellow-bishops Heros and Lazarus, which we enclose. These having been read, we perceive that Pelagius and Celestius were accused of being authors of a wicked error, which must be anathematized by all of us. Wherefore we asked that all which had been done with regard to Celestius here in Carthage about five years ago should be gone through. This having been read, as your Holiness can perceive from the acts which we append, although the decision is clear, by which so great a wound was shown to have been cut away from the Church by an Episcopal judgement, yet we thought it good by a common deliberation, that the authors of this persuasion (although it was said that this Celestius had arrived since then at the priesthood), unless they are openly anathematized in order that, if their salvation cannot, at least that those who may have been or may be deceived by them may be procured, when they know the sentence against them......(ut statutis

---

143   See Ibid – Pelagius Acquitted at Diospolis; See also an article by White, James, "Catholic Legends And How They Get Started: An Example, April 11, 2000, where Dr White quotes B.B. Warfield wrote concerning the history of the Pelagian Controversy, and especially of St Augustine's response to Zosimus, bishop of Rome: http://www.freerepublic.com/focus/f-religion/1689492/posts

144   See "Pelagius Acquitted at Diospolis" Ibid in footnote 132.

nostrae mediocritatis etiam apostolicae sedis adhibeatur auctoritas) for the preservation of the safety of many, and the correction of the perversity of some."[145]

In a concerted effort to stop Pelagius and Celestius from continuously spreading their erroneous teachings and in order to put an end to this heresy they stated:

> "For all must of necessity become more cautious when they see that the inventors of evil, at the relation of two synods, have been cut off by our sentence from ecclesiastical communion. Your charity will therefore do a double good. For you will obtain the grace of having preserved the canons, and the whole world will share your benefit.

> "We judge by the authority of Apostolic power (apostolici uigoris auctoritate) that Pelagius and Celestius be deprived of ecclesiastical communion, until they return to the faith out of the snares of the devil..."[146]

The African bishops intensified their charges against Pelagius and brought the pressure to bear upon the issue in their address to Pope Innocent I.

Following the letter of the sixty-eight African Bishops at the Council of Carthage, another sixty-one African Bishops which included St Augustine held a provincial council of Numidia at Milevis and also wrote a letter to Pope Innocent I exposing the heresy in the teachings and writings of Pelagius and Celestius. They implored Pope Innocent I in their letter to act swiftly against Pelagius and Celestius by telling him the dangers that those members with weak faith and understanding in the Church face with Pelagius and Celestius being at liberty to carry on their erroneous theological teachings and writings:

> "The authors of this most pernicious heresy are said to be Pelagius and Celestius, whom, indeed, we should prefer to be cured with the Church, rather than that they should be cut off from the Church, if no necessity compels this.

---

[145]   See "Sixty-Eight Bishops at Council of Carthage to Pope Innocent I" Ibid footnote 131 above.

[146]   Ibid.

One of them, Celestius, is even said to have arrived at the priesthood in Asia. Your Holiness is better informed by the Council of Carthage as to what was done against him a few years back. Pelagius, as the letters of some of our brethren say, is in Jerusalem, and is said to have deceived many there. Many more, however, who have been able to examine his views more closely, are fighting him on behalf of the Catholic Faith, but especially your holy son, our brother and fellow-priest, Jerome. But we consider that with the help of the mercy of our God, whom we pray to direct your counsels and to hear your prayers, those who hold such perverse and baneful opinions will more easily yield to the authority of your Holiness, which has been taken from the authority of the Holy Scriptures (auctoritati sanctitatis tuae, de sanctarum scripturarum auctoritate depromptae facilius...esse cessuros), so that we may be rather rejoiced by their correction than saddened by their destruction. But whatever they themselves may choose, your Reverence perceives that at least that those many must be cared for whom they may entangle in their nets if they should not submit straightforwardly. We write this to your Holiness from the Council of Numidia, imitating our fellow bishops of the Church and province of Carthage, whom we understand to have written of this affair to the Apostolic See which your Blessedness adorns."[147]

Pope Innocent I replied the African Bishops' letters in a letter dated January 27, 417, with the following answers and appreciation of their due regards and pious stance:

"For you decided that it was proper to refer to our judgement, knowing what is due to the Apostolic See, since all we who are set in this place, desire to follow the Apostle (Peter) from whom the very episcopate and whole authority of this name is derived. Following in his steps, we know how to condemn the evil and to approve the good. So also, you have by your sacerdotal office preserved the customs of the Fathers, and have not spurned that which they decreed

---

[147] Letter from the Sixty-One Bishops at Council of Milevis (Numidia) to Pope Innocent I. Ibid as in footnote 129.

by a divine and not human sentence, that whatsoever is done, even though it be in distant provinces, should not be ended without being brought to the knowledge of this See, [39] that by its authority the whole just pronouncement should be strengthened, and that from it all other Churches (like waters flowing from their natal source and flowing through the different regions of the world, the pure streams of one incorrupt head), should receive what they ought to enjoin, whom they ought to wash, and whom that water, worthy of pure bodies, should avoid as defiled with uncleansable filth."[148]

While Pope Innocent I took a firm stance in siding the decision of the African Bishops for the edification of the Church and condemned Pelagius and Celestius' heresy, the matter did not simply end with Pope Innocent I's decision to acquiesce the decision of the African Bishops. Because when error has gained root in the hearts of men and has occupied the place of truth, the spirit of the error will always seek to manifest itself, so that others may embrace it. This may be one reason why people repeat their mistakes as well as wrongdoings carried out as human weakness of the will for which Pelagius did not give due consideration in his estimation of man as a perfect being even without divine grace. Just as the scripture says:

"For God is not the author of confusion"

- Holy Bible, 1 Corinthians 14:33 (KJV).

It also says:

"But evil men and seducers shall wax worse and worse, deceiving, and being deceived."

- Holy Bible, 2 Timothy 3:13 (KJV).

That God is not the author of confusion does not mean the devil will not plant evil men in the Church to cause confusion. And so upon the death of Pope Innocent I, Pelagius and his disciple Celestius re-invented themselves to gain relevance by entreating Pope Zosimus the successor of

---

[148]   "The Answers of Pope Innocent to the African Bishops." Ibid.

Innocent I, to exonerate them from the heresy of pelagianism for which they were condemned and expelled out of the Catholic Church. And as if to prove that men are men even if they hold the high office of a pontiff that requires piety and decisions dictated by the Spirit of God; in a way that will make some people wonder whether indeed the Holy Spirit or in fact even the Spirit of Peter automatically rests upon anyone elected to the exalted Office of a Pope, Zosimus in his exalted position as pontiff, without due regards to the sanctity of the Church re-opened the case of Pelagius and Celestius following entreaties from Celestius who appeared before him to deny the charges for which Pelagius and him were condemned.

According to Warfield as quoted by White, while Pope Innocent I agreed with the African Bishops' decisions:

> "asserting the necessity of inward grace, rejected the Pelagian theory of infant baptism, and declared Pelagius and Coelestius excommunicated until they should return to orthodoxy. In about six weeks more he was dead: but Zosimus, his successor, was scarcely installed in his place before Coelestius appeared at Rome in person to plead his cause; while shortly afterwards letters arrived from Pelagius addressed to Innocent, and by an artful statement of his belief and a recommendation from Praylus, lately become bishop of Jerusalem in John's stead, attempting to enlist Rome in his favor. Zosimus, who appears to have been a Greek and therefore inclined to make little of the merits of this Western controversy, went over to Coelestius at once, upon his profession of willingness to anathematize all doctrines which the pontifical see had condemned or should condemn; and wrote a sharp and arrogant letter to Africa, proclaiming Coelestius "catholic," and requiring the Africans to appear within two months at Rome to prosecute their charges, or else to abandon them."[149]

Having set aside, his predecessor's decision to ex-communicate Pelagius and Celestius, Zosimus went further to display what could be clearly understood as his act of superiority over the African Bishops by summoning them to appear before him for prosecution of their charges

---

[149]   White, James, "Catholic Legends And How They Get Started: An Example." Ibid. footnote 129.

against Pelagius and Celestius or to abandon such charges indefinitely. His conduct did not only leave a sour taste about the person of Zosimus but also begs understanding as to whether he was operating by the Spirit of God or there was another spirit behind the conduct of someone in his position, who had attained the exalted and spiritually highly esteemed office of the Bishop of Rome and the Apostolic See as Pope of the Catholic Church?

But reasons precede every human conduct. It is either that a reason drives someone to act in a particular way or someone acted in a particular way because he could not see any reason for acting otherwise. Either way, reason has a role in every action or inaction of human conduct. For Pope Zosimus, the reason he acted the way he did almost immediately he assumed the office of Pope of the Catholic Church was as a result of his own inadequacies; as we shall see from White's article already quoted, he further stated:

> "It is difficult to understand Zosimus' action in this matter: neither of the confessions presented by the accused teachers ought to have deceived him, and if he was seizing the occasion to magnify the Roman see, his mistake was dreadful. Late in 417, or early in 418, the African bishops assembled at Carthage, in number more than two hundred and replied to Zosimus that they had decided that the sentence pronounced against Pelagius and Coelestius should remain in force until they should unequivocally acknowledge that "we are aided by the grace of God, through Christ, not only to know, but to do what is right, in each single act, so that without grace we are unable to have, think, speak, or do anything pertaining to piety.
>
> This firmness made Zosimus waver. He answered swellingly but timidly, declaring that he had maturely examined the matter, but it had not been his intention finally to acquit Coelestius; and now he had left all things in the condition in which they were before, he claimed the right of final judgement to himself. Matters were hastening to a conclusion, however, that would leave him no

opportunity to escape from the mortification of an entire change of front."[150]

So the matter of Pelagius, Celestius and the heresy of pelagianism was eventually put to rest, but after Pope Zosimus had been made to be seen as a pontiff who did not have the theological knowledge and spiritual maturity to discern between honesty and deception at the onset of his papacy. That over two hundred African bishops in their resolve informed him that they would sustain their decision to excommunicate Pelagius and Celestius until they realised that "we are aided by the grace of God, through Christ, not only to know, but to do what is right, in each single act..."[151] was an indictment of the Spirit by which Pope Zosimus was operating by, at least on the serious matter of dealing with heresy which as an overseer of the Catholic Church, he as Pope was expected to be attentive to. Pope Zosimus's initial decision to exonerate Pelagius and Celestius reveal a fundamental problem of disconnection between the decisions men of God make with human understanding without the guidance of the Holy Spirit and the crisis of truth that follows such decision through history. In this regard, the writing of Pope John Paul II provides some illumination. In his Encyclical Letter he stated thus:

> "...many of the problems of the contemporary world stem from a crisis of truth. "once the idea of a universal truth about the good, knowable by human reason, is lost, inevitably the notion of conscience also changes. Conscience is no longer considered in its prime reality as an act of a person's intelligence, the function of which is to apply the universal knowledge of the good in a specific situation and thus to express a judgment about the right conduct to be chosen here and now."[152]

One of the twentieth century's great Christian apologists, C.S. Lewis, remarked in his book, The Screw Tape Letters, that: "men are not angered by mere misfortune but by misfortune conceived as injury. And

---

[150]   White, James quotes B.B. Warfield, in his article "Catholic Legends And How They Get Started: An Example." Footnotes 113 and 114.

[151]   Ibid

[152]   John Paul II, Encyclical Letter of John Paul II, Fides Et Ratio, On the Relationship between Faith and Reason. Copyright (c) 1998, Libreria Editrice Vaticana, Citta del Vaticano. Published by Pauline Books & Media. P. 120.

the sense of injury depends on the feeling that a legitimate claim has been denied."[153]

Some of the problems of the Catholic Church that were to eventually give birth to Protestant Church were the tolerance of false doctrines such as Arianism and to some degree Pelagianism. Beyond toleration of false doctrines in the cases that were discussed above, the other issue is probably the tendency to exalt the person of the Pope beyond the level of his humanity as the incident of Pope Zosimus. While the Pope must be accorded the honour of his position he cannot take the place of Christ who is his Lord and Master, which is why Christ alone is to be "lifted high and so that he will draw men onto himself".[154]

The controversies certainly created cracks in the Catholic Church, splitting those who just want to follow the orders of the Pope and those who want to know God for themselves. The seed for protestantism was then sown and though it would take several hundred years for it to erupt and produce fruits, it was definitely going to germinate.

The Holy Spirit in his work to aid the believers move in the hearts of those who wanted God and his Son Jesus Christ to be glorified to initiate the reforms which gave birth to Protestantism and its various forms of Evangelical and Pentecostal Christian denominations. But more than a few number of spirit led men of God being determined to make the Name and the Word of God known and understood by future generations of Christians like the Berean[155] Christians that the Apostle Paul extolled for their diligence in searching to understand the Scriptures, God's Word was also be fulfilled. Whether for the salvation of humanity or the judgement of wicked people and nations, God's plan and purpose for humanity was not going to be altered because it is written:

> "I have a plan for the whole earth, a hand of judgement upon all the nations. The LORD of Heaven's Armies has

---

[153]   C.S. Lewis, The Screw Tape Letters, p.81.

[154]   See Holy Bible, John 12:32: http://biblehub.com/nlt/john/12.htm

[155]   "And the people of Berea were more open-minded than those in Thessalonica, and they listened eagerly to Paul's message. They searched the Scriptures day after day to see if Paul and Silas were teaching the truth." – Holy Bible, Acts of the Apostles 17:11- http://biblehub.com/nlt/acts/17.htm

spoken - who can change his plans? When his hand is raised, who can stop it?"[156]

4.4 The Four Great Reformers

And so against the wishes of the Pope and the Council of Rome whose powers then sometimes surpassed the powers of some of the Christian Emperors of the Holy Roman Empire, men such as (A) John Wycliffe; (B) Erasmus Desiderius; (C) William Tyndale; and (D) Martin Luther, like the apostle Paul in the face of threats to their liberty and security, considered their lives of no value[157] except for the advancement of the freedom that comes with the true knowledge of God through his son Jesus Christ.

This was how each of these four men played a role in the birth of the Protestant Church and the proclamation of true freedom of the Christian religion within the tenets of the Word of God as stated in the Holy Bible.

A. John Wycliffe[158]

John Wycliffe, referred to by some people of his time as the "Morning Star" was a fourteenth century English theologian, philosopher, and promoter of his first complete translation of the Bible in English."[159] Wycliffe doubled as a lay preacher while he was teaching at Oxford University. But he went further than lay preaching to demonstrate "the marks of moral earnestness and a genuine desire for reform"[160] of the Church. His passion for translating the Holy Bible into English was driven by his desire "to make the law of God available to every man who

---

[156]   Isaiah 14:26-27. See also http://biblehub.com/nlt/isaiah/14.htm

[157]   The apostle Paul stated:"But I do not account my life of any value nor as precious to myself, if only I may finish my course and the ministry that I received from the Lord Jesus, to testify to the gospel of the grace of God." Holy Bible, Acts 20:24 http://biblehub.com/esv/acts/20.htm

[158]   John Wycliffe (c. 1330 – 1384), was an English Philosopher, theologian and reformer. See entry on Wycliffe, John in The Oxford Dictionary of the Christian Church © 1974 Oxford University Press. Pp.1502-1503. Also see John Wycliffe in 131 Christians Everyone Should Know © 2000 Christianity Today, Inc. pp.211-213

[159]   On John Wycliffe, see http://www.britannica.com/EBchecked/topic/650168/John-Wycliffe

[160]   See   http://www.britannica.com/EBchecked/topic/650168/John-Wycliffe/8039/Wycliffes-attack-on-the-church

could read."[161] But for this the Pope and the Roman Catholic Church took great offence for which they did not forgive Wycliffe. Even forty-four years after his death, Pope Martin V, decided to execute what to him was vengeance on Wycliffe by ordering that his bones should be dug up and burned[162] and the ashes spread on the river Swift to satisfy the Roman Catholic Church's quest to punish Wycliffe who defied their authority and proceeded to honour God and advance the proclamation of the word of God.[163]

After the death of Wycliffe in 1384, there were no known noticeable protestant reformers until the mid fifteenth century through to the mid sixteenth century when three men surfaced on the horizon from across Western Europe. The three men already mentioned: Erasmus Desiderius; William Tyndale and Martin Luther emerged in the fifteenth and sixteenth centuries, respectively. Though their missions were the same in that they were reformers, their approach and their fate in the hands of the powerful Catholic Church of their time was quite different.

B. Erasmus Desiderius[164]

Erasmus was born in Rotterdam and took on the name Desiderius[165] in his adult life. He was ordained a priest in 1492 and thereafter studied theology.[166] Erasmus had an ambition to have everyone read the Bible, so he went on to edit and translate the New Testament in the original Greek and published his own edition of translation of the Bible in 1516.[167] His objective as already stated:

---

[161]   Ibid

[162]   See the story on John Wycliffe in the article "History of the English Bible": http://www.wayoflife. org/database/history_of_the_english_bible_wycliffe.html

[163]   Ibid.

[164]   Erasmus, Desiderius (c.1466 – 1536), known as a humanist and a leading light for the reformation.

[165]   See entry on Erasmus in 131 Christians Everyone Should Know Editors: Galli, Mark and Olsen, Ted © 2000 Christianity Today, Inc. pp.342-344; See also entry on Erasmus, Desiderius (prob. 1469 – 1536) in The Oxford Dictionary of the Christian Church, pp. 466 – 467.

[166]   Ibid.

[167]   Ibid.

"Would that these were translated into each and every language …..Would that the farmer might sing snatches of Scripture at his plough and that the weaver might hum phrases of Scripture to the tune of his shuttle that the traveller might lighten with stories from Scripture the weariness of journey."[168]

Erasmus was critical of the theologians of his day and the practices of the Roman Catholic Church of his time. He wrote:

"Had I not seen it, nay, felt it myself,.. I should never have believed anyone who said theologians could become so insane."[169]

He demonstrated his displeasure with the state of things in the Roman Catholic Church in a satire he wrote titled: In Praise of Folly in which:

"he attacked the monastic and ecclesiastic corruption. He lambasted miracles supposedly performed by images, indulgences, and what he felt were useful church rites."[170]

Martin Luther who will be discussed here was notably impressed by the writings of Erasmus and wrote to him for support.[171]

Erasmus was also noted to have been impressed by Martin Luther to the extent that he described him to Pope Leo X as:

"a mighty trumpet of gospel truth."[172]

In the entry against his name in The Oxford Dictionary of the Christian Church, Erasmus is said to have been:

"The most renowned scholar of his age…a man of vast if not always deep erudition, of uncommon intellectual

---

[168]   Ibid.

[169]   Ibid.

[170]   Ibid.

[171]   Ibid.

[172]   Ibid.

powers, but averse to metaphysical speculation, esp. in its medieval and scholastic forms. Though he had himself paved the way for the Reformation by his merciless satires on the doctrines and institutions of the Church, his scholarly character, which abhorred violence and sought tranquillity, prevented himself from joining the Protestants, and threw him back on the tradition of the Church as the safeguard of stability."[173]

In the commentary on Erasmus in the 131 Christians Everyone Should Know, the Editors summed him up thus:

"[his] writings and scholarship started a theological earthquake that didn't stop until western European Christendom was split."[174]

Today, by the sacrifices and foresights of John Wycliffe, Erasmus Desiderius and William Tynedale that will be discussed below following Martin Luther, according to the Christian Lingua as at September 11, 2018, the Holy Bible has been translated into approximately 700 languages.[175]

C. William Tyndale[176]

William Tyndale, was passionate about getting people to have understanding of the good news of justification by faith which he discovered when he read Erasmus Greek Edition of the New Testament.[177] He was especially, inspired by Erasmus statement that:

"Christ desires his mysteries to be published abroad as widely as possible. I would that [the Gospels and the

---

[173]   Ibid. p.467

[174]   Ibid. p.342.

[175]   See "Into how Many Languages has the Bible Been Translated", Christian Lingua, September 11, 2018 https://www.christianlingua.com/into-how-many-languages-has-the-bible-been-translated/

[176]   William Tyndale (1494 – 1536) English Translator of the New Testament of the Holy Bible and a reformer. See entry under William Tyndale in 131 Christians Everyone Should Know © 2000 Christianity Today, Inc. pp.348-350; See also entry on William Tyndale, The Oxford Dictionary of the Christian Church, Second Edition Edited by F.L. Cross and E. A. Livingstone © 1958, 1974 Oxford University Press pp. 1400 – 1401.

[177]   Ibid. 131 Christians Everyone Should Know p.348.

epistles of Paul] were translated into all languages, of all Christian people, and that they might be read and known."[178]

However, England was unfair and harsh to him and the early reformers. After the sad end of John Wycliffe discussed earlier, William Tyndale who became a subsequent English reformer met a harsh and cruel end in the process of carrying out his reformation agenda by way of the Holy Bible into English. Tyndale had Oxford and Cambridge Universities education before being ordained into the Catholic Priesthood in 1521.[179] Against the policy of the Roman Catholic Church in England prohibiting the translation of the Bible, Tyndale started translating English New Testament in 1523 and went on to meet with Martin Luther in Wittenberg before settling in Worms, Germany, where he eventually translated and published the English New Testament in 1525 and then smuggling copies into England. While he was been hunted for by King Henry VIII of England and the Roman Catholic Church in England for an act prohibited by the kingdom, he went into hiding and started translating the Old Testament. He was yet to complete his translation of the Old Testament before his 'odd' friend Henry Phillips betrayed him and he was arrested in August 1535 and was tried and convicted for heresy and treason and executed on the 6th October 1530. He was strangled on the stake and put to death by burning.[180] Nevertheless, his cry before his death: "Lord, open the King of England's eyes" was doubtlessly answered as King Henry VIII used his work to publish the "Great Bible" and his work was also used for the King James Version of the Bible published in 1611.[181] And indeed, time has exposed the spiritual myopia of the Pope and King of England who opposed and eventually killed William Tyndale as he is now known to had embarked on a good cause for the gospel of Christ and honoured for his contribution to the reformation.

---

[178] Ibid. pp.348-9.

[179] See BBC History on William Tyndale: http://www.bbc.co.uk/history/people/william_tyndale/ See also the William Tyndale, Christian History Facts: http://www.christianity.com/church/church-history/timeline/1501-1600/translator-william-tyndale-strangled-and-burned-11629961.html

[180] Ibid.

[181] Ibid.

D. Martin Luther[182]

Martin Luther had a doctor of theology degree and was a professor of Scripture at the University of Wittenberg from 1511.[183] He became the man whom God would use to bring about the great reformation of the Church that gave birth ultimately to Protestantism and what today has metamorphosed into various denominations such as the Evangelical and Pentecostal Church. While Erasmus who was discussed above worked inside the Church to bring about reforms and freedom from abuses, Luther raised the alarm to the hearing of the world by his 95 Theses[184] to expose the abuses in the church even by the way that the truth of the Word of God was being diluted and misrepresented in presentation and preaching by the Roman Catholic Church priests of his day. Perhaps, one reason for Luther's pragmatic action on church reformation in order to secure genuine religious freedom of the Christian believers to know and worship God in truth was as a result of the manner of his conversion into Catholicism and Christianity.

A brilliant and somewhat concise account of how Martin Luther went into the priesthood and inspired the reformation of the Church to deliver Protestantism is given by the writer of the English Bible History on Martin Luther as well as in the Oxford Dictionary of the Christian Church © 1958, 1974 under the entry on Luther as already quoted and in the 131 Christians Everyone

Should know also already quoted.[185] In these accounts there are things that are more than the ordinary which could have driven Luther to do the extraordinary. In the account of his early life, it is stated that Martin Luther:

> "At the age of seventeen in 1501 he entered the University of Erfurt. The young student received his Bachelor's

---

[182]   Martin Luther (1483 – 1546) see entry on Martin Luther, 131 Christians Everyone Should Know © 2000 Christianity Today, Inc. pp.33-36; Also see entry on Luther, Martin, in The Oxford Dictionary of the Christian Church, Second Edition, Edited F.L. Cross and E.A. Livingstone © 1958, 1974 Oxford University Press pp.846-848.

[183]   Ibid. The Oxford Dictionary of the Christian Church. P. 846.

[184]   95 Theses by Martin Luther, Translated by Adolph Spaeth, First Rate Publishers.

[185]   For this account of Martin Luther by the English Bible History see http://www.greatsite.com/timeline-english-bible-history/martin-luther.html

degree after just one year in 1502! Three years later, in 1505, he received a Master's degree. According to his father's wishes, Martin enrolled in the law school of that university. All that changed during a thunderstorm in the summer of 1505. A lightning bolt struck near to him as he was returning to school. Terrified, he cried out, "Help, St. Anne![186] I'll become a monk!" Spared of his life, but regretting his words, Luther kept his bargain, dropped out of law school and entered the monastery there."[187]

Martin Luther who joined the monastic order in 1505 was ordained in 1507. However, he soon got frustrated "about the clergy selling "indulgences" – promised remission from punishments for sin, either for someone still living or for one who had died and was believed to be in purgatory. The departure from preaching the authentic gospel of Jesus Christ and the substitution of indulgences for repentance and renouncement of sins was becoming an established pattern authorised by the Pope as the head of the Roman Catholic Church and Reverend Dr Martin Luther could no longer bear it. Luther's extraordinary conversion has not only led him to be a great theologian but also as one passionate for things of the kingdom of the God that he had given his life to serve.

The Pope and the Roman Catholic Church of Luther's day equated or elevated the sacramental penance to the height of the poenitentiam agite. To Luther it mattered that the gospel should be preached and the word of God be made known as the only truth gives life over and above indulgences.

For this reason when on All Saints' Eve in 1517, the preacher Johann Tetzel was preaching on the granting of Indulgences by Pope Leo X, in other words was selling indulgences:

---

[186] Martin Luther was said at the time to have called on Anne the mother of the Virgin Mary, the mother of Jesus Christ to come to his rescue to avoid the thunder bolt striking killing him. In the Catholic Church the parents of the Virgin Mary the mother of Jesus Christ have been canonised even though they are not mentioned in the Holy Bible, hence Luther appealed to St Anne for help. See http://www.catholicculture.org/culture/liturgicalyear/activities/view.cfm?id=1094

[187] Martin Luther's Early Life, English Bible History. Ibid.

"for contributions to the renovation of St. Peter's in Rome"[188]

and he went on to say:

"Once the coin into the coffer clings, a soul from purgatory heavenward springs!"[189]

Irked by Tetzel's preaching and deception with the indulgences, Luther stood up to expose the deceits of the indulgences and called for a debate of his:

"95 Theses, which he affixed to the door of the Schlosskirche at Wittenberg. Within a fortnight they had spread throughout Germany, where they were welcomed esp. by the Humanists and other circles desiring the reform of the Church."[190]

In his 95 Theses, Luther had differentiated between poenitentiam agite and sacramental penance and amplified the teachings of Jesus Christ on salvation and eternal life by stating inter alia, thus:

"1. Our Lord and Master Jesus Christ, when He said Poenitentiam agite, willed that the whole life of believers should be repentance."

"2. This word cannot be understood to mean sacramental penance, i.e., confession and satisfaction, which is administered by the priests.

"33. Men must be on their guard against those who say that the pope's pardons are that inestimable gift of God by which man is reconciled to Him;

"34. For these "graces of pardon" concern only the penalties of sacramental satisfaction, and these are appointed by man.

---

[188]   Luther, Martin, The Oxford Dictionary of the Christian Church © 1974. p.847.

[189]   Martin Luther, 131 Christians Everyone Should Know © 2000 Christianity Today, Inc. p.35

[190]   Luther, Martin, The Oxford Dictionary of the Christian Church © 1974 Oxford University Press. p.847.

"35. They preach no Christian doctrine who teach that contrition is not necessary in those who intend to buy souls out of purgatory or to buy confessionalia.

"36. Every truly repentant Christian has a right to full remission of penalty and guilt, even without letters of pardon.

"43. Christians are to be taught that he who gives to the poor or lends to the needy does a better work than buying pardons;

"44. Because love grows by works of love, and man becomes better, but by pardons man does not grow better, only more free from penalty.

"45. Christians are to be taught that he who sees a man in need, and passes him by, and gives [his money] for pardons, purchases not indulgences of the pope, but the indignation of God.

"52. The assurance of salvation by letters of pardon is vain, even though the pope himself, were to stake his soul upon it.

"54. Injury is done to the Word of God when, in the same sermon, an equal or a longer time is spent on pardons than on this Word.

For the above theses and all that is stated in Luther's 95 Theses, he was summoned to Worms, Germany, in 1521, to appear before Charles V, Holy Roman Emperor. Luther had thought he would be given an opportunity to debate his theses but he found out that he was going to face a trial at which he would be asked to recant his views. He resisted the pressure on him to do so because there was no Scriptural evidence to convince him to do so. He went on to say that it was:

"neither safe nor wise to act against conscience."[191]

---

[191] Martin Luther in 131 Christians Everyone Should Know © 2000 Christianity Today, Inc. p.35.

Luther escaped to Wartburg castle before he was convicted for heresy by an imperial edict. However, he returned to Wittenberg in 1522 and led the reformation movement. He married a nun Katharina von Bora. Luther's determination to take the gospel to people even right into their houses led him to translate the Bible into the German language in 1534 and that helped in the understanding of the Word of God outside the Church in Germany and elsewhere in Europe before his death 1546.[192]

4.5 Evaluation and Summary

The overriding fact that can be conspicuously seen in the sequence of events that followed the trials and convictions of the reformers which in the case of William Tyndale led to a cruel execution is the fact that the Pope and the Council of the Roman Catholic Church were more prepared to see that the authority of the Pope even when he was in error was not challenged. It was neither God nor His Word that was given the pre-eminence but the Pope.

The idea that people should abdicate the use of their senses and reliance on their consciences as a guide and just believe the head of the Church even when the Word of God does not support the position of the head of the Church is what is undermining the place of Christianity in the world even today. It is what is making churches empty in the western nations especially as a sense of individuality and independence is taken seriously. It also gave way to the undoing of Christianity in middle centuries especially between the seventh century and the nineteenth century when Islam was embraced and it spread by conquest over places that were once Christian strongholds such as Turkey and North Africa as the discussion in the next chapter will show.

---

[192] See http://www.bbc.co.uk/history/historic_figures/luther_martin.shtml

5

ISLAM, SLAVE TRADE, AND THE ECLIPSE OF CHRISTIANITY IN AFRICA FROM THE 7TH - 19TH CENTURY AD

"The human heart is the most deceitful of all things, and desperately wicked. Who really knows how bad it is?" Jeremiah 17:9 [NLT]

"but you are the very ones who hate good and love evil. You skin my people alive and tear the flesh from their bones." - Micah 3:2 [NLT].

While the theological controversies and conflicts that followed the freedom and legal protection of Christians from the fourth century ensued as discussed in chapters 3 and 4, the unity of the Church became increasingly weakened and divided following the heresies of Arius and Pelagius. This was especially damaging in Africa since Bishop Arius was an African and the Arianian controversy left its effect on the African Church. It was compounded by the Pelagian heresy in which 214 African Bishops took part in the decision to write a letter to the Pope that clarified what the theological position of the Church should be. At the same time, the effect of the Donatists' position in Tunisia and in other African countries such as Algeria, Libya and Egypt, damaged Church unity. In all, mistrust overshadowed love and trust in the Church as the two central pillars of the Christian faith which Jesus set out in Matthew 22:37, 39, as:

"'...You must love the Lord your God with all your heart, all your soul, and all your mind. This is the first and greatest commandment. A second is equally important: 'Love your neighbour as yourself'"

It was substituted for doctrinal expositions amid heresies and conflicts. Against the backdrop of these incidents, and its cumulative negative impact on the Church which had a strong Christian community in Africa from the 1ˢᵗ to the 7ᵗʰ century, Islam emerged in Mecca, Saudi Arabia and spread within the Arab nations within the axis of the European continent and next to Africa.

5.1 The Prophet Muhammad[193] and Islam

Although Muslims generally believe that Islam as a religion has always existed, they unanimously also hold the belief that Muhammad was the final messenger and prophet of God [Allah] who received the Qu'ran by angelic revelation in the first decade of the 7ᵗʰ century.[194] Upon receiving the revelations that formed the text of the Holy Qu'ran in 610, he began preaching what Allah [God] has revealed to him. He asked people to submit to the will of God completely [Islam].[195]

5.2 Islamic Conversions and Migrations

The preaching of the leader of the Islamic faith, the prophet Muhammad was said to have been quite successful with many people converting to Islam following his preaching in the early seventh century. However, by AD622 those who were in power in Mecca, felt threatened by the

---

[193] Muhammad (570 – 632), the prophet and founder of the Islam religion was born in Mecca in Saudi Arabia and is believed by Muslims as the messenger and prophet of [God] Allah. See entry on Islam in The Oxford Dictionary of The Christian Church Second Edition Edited by F.L. Cross and E.A. Livingstone (C) 1974 Oxford University Press. pp.717-8. See also BBC Introduction to the Prophet Muhammad: https://www.bbc.co.uk/religion/religions/islam/history/muhammad_1.shtml#:~:text=Muslims%20believe%20that%20Islam%20is,in%20the%207ᵗʰ%20century%20CE.

[194] Ibid. BBC Introduction to the Prophet Muhammad.

[195] Ibid.

increasing popularity of the prophet Muhammad and mounted opposition against him as well as intensifying persecution

against those who had converted to Islam. Consequently, Prophet Muhammad decided to migrate from Mecca to Medina with his followers. However, within 10 years he returned to conquer Mecca and settle there until his death in AD632.[196]

5.3 Islamic Conquests of North Africa

The first Muslims that arrived in Africa got into North Africa while fleeing from the persecution that those in power in Saudi Arabia directed at them for converting to Islam. They entered North Africa through the Arabian Peninsula. However, in 639 an Islamic military conquest campaign led by a Muslim General by the name of Amr ibn al-Asi invaded North Africa.[197] The Christians in Egypt, Libya, Tunisia and Algeria etc. were forced to convert to Islam, die as martyrs or flee.

5.4 The Slave Trade and the Poison of Racial Tensions

Europeans practised slavery between themselves which was why Emperor Constantine denounced it in 312 as already discussed. The Africans also practised slavery among themselves. However, slavery took a barbaric dimension when it was commercialised as a transatlantic trade by the middle of the fifteen century. Prior to its transatlantic commercialisation, Arab- mullahs otherwise known as Muslim scholars and teachers were already engaged in slave trading following the Islamic conquest of Africa in the seventh century.[198] They were selling some of the African slaves that they seized by force of terror or they bought from some African kings who traded their people as slaves and sold them to Europeans.

---

[196] Ibid.

[197] BBC World Service: Islam, The Story of Africa written by Edward W Blyden: http://www.bbc.co.uk/worldservice/africa/features/storyofafrica/index_section7.shtml

[198] Thomas, Hugo, The Slave Trade © 1997 Picador. At pages 12-13, Thomas stated thus: "If one is critical of Islam as Mr Farrakhan is of Jewry, one can explore how far the medieval trans-Saharan trade in black Africans, from the coast of Guinea, was managed by Arab mullah-merchants in the first centuries after the Muslim penetration of Africa, long before Prince Henry the Navigator's ships were seen in West Africa."

Eventually, the Europeans entered into the slave trade market and engaged directly with the African kings and merchants involved in the inhuman trade of their people. By the middle of the fifteenth century the demand for agricultural labour was high and the Portuguese who were the first to sail into West Africa indulged in large scale slave trading that ultimately exceeded the Arab mullahs' deals. The slaves were bought from Africa and sent to plantation farms in the Caribbean region of America where the climate and soil quite understandably were more suitable for agricultural farming mainly for the production of sugar and cottons that cannot be obtained in European nations' climate and soil. The other European nations such as the French and the British eventually joined and overtook the Portuguese in the slave trade business of shipping thousands of Africans to the Caribbean and South American countries such as Cuba and Brazil for plantation farming and later to North America.

The British became the most vicious and inhumane when they entered into the commerce of slave trading.[199] According to Hugo Thomas in his book, The Slave Trade:[200]

> "Britain's substantial participation in the slave trade during the eighteenth century – the country's slave captains were carrying about 35,000 captives across the Atlantic every year in the 1780s, in about ninety ships – was compensated for by the lead which British statesmen later gave in abolishing the commerce and, turning gamekeeper to the world after having been its poacher-in-chief, dedicated diplomacy, naval power, guile, financial subsidies to bring the trader to a conclusion? In this connection, one can ask whether that British policy was the decisive element in concluding Brazilian slave trading in the 1850s or Cuban in the 1860s."[201]

The hypocrisy of the claim of Christianity and godliness of the slave traders and slave owners took several heights of ungodly proportions. For example, following the reformation in Europe, the English Christians

---

[199] Thomas, Hugo, The Slave Trade © 1997 Picador. Read Chapter "13 No Nation Has Plunged So Deeply Into This Guilt As Great Britain." Pp. 235 – 261.

[200] Ibid.

[201] Ibid. p. 12

who believed they were purer and holier and called themselves the puritans left England for America in the sixteen century because they did not want to do the King's bidding of joining the Church of England.

But these same English Christians when they settled in America did not live by the Christian injunction of 'love your neighbour as yourself.' Instead they set out to discriminate and direct hatred at Irish Catholics in America and worst of all, to exhibit the barbarism of passing laws that would free them from the murder of their slaves. The colony of Virginia Act of casual killing of slaves 1669 which was passed by the General Assembly of Virginia in October 1669, inter alia says:

> "masters who kill their slaves in the act of punishing them are held not to be responsible of murder."[202]

Upon that lofty height of hypocrisy and cruelty, human beings who were unfortunately, slaves were reduced to the value of cheap merchandise items.

Under the yoke of a dreadful oppression, the slaves began to look for ways of freeing themselves. A major significant breakthrough came with a revolt in Saint-Domingue towards the tail end of the eighteenth century and it eventually led to Saint-Domingue becoming an Independent Haita in 1803. According to Jeremy D. Popkin in his book, You Are All Free, The Haitan Revolution and the Abolition of Slavery © 2010 Cambridge University Press:

> "June 20, 1793 would be forever associated not with the end of slavery, but with the violent destruction of a major city, a proud symbol of European civilization in the tropics. The fighting that broke out in the city of Cap Français on that hot Caribbean morning set off, over the next three days, a conflagration that cost thousands of lives and reduced the wealthiest port in the French colonies to ashes. The destruction of Cap Français was bloodier than any of the episodes of urban violence in revolutionary Paris, claiming at least twice as many victims as the journee of August 10, 1792 or the September massacres of that year in

---

[202] See "An Act about Casual Killing of Slaves (1669): https://www.encyclopediavirginia.org/ An act about the casuall killing of slaves 1669

Paris, and the death toll – somewhere between 3,000 and 10,000 – makes it the most murderous instance of urban conflict in the entire history of the Americas. The flames that consumed Cap Français had a devastating impact on the overseas trade that had fueled France's prosperity since the beginning of the eighteenth century. No single event in the history of France's second overseas empire, not even the Algerian war of 1954-62, delivered such a sudden and massive jolt to the metropole's prosperity as the destruction of Cap Français in 1973."[203]

"The events of June 20, 1793, drove thousands of survivors – whites, blacks, and free people of color – to the shores of the new republic of the United States, producing the country's first refugee crisis. The horrifying stories the white colonists brought with them changed the American debate about slavery, convincing southerners that their "peculiar institution" needed to be defended in the most intransigent terms. The refugees of color, many of whom settled permanently in cities such as Philadelphia and New York, had their own versions of events in Saint-Domingue and brought a new spirit of self-assertion to the growing African-American communities there. Fear of the effect that their testimonies might have on slaves in the United States led to the first American panic about foreign subversion"[204]

Against that historic backdrop, it can be said that the abolition of slavery and slave trade was not necessarily an act done to protect

and return the human dignity of the African slaves back to them, but in actual fact, it was an act done to salvage humanity from the monumental destruction of human lives across the black and white races that was staring humanity in the face while slave trade lasted. Masters and slaves alike, as the evidence of the Cap Français event of June 20, 1793 showed, would have been destroyed in bloodbath and various cities would have been awash with wasted human lives in the transatlantic nations where slaves were in high numbers and could rise to resist their oppressors or owners.

---

[203]   Popkin, Jeremy D., You Are All Free The Haitan Revolution And The Abolition of Slavery © 2010 Cambridge University Press. p. 2.

[204]   Ibid. pp.3-4.

5.5 Evaluation and Summary

Following the Islamic conquest of Africa in the 7th century only 'pockets'[205] of Christians were said to have been left in African nations such as Egypt, Sudan and Ethiopia. It can be easily imagined that most of the African Christians from the 7th century onwards who were not prepared to convert to Islam during the Islamic invasion of Algeria, Tunisia, Libya and Egypt must have fled from the conquered North African region which became the stronghold of Islam to the East, South and West African regions, while some who remained might have simply converted to Islam or died in the process of resistance. It should also be said that Islam did not secure converts solely by force. There were those who were attracted to the Islam faith because it allowed them to marry more than one wife[206] and also to maintain some of their traditional values which Christianity did not allow them to hold onto. There were also others who might have found Islam more preferable as a religion because it requires submission to God with punitive measures for disobedience to laws. People generally want to see those who deviate from societal norms and disobey the laws penalised instantly, and sometimes drastically, too, depending on the severity of the offence; and Islam offered such through its Sharia Court, so some were attracted to the Islamic faith as a result of it. However, in the twentieth century, there had been instances of people who were born into Christian families converting to Islam and vice versa Muslims converting to Christianity without the use of force or even human persuasion, but instead, by pure conviction, voluntary intent or interest to convert to another religion. Yet interestingly, the basis of such conversions has been dramatically different. In the United States for example, the twentieth century saw conversion of some African Americans who were born into Christian families converting to Islam. One of such persons was the most famous boxer of the twentieth century Cassius Marcellus Clay, Jr who in his adult life converted to Islam and changed his name to Muhammad Ali[207] because of racial discrimination meted out to him by white American Christians whose religion he did not want to be identified with. Black

---

[205] See Islam: The Story of Africa, BBC World Service by Edward W. Blyden: http://www.bbc.co.uk/worldservice/africa/features/storyofafrica/index_section7.shtml

[206] Ibid.

[207] Muhammad Ali (Cassius Marcellus Clay Jr.): https://www.britannica.com/biography/Muhammad-Ali-boxer

Africans suffered racial discrimination in the United States in spite of the Civil Rights Act 1875which was intended to end the Jim Crow laws[208] which enforced racial segregation in the nineteenth century. On the other hand, in the heart of the Islamic Republic of Pakistan, a committed Muslim woman whose family's religious foundation was well known and respected within the Islamic community converted to Christianity when she had a series of extraordinary spiritual encounters that led her in 1966 to convert to Christianity. She tells the story of extraordinary experiences and her conversion in her book titled, I DARED TO CALL HIM.[209]

Bearing in mind that only bishops and preachers had access to the Holy Scriptures in the 7th century because the Holy Bible was not printed until "1455 when Gutenberg produced the first printed Bible"[210], the African Bishops and Christian believers who were dispersed across the African continent during the Islamic conquest could not have been able to pass on their Christian faith to their descendants through the subsequent generations in its pure essence. However, practical Judeo-Christian practices such as naming of a child on the 8th day after birth and circumcision which could be traced to Judaism and Christianity was traditionally maintained even when people were not calling themselves Christians well before the Christian renaissance following European colonisation and missionary settlements in Africa in the nineteenth century through to the twentieth century when most African nations secured independence from their colonial masters. However, those who practiced these Christian customs also practiced paganism and traditional African religions not too dissimilar to the idolatry that the Israelites practiced when they deviated from the worship of God.[211]

---

[208] Melvin I Urofsky, "Jim Crow Law United States [1877 – 1954]" in Encyclopaedia Britannica: https://www.britannica.com/event/Jim-Crow-law

[209] Sheikh, Bilquis, I dared to Call Him Father © 2003 Chosen Books 25th Anniversary Edition.

[210] See Christian History "Guttenberg produced the first printed Bible in 1455". See: https://www.christianitytoday.com/history/issues/issue-28/1455-gutenberg-produces-first-printed-bible.html

[211] Exodus 32:2-10; 2 Kings 17:5-17.

In what was obviously an act of divine reversal, the Europeans such as the British who were sold as slaves in a Roman market[212] and who were largely practicing idolatry in Britain between the first and sixth century when Africa already had hundreds of bishops such as Alexander, Athanasius and Augustine as discussed above, became colonisers of African nations, with re-Christianisation, mainly by the British, but also by the French and Portuguese, in the nineteenth and twentieth century. This was following a period of over four hundred years in which they had traded and owned Africans as slaves. The invention of machines which were more efficient than human beings in agricultural production led to the industrial revolution[213] which partly made the abolition of the slave trade in 1807[214] possible, even though the events in Saint-Domingue in the 1790s as discussed had led slaves becoming free persons and Haiti also becoming independence in 1803.

However, some men of good conscience such as William Wilberforce[215] and Lord Grenville[216] rose up in the British establishment which was a dominant power in the world order at the time to argue for the abolition of the slave trade against those who had vested interested and benefitted

---

[212] Mark Galli and Ted Olsen in their account of Gregory the Great in their book 131 Christians Everyone Should Know © 2000 Christianity Today, Inc.. quoted in passim stated thus: "Gregory, before he became pope, happened to see some Anglo-Saxon slaves for sale in a Roman market place. He asked about the race of the remarkable blond men and was told they were "Anglos." "Not Anglos, but angels," he was said to reply. As a result, it said, Gregory was later inspired to send missionaries to England…His frequent correspondence across the world shows him well aware of evangelistic opportunities in Britain. So
it is not surprising that in in 596 he sent Augustine, along with 40 monks, on a mission to "this far corner of the world." Pp.317, 319 of 131 Christians Everyone Should Know.

[213] The food with which the world was fed prior to the industrial revolution was produced by the slaves by hand farming in plantations in faraway South America where the slaves were taken to for farming. The European climate and soil as it were was not suitable for the agricultural farming of the various ranges of world. Once the Industrial Revolution started in the latter half of the 18th century, and machines could be used for agricultural farming and to produce far more food than men and women could do with their hands, it became unnecessary to use slaves for agricultural farming, and by the early 19th century, in 1806 slave trade was abolished by the British Empire who committed the most vicious form of the slave trade. See: Industrial Revolution. https://www.history.com/topics/industrial-revolution/industrial-revolution.

[214] For "Abolition of the Slave Trade Act 1807 by the British Parliament" see The National Archives: https://www.nationalarchives.gov.uk/pathways/blackhistory/rights/abolition.htm

[215] Thomas, Hugh, The Slave Trade, The History of the Atlantic Slave Trade 1440 – 1870 © 1997 Picador. At page 526: William Wilberforce's eventual winning bill for the abolition of the slave trade in April 1792 was presented to the House of Commons with a cry from Wilberforce saying: "Africa, Africa, 'your sufferings have been the theme that arrested and engaged my heart. Your sufferings no tongue can express, no language impart.'

[216] Ibid. pp.553-4.

from the slave trade that were opposing the bill for its abolition in the British Parliament.

The politicised Christianity that the British and French as well as the Portuguese practiced became part of the colonial tools that they brought to the African territories that they apportioned to themselves at the Berlin Conference of 1884-1885.[217] Christian Protestantism which was mainly Anglicanism was brought by the British that had a larger number of territories across the West, South and East Africa nations. While on the other hand, the French and Portuguese brought Catholicism, otherwise known as the Roman Catholic Church version of Christianity, to the territories that were under them for colonisation. In actual Christian practice, both the Catholicism and Protestant Anglicanism denominations of the Christian religion that the colonialists brought to Africa, was a bad marriage of political and religious forms of Christianity, which attempted to strip off the heart and soul of true Christianity. But for the godly sacrifices and acts of a few genuine godly missionaries, who evangelised the people and demonstrably sought to practice Christianity void of colonial religiosity and politics. They built missionary schools, hospitals and did other charitable acts. But the fact that both the Catholic and Anglican Churches had participated in the slave trade and that was known to the indigenous people of Africa made both the genuine missionaries and the administrative and political agents of the colonial masters clothed in religious garments to be treated with suspicions. The edifices built with the financial gains of the slave trade are still manifestly visible in most British cities. There are even statues of slave merchants in the Church of England, so the people who were still mindful of the degradations they had suffered during the slave trade which was less than a hundred years before were not easily persuaded in the Christianity that the British were presenting to them, even as their natural resources were being exploited during the colonisation.[218]

---

[217] See "Berlin Conference 1884-1885 Meeting at which the major European powers negotiated and formalized claims to territory in Africa" by Elizabeth Heath in Oxford Reference: https://www. oxfordreference.com/view/10.1093/acref/9780195337709.001.0001/acref-9780195337709-e-0467

[218] Following the "Black Lives Matter" protests across various nations of the world in reaction to the United States city of Minneapolis Police brutal killing of George Floyd, an African American, on the 25 May 2020, the Archbishop of Church of England, Justin Welby, in response to destruction of monuments of slave merchants in the UK stated on 26 June 2020 that "Church of England needs to review statues over slavery": https://www.reuters.com/article/ us-minneapolis-police-britain-church-idUSKBN23X1B5

In the United States of America, whose preamble to the declaration of independence stated thus:

> "We hold these truths to be self-evident, that all men are created equal, that they are endowed by their creator with certain inalienable Rights, that among these are Life, Liberty and the Pursuit of Happiness."[219]

And also went on to state the following in their Constitution:

> "We the people of the United States, in order to form a more perfect union, establish justice, insure domestic Tranquillity, provide for the common defence, promote the general welfare, and secure the Blessings of Liberty to ourselves and our Posterity, do ordain and establish this Constitution for the United States of America."[220]

In spite of the clear and unambiguous statement of "all men are created equal" in the declaration to independence and forming 'a more perfect union, establish justice' in their constitution, the courts still discriminated against African Americans until well into the late twentieth century. In one of its most famous and dehumanising decisions, the Supreme Court of America's judges violated the US constitution even as they swore with the Holy Bible professing their Christian faith and giving the impression that they would uphold the truth and do justice, they did the contrary, in the case of Dred Scott v. Sandford, 60 U.S. 393 (1857). In it, the United States Supreme Court decided that Scott who was a freed slave was not an American citizen because his:

> "ancestors were brought to this country and sold as slaves, is not a "citizen" within the meaning of the Constitution of the United States"[221]

The absurdity of the decision of the U S Supreme Court in the Dred Scott case stood as an embarrassment to the United States founding

219   See Preamble to the declaration of Independence: https://www.archives.gov/founding-docs/declaration
220   See the Constitution of the United States of America: https://www.archives.gov/founding-docs/constitution-transcript
221   Dred Scott v Sandford, 60 U.S. 19 How. 393 (1857) at paragraph 4.

fathers dream of what the nation should be until it was reversed by the Thirteenth and Fourteenth Amendments of the Constitution of the United States of America. However, it had left a gap on how people could understand the practice of Christianity if those who swore by the Bible to uphold justice in the name of Christianity find it convenient to dehumanise and abuse other human beings by their rulings and decisions.

However, colonialism recovered some lost ground in re-evangelising Africa and repositioning it as a major Christian continent as it pushed back Islam from areas it had intended to reach but met with resistance before the arrival of European colonial masters.

6

CHRISTIAN RENAISSANCE AND THE EMPIRES THAT SUCCEEDED THE ROMAN EMPIRE

"Even perfection has its limits, but your commands have no limit." – Psalm 119:96 (NLT)

Africa was not the only conquered territory of Islamic advance. The theological controversies and divisions in the Catholic Church as far back as the fourth century as discussed in the previous chapters of this book increasingly weakened the unity of the Church over several centuries and effectively led to the fall of Christianity in some of its strongholds. The very land comprising of many Biblical cities such as Antioch, Ephesus etc. which was the cradle of Christianity fell into the hands of the Ottoman Empire when Osman Ghazi otherwise Osman I, fought the Byzantine Empire which was the Eastern half of the Roman Empire and took Constantinople and the entire territory which is known as Turkey today that comprised those Biblical cities. The names have been changed in some cases to bear Islamic names.

Constantinople for example is now Istanbul.[222] However, besides Turkey, Christianity largely recovered from Islamic conquests both in Europe and Africa.

---

[222]   See Origins and expansions of the Ottoman State, c.1300 – 1402 by Malcolm Edward Yapp, professor of the Modern History of West Asia in Britannica: https://www.britannica.com/place/Ottoman-Empire

6.1 The Spanish Empire and the Spread of Christianity

Prior to the Spanish Empire, Spain had three monotheistic religions: Jews, Christians and Muslims lived in Spain and practiced their religious beliefs. Spain was one of the first European nations to be reached by Christianity to the extent that the Christians in Spain were affected by the great persecutions with some dying as martyrs.[223] As at the fourth century, Spain already had Christian councils in Zaragoza (Saragossa) 380[224], Elviria c.306[225], and Toledo 400.[226] But Christianity in Spain took a downward turn following Islamist conquest of Spain after the behest of one Christian Chief who felt oppressed. In AD 711, an aggrieved Spanish Christian Chief Julian was said to have appealed to Musa ibn Nusair, a governor of North Africa for help against the tyrannical Visigoth ruler of Spain, Roderick.[227] While the story of Julian's appeal to Nusair is said to be contentious, the indisputable fact is that General Tariq bin Ziyad with an army of 7000 troops did successfully invade and conquer Spain and made Spain a Muslim nation between AD711 and AD1492. However, after several wars and rebellions, the Christians under the rule of Ferdinand V and Isabella defeated the Moorish Kingdom, otherwise the Muslims and returned Spain to a Christian nation by the early sixteen century.[228] It has to be said that this was possible because of the influence of Pope Sixtus IV who in 1478 authorised an inquisition[229] in Spain and many Muslims found it rather convenient to convert to Christianity by 1492. However, just as Spain emancipated herself from some centuries of Muslim domination between AD 711 and AD 1492, she went on to become an empire that lasted for three centuries between the sixteenth and eighteenth century. And the Spanish empire did not only impose the Spanish language and its version of Christianity upon the Americas which Christopher Colombus 'discovered' but also upon

---

223   See entry on Spain in The Oxford Dictionary of the Christian Church Second Edition © 1958, 1974 Oxford University Press at page 1296.

224   Ibid.

225   Ibid.

226   Ibid.

227   See BBC – Religions – Islam: Muslim Spain (711-1492): http://www.bbc.co.uk/religion/religions/islam/history/spain_1.shtml

228   See Roger Boase, "The Muslim Expulsion From Spain" Published in History Today, Volume: 52, Issue 4 2002 http://www.historytoday.com/roger-boase/muslim-expulsion-spain

229   Supra in the article quoted in footnote 60.

its colonies in Africa, Asia and the Oceanic territories. The language and religion remained even after the independence of these nations between the nineteenth and twentieth century. So the spread of European version of Christianity and religion as well as its domination of the world at the time was enhanced by imperial and colonial masters such as Spain.

6.2 The French Empire and the Spread of Christianity

In what was obviously the succession of empires by western European nations, France took on the baton of being an empire from Spain, so to speak, from 1804, when Napoleon I was crowned the Emperor of France to the middle of the twentieth century. The French empire took French culture and Christianity to various French colonies and territories. But unlike in Spain that the date of Christianity can be traced to the fourth century in AD 360, France is said to have received Christianity directly from Jerusalem in the first century because the apostle Philip[230] settled there and Joseph of Arimathea[231] and Mary Madgalene[232] who were exiled from Jerusalem by persecutors miraculously sailed to France by a boat without a sail.[233]

6.3 The British Empire,[234] Slave Trade and the Spread of Christianity

The British Empire was the last and most domineering of the European empires and it bore several phases. Historians differ on when the

---

[230] This is the same Philip the disciple of Jesus Christ discussed above and referred to in the Holy Bible, Acts 8:26-39. See: See Christian Assemblies International write up entitled: "The Christian History of France" and see the section on The First Christians in France: https://www.cai.org/bible-studies/christian-history-france

[231] Joseph of Arimathea was a man of influence who was also a secret disciple of Jesus Christ and he went to Governor Pontius Pilate and asked for the body of Jesus Christ after his crucifixion. See Holy Bible, John 19:38 http://biblehub.com/kjv/john/19.htm

[232] Mary Magdalene was the woman who was told by the angel that Jesus Christ had resurrected when she went to his tomb on the third of his burial. See Holy Bible, Matthew 28:1-7 http://biblehub.com/esv/matthew/28.htm

[233] Supra as in footnote 222 - See Christian Assemblies International write up entitled: "The Christian History of France" and see the section on The First Christians in France: https://www.cai.org/bible-studies/christian-history-france

[234] See inter alia on the topic the book by James, Lawrence, The Rise and Fall of the British Empire © 1994, 1998 Abacus, An imprint of Little, Brown Book Group.

empire started with some saying it started in the 1490s and others saying it started in early 1600s. However, it sounds more plausible or rather indisputable to say the British Empire became transparently on course in the early sixteenth century following King Henry VIII's[235] split from the Catholic and his passing of Act of Succession and Act of Supremacy in 1534 which made him the head of the Church of England.[236] Following that Queen Elizabeth I of England, in 1583, began her quest for world domination and went on to colonise the thirteen colonies in North America and India while engaging in slave trade in Africa and Asia. In addition to the success that the enterprise of Queen Elizabeth I of England had in the quest to make England an empire came reinforcement when the union between England and Scotland which produced Great Britain was formed in 1707. However, even with the union there came a threat to the world influence of the British Empire because of the victory that the thirteen colonies in North America had when they won their battle for independence in 1783.[237] France also had a long standing rivalry with Britain but this came to a halt with the victory of Britain over France when she defeated the French Emperor Napoleon at the Battle of Waterloo in 1815 and reinforced her position of power and influence in the world. Great Britain became the most powerful and enduring empire during the nineteenth century and until the first half of the twentieth century following the end of the Second World War. With the Church of England as its Christian religious denomination, the British Empire took an alternative Christianity to the Spanish and French Empires that promoted the Catholic Church. The British even went on to coin and append the name "Roman" to the Catholic Church, hence what was the Catholic Church and still is the Catholic Church

---

[235] See Henry VIII in 131 Christians Everyone Should Know quoted in passim at pp. 329-331. See also entry on Henry VIII in The Oxford Dictionary of the Christian Church quoted in passim at pp. 634 – 635.

[236] Ibid. The Oxford Dictionary of the Christian Church. See also Church of England, History and role, BBC Religions: https://www.bbc.co.uk/religion/religions/christianity/cofe/cofe_1.shtml

[237] James, Lawrence, The Rise and Fall of the British Empire © 1994, 1998 Abacus chapter 5 The World Turned Upside Down: The American War of Independence 1775 – 1783. pp. 107-121.

took a new name now often referred to as the Roman Catholic Church.[238] Understandably, the act of calling it the Roman Catholic Church was done not only in jest but to possibly spite the Catholic Church of any claim to being the universal church in the world especially following the reformation. So in this way, the influence of the British Empire on Christianity was grossly enlarged in spite of the fact that in some of their colonies and territories, the Catholic Church was already in existence either because of the Portuguese, Spanish or French visit prior to the British. Furthermore, because the empire had colonies that were made of a third of the world's population and they established Church schools which inevitably promoted Christianity, the effect and legacy of the British Empire, unlike the Spanish Empire and French Empire, became more evidentially enduring to this day because the Spanish and French Empires had no national church of their own and therefore took the Catholic Church to their colonies. But the positive influence of British Christianity was not only limited to what the Church of England did in their colonies and territories. Some English evangelical Christians such as William Wilberforce, already discussed in the previous chapter, who as a Member of the House of Parliament, gave British Christianity and the Christian religion a good name and doubtlessly inspired people to see British Christians in a positive light. William Wilberforce had a Cambridge University education and became an evangelical Christian and used his position as a Member of Parliament to lead the campaign for the abolition of slavery at a time in the eighteenth century that many could not summon courage do so. He is quoted to have written in his diary in 1818 that: "In Scripture, no national crime is so condemned so frequently and few so strongly as oppression and cruelty, and the not using our best endeavours to deliver our fellow-creatures from them."[239] Wilberforce extended his freedom in Christ to freedom from slavery for those who by human cruelty were subject to barbarism and abuse in

---

[238]   See Kenneth D. Whitehead, "How Did the Catholic Church Get Her Name?" Whitehead says in this article that "The term Roman Catholic is not used by the Church herself..." Read the full article at: https://www.ewtn.com/faith/teachings/churb3.htm ; See also Catholic.com quick questions and answers website where they trace the origin of the term "Roman Catholic Church" to the birth of Anglican Church: http://www.catholic.com/quickquestions/when-did-the-term-roman-catholic-church-first-come-into-being. It is worth adding that prior to appending the name Roman to the Catholic Church it was referred to as the Roman Church in the same way as the Church in Africa was referred to as the African Church in the first millennium of Christianity and into the first half of the second millennium.

[239]   See William Wilberforce and the abolition of the Slave Trade: Did You Know? "In Christianity Today, 1997, Issue 53: http://www.christianitytoday.com/ch/1997/issue53/53h002.html

their dispensation of labour and service to others who thought they were superior human species.

While it is sometimes said that the end of the British Empire came with the British handover of Hong Kong to China in 1997, in a sense, the empire did not end, but metamorphosed into being a friendly master of her former colonies and territories through the Commonwealth of Nations, the organisation of 53 independent member states of former Britain colonies and territories.[240] The organisation though based on equality of the independent states that are drawn from its members' states has the British Monarch, His Majesty King Charles III as the ceremonial head of the organisation.

6.4 The United Nations Organization Effect

The teachings of Christianity and its good and benefits for humanity found bearings in the laws and rules that have helped to shape human lives and affairs universally through the United Nations Organization, because at the time of its formation on 24 October 1945, the dominant powers such as the United States of America, United Kingdom of Great Britain and Northern Ireland, and France, were emphatically Christian nations and they more or less dictated the principles enshrined in the UN Charter.

While war must be discouraged and avoided by every moral and legitimate means possible, sometimes the sobriety and reality that the aftermath of war brings to human conscience tend to produce immediate good and benefit for humanity. That in essence partly explains the godly face of the United Nations (UN) Charter 1945[241] which was the product of the end of the Second World War.

The UN Charter has several clauses and articles with resemblances of the precepts that are in the Christian Holy Bible such as "love your neighbour as yourself."[242] And in many ways, it is the United Nations

---

[240]   See the Commonwealth member countries, the Charter of the Organisation and the work of the Commonwealth Organisation at: http://thecommonwealth.org/member-countries

[241]   See the United Nations Charter at: https://treaties.un.org/doc/publication/ctc/uncharter.pdf

[242]   See Holy Bible, Mark 12:31 http://biblehub.com/esv/mark/12.htm

Organization in implementing of the contents of its charter which is legally binding on its member states that brought the freedom and the liberty which the Church could not get the emperors and the political leaders they had influence on to effect. For even after the end of some of the European state empires such as the end of the Spanish Empire, French Empire, and the British Empire, these nations still had colonial territories that they dominated and exploited for their pleasure, especially in Africa and Asia. But all that came to a certain limitation, if not an outright end, once the United Nations Organisation Charter was signed. Article 73 in Chapter XI of the UN Charter stripped colonial masters of their dominion and power over most of the nations and territories that they took control of or commandeered in some cases:

Article 73

Members of the United Nations which have or assume responsibilities for the administration of territories whose people have not yet attained a full measure of self-government recognize the principle that the interests of the inhabitants of these territories are paramount, and accept as a sacred trust the obligation to promote to the utmost, within the system of international peace and security established by the present Charter, the well-being of the inhabitants of these territories, and to this end:

a.   to ensure, with due respect for the culture of the peoples concerned, their political, economic, social and educational advancement, their just treatment, and their protection against abuses;

b.   to develop self-government, to take due account of the political aspirations of the peoples, and to assist them in the progressive development of their free political institutions, according to the particular circumstances of each territory and its people and their varying stages of advancement;

c.   to further international peace and security;

d.   to promote constructive measures of development, to encourage research, and to co-operate with one another and, when and where appropriate, with specialized international bodies with a view to the practical achievement of the social, economic, and scientific purposes set forth in this Article; and

e. to transmit regularly to the Secretary-General for information purposes, subject to such limitation as security and constitutional considerations may require, statistical and other information of a technical nature relating to economic, social, and educational conditions in the territories for which they are respectively responsible other than those territories to which Chapters XII and XIII apply.[243]

By the contents of Article 73 of the UN Charter as stated above, colonization became a burden for the colonial masters to bear. Where economic exploitations and abuses of human labour was carried out without questions in the colonial territories, under the UN Charter the burden to protect the inhabitants of such territories from such abuses and exploitations became the legal obligations of the colonial masters. Furthermore, there was also the legal burden on the colonial masters to educate and improve the social standing of people who were inhabitants of the territories they were colonising. With that legal demand and obligation, the colonial masters, mostly, Spain, France and Britain hurriedly granted independence to most of their colonial territories between 1945 and 1997.

6.5 Evaluation and Summary

While it is indisputable that the Catholic Church through the Popes and the Council of Rome dominated and influenced world affairs from the fourth century through the first half of the sixteenth century when the Church of England was established, it did not succeed in making Christianity the religion of love and freedom as Jesus Christ taught as discussed in chapter 3. Nevertheless, Church patriarchs such as Athanasius remain example of how godly leadership can prevail. As for Christianity, individual Christians such as William Wilberforce in the nineteenth century that was discussed earlier, or the twentieth century outstanding humanitarian Christian nun Agnes Gonxha Bojaxhu widely known as Mother Teresa of Calcutta and now canonized by the Catholic Church as Saint Teresa of Calcutta[244], who spent her life to give

---

[243] UN Charter, Chapter XI, Article 73: https://treaties.un.org/doc/publication/ctc/uncharter.pdf

[244] See Mother Teresa, Roman Catholic nun in Encyclopaedia Britannica: https://www.britannica.com/biography/Mother-Teresa

help to the poor and to give hope to orphans in India, and several other individual Christians, have showed a measure of Christian love and what it means to be a Christian in ways that were liberating and enriching to humanity. Even people of other religions other than Christianity do not deny the fact that Christians such as William Wilberforce and Mother Teresa were good and exemplary Christians whose faith brought love and hope for humanity. The problem of Christianity from the above therefore is the temptation of its leaders to forget that they are called to show the love of Jesus Christ and not to appropriate power and authority vested on them for the deprivation of the freedom of others and thus resulting in the enactment of human rights law to guarantee some individual rights to freedom.

The Empires that came after the Roman Empire such as the Spanish, French and British Empires as discussed did not do Christianity and indeed the world much good with respect to how it indulged in acts of cruelty to humanity such as advancing dubious causes like the slave trade. All of the above had led humanity to believe that relating with one another according to law instead of according to the teachings of godliness and love as the Christian Bible says is the way to peace. So rather than people looking to God for justice they turn to the Courts of law to pursue justice. The mechanism for such legal redress for those who look to the law for justice is the subject of discussions in the subsequent chapters.

PART II

LEGAL FOUNDATIONS OF HUMAN RIGHTS AND RELIGIOUS FREEDOM

7

THE SEVENTEENTH CENTURY CHRISTIAN DENOMINATIONAL RELIGIOUS WARS IN EUROPE

"Great was the turmoil and many the monstrous crimes committed in the name of Christ in the wake of the Reformation in Europe. Religious passion quickly passed into political conflict."[245]

As the discussions in the previous chapters have shown everything possible was done to annihilate the Christian faith and religion in the first three hundred years of it coming into being following the death and resurrection of Jesus Christ.[246] The desperation to eradicate the Christian faith and religion was so intense in the first century AD that to dissuade people from becoming Christians and to get those who were Christians to recant their faith, the authorities of the Roman Empire often arrested those who were identified as Christians and got them thrown as food to feed hungry wild beasts. The account of how

---

[245] Dan Graves, MSL, Peace at Augsburg: https://www.christianity.com/church/church-history/timeline/1501-1600/peace-at-augsburg-11629989.html

[246] The account of the death and resurrection of Jesus Christ, can be read in each of the four gospels namely Matthew, Mark, Luke and John in the New Testament of the Holy Bible.

Emperor Septimius Severus[247] of the Roman Empire condemnation of a young African woman called Perpetua[248] and her fellow converts to Christianity after the emperor had forbidden conversion into Christianity in AD 202 is demonstrable of the cruel and degrading way Christians were tortured and executed for their faith and religious belief. That Emperor Septimus Severus who was an African too, of Libyan[249] origin by birth could have been so brutal to Perpetua, a mother still nursing her baby shows just how barbaric emperors were in the first, second and third centuries, in their desperation to stamp out Christianity. It is stated that when Perpetua was asked to recant her Christian faith and religion and offer a sacrifice to the gods of Rome for the health of the Emperor and she refused, she and her fellow converts were condemned to a humiliating public death. Her fellow Christian converts who were male were thrown to wild beasts and were mauled and chewed to death by a leopard and bear. As for Perpetua and her fellow lady convert, Roman gladiators killed them with swords.[250]

However, in spite of these despicable and cruel efforts to frustrate and obliterate the Christian faith and religion, it turned out as had been discussed above that by the fifth century AD, as a result of the conversion of Constantine the Great, the Christian religion became the religion of the Roman Empire and the entire empire itself became known as the Holy Roman Empire with everyone in the world then under its control obligated to profess the Christian faith and be affiliated to it by religious association.

---

[247] See Septimius Severus in Ancient History Encyclopedia: https://www.ancient.eu/Septimius_Severus/; See also account of Septimius Severus treatment of Christian converts following his prohibition of conversion to Christianity in AD 202 in

[248] See Perpetua in The Oxford Dictionary of the Christian Church, Edited by F.L. Cross and E.A. Livingstone, Second Edition, © 1974 Reprinted 1977 (with correction), p.1064.

[249] See the biography of Emperor Septimus Severus detailing his place of birth in Libya and how he moved to Rome and became Emperor in the Encyclopaedia Britannica: https://www.britannica.com/biography/Septimius-Severus

[250] See the Early Christians – The Martyrdom of Perpetua: http://www.jaysromanhistory.com/romeweb/christns/perpetua.htm

7.1 Conflicts between Catholics and the Protestants and the Peace of Augsburg 1555

Following the reformation as already discussed above in the sixteenth century, the Christian church was divided at into various protestant denominations namely then as the Catholic[251] Church, the Lutheran[252] Church, Anabaptists[253], the Church of England[254], and Calvinism.[255]

However, the freedom for individual Christians to belong to any of these denominations vexed various rulers in European nations, especially, if the person asserting such denominational affiliation was in their realm and claiming a denomination such as Roman Catholicism or Lutheranism when such was not that of the ruler of the realm. For instance, Emperor Charles V, who was both the ruler of the Holy Roman Empire and Spanish Empire sought to outlaw the Christians who identified themselves as Lutherans following the reformation of Martin Luther, by stating in 1521 at the assembly of princes known as the Diet of Worms that he intended to outlaw the Lutherans.[256] Charles V desire then was for all Christians to be identified as Catholics and not by any other Christian denomination. And because he did not achieve his goal in 1521, he went on to proclaim in 1529 with the authority vested on him as an Emperor that Catholicism should be restored everywhere in Germany. However, his order was met with an immediate resistance protest that was carried out by not only Lutherans but by all the other Christian denominations such as the Anabaptists and Calvinists; and the success of that protest led to non-Catholics' evangelical Christians being called Protestants[257] till this day.

---

[251]   Universal. The Catholic Church was originally the universal church until the reformation. It should not be mistaken with the Catholic Apostolic Church. See The Oxford Dictionary of the Christian Church quoted in passim at pp.254 – 255.

[252]   Lutheranism which is the teaching of Martin Luther on 'justification by faith alone' led to formation of the Lutheran Church. Ibid. Pp. 848-849.

[253]   Ibid. p. 47.

[254]   Ibid. pp. 290-291

[255]   A Church that is based on the teachings of John Calvin. Ibid. pp.223-224

[256]   Supra. Also see Augsburg in The Oxford Dictionary of the Christian Church. Second Edition Edited by F.L. Cross and E.A. Livingstone. Oxford 1974.

[257]   The libel 'Protestant' is only used for non-Catholics Christians. Even Christian denominations that did not exist at the time have come to bear the name Protestant because they are not of the Catholic denomination.

Nonetheless, the apparent resistance demonstrated by the protest in 1529, did not convince Emperor Charles V, to yield for the Lutherans and the other denominations to co-exist as Christian Churches alongside the Catholic Church. Even though the Lutherans took their confession of faith to the Emperor in 1531 in the bid to convince him that they were Bible believing Christians Emperor Charles V was still not persuaded by their Biblical Confessions to accede to their demands for legal standing as a body of Christian believers.[258] It took the declaration of war in 1552, and the glaring prospect of the Emperor losing that war before he yielded to the Lutherans to have the peace arrangement which became known as the September 25, 1555 Augsburg Peace that gave the Lutherans legal standing to exist as a Church alongside the Catholic Church. But the Anabaptists and Calvinists were excluded.

In fact, more seriously was the fact that the religious freedom that was agreed at the Augsburg Peace 1555 was not for the individuals who held Christian religious beliefs as Roman Catholics or Lutherans but for the rulers who were in charge of the realm. Cuius regio eius religio – the religion of the ruler determines the religion of citizens - was the pillar of the agreement. And even so, the rulers and princes themselves were limited generally to either be Roman Catholics or protestant Lutherans.[259]

With limitations in the religious freedoms that were reached at the Peace of Augsburg with Emperor Ferdinand I in 1555, Emperor Ferdinand II of Germany some years later still wanted to renege on that agreement. He wanted to stamp out the evangelicals who had become known as Protestants. He attempted to get everyone in every realm of the Holy Roman Empire to profess only the faith of the Catholic Church. This attempt of Ferdinand II led to the three decades of wars that ripped Central European nations apart between 1614 and 1648. The worst affected of these was Germany whose population was reduced from 16 million in 1620 to 10 million in 1650[260] as a result of those who lost their

---

[258]   Supra as in footnote 192.

[259]   See The Oxford Dictionary of the Christian Church. Second Edition Edited by F.L. Cross and E. A. Livingstone © OUP 1974. Augsburg, Peace of (1555). P.108

[260]   Fassbender, Bardo, Westphalia, Peace of (1648), A. Introduction, at paragraph 4 in the Oxford Public International Law published under the auspices of the Max Planck Foundation for International Peace and the Rule of Law under direction of Rudiger Wolfrum http://opil.ouplaw. com/view/10.1093/law:epil/9780199231690/law-9780199231690-e739

lives in the cause of the war and also because of economic hardships and starvation occasioned by the years of war.

7.2 The European Nations War of Religious Conflicts and Political Interests 1618 - 1648

Until the war began in 1618, Spain had been in control of the Holy Roman Empire since 1494 and therefore determined the political direction of the empire in alliance with the Pope with whom together they ruled not only Europe but to a large extent the entire world. Whilst the wars were triggered by religious conflicts and intolerance of the Holy Roman Emperor under the leaderships of the Emperor and the Pope, intrinsic to the cause of the war was also national and political interests of the major central European nations such as Germany, France, Sweden, Spain, Italy and the Netherlands.

Tensions were exasperated in 1618 when Ferdinand II in disregard to the Peace of Augsburg 1555 sought to abolish Protestantism by ordering that only Roman Catholicism should be the Church that all Christians in the empire should belong to. In reaction to the Emperor's decree to take away their religious freedom as Protestants, the then Bohemian states who today are the people of the nations of Austria and Czech Republic demonstrated their rejection of Emperor Ferdinand II's decree by throwing out his representatives at the Prague Castle, in an act that became known as the defenestration of Prague.[261] following the defenestration of Prague, the Bohemian states went on to form alliances with other Christian States within the Germany territories. On the other hand, the Holy Roman Emperor Ferdinand II, also engaged the support of King Philip IV of Spain. The Bohemian States Protestant forces fearing defeat in the hands of Ferdinand II forces acted in a manner consistent with national political interest but averse to the Christian

---

[261] Asch, Ronald G. The Thirty Years War, The Holy Roman Empire and Europe 1618 – 1648 © 1997 MacMillan Press Ltd. Pp.47-54.

religious admonition[262] by engaging the Islamic forces of the Ottoman Empire[263] to push back the Poles who were fighting in support of Ferdinand II.

Emperor Ferdinand II further engaged forces of the Catholic nation states of Belgium, France and Germany. The Protestant forces were also expanded by the joining of Protestant States such as Denmark and Norway. In the battles that followed the Catholic forces defeated the Protestant armies. However, in 1630 the leader of Sweden, Gustavus Adolphus, joined the Protestant forces and led them to some victories in which they took over territories previously seized by Catholic forces. But the victory of the Protestant Armies gained through the support of Gustavus Adolphus was short-lived because he was killed in the Battle of Lutzen in 1632.[264]The Protestant forces however did not surrender. They fought on and the war might well had ended in 1635 with the Peace of Prague but for the fact that the treaty of Prague only conceded territories to the rulers of the Lutherans and Calvinists and it was not extended to the Protestants of Austria and Czech Republic.

More damaging to the terms of the treaty that led to the Peace of Prague 1635, was the deliberate modification of the terms by Ferdinand II "to further his own and the Catholic princes favour."[265] And if that was not bad enough to warrant the failure of the treaty and the Peace of Prague, as we see from Asch's historic account in his book, The Thirty Years War:

> "Pope Urban VIII continued to advocate a strict Counter-Reformation policy, not just for religious reasons but also because he was opposed to Spain."[266]

---

[262]   The idea of engaging non-Christian soldiers such as the Islamic forces of the Ottoman Empire in the war, was an anti-Christian act as in 1 Corinthians 6:1-8 in the Holy Bible, the Apostle Paul admonished the believers not to take their disputes to unbelievers to judge them, let alone engage unbelievers to help them kill their fellow believers but the war was not just about religious beliefs. But the war was not only about religious freedom but about supremacy, hence it was more important to them to win the war than comply with the scriptural admonition of not engaging unbelievers in the fight between Christians.

[263]   A very helpful and easily understood account of the causes of 'The Thrity Years' War' in Europe between 1618 and 1648 can be read on the History.com site: https://www.history.com/topics/reformation/thirty-years-war

[264]   Asch, Ronald G., The Thirty Years War 1618 – 1648, pp. 106 -

[265]   Ronald G. Asch, THE THIRTY YEARS WAR The Holy Roman Empire and Europe, 1618 – 1648 © 1997 MacMillan Press. P.112

[266]   Ibid.

Often people pursue their personal ambitions as Ferdinand II and Pope Urban did under the synthetic guise of their religious stance, to the detriment of humanity leading to human rights violations and abuses and in extreme cases, as it is in this instance, to the wanton destruction of human lives and crimes against humanity. There was nothing that Emperor Ferdinand II did in modifying the terms of the Peace of Prague that intended to honour the God that the Catholic Christians believed in other than the desire for the Roman Empire to remain a super power. If Emperor Ferdinand II was worldly and lacking in piety by his acts of modifying the terms of the treaty of the Peace of Prague, then Pope Urban VIII, in spite of his spiritual position as the head of the Catholic Church did not see any reason at the time to be different by been pious as his reasons for taking a counter-reformation policy was not based on religious consideration but his worldly desire to oppose Spain on grounds that Spanish possessions in Italy were overshadowing his position and his rule.[267]

Compounding the vested interests that Ferdinand II and Pope Urban VIII had advanced over and above securing peace by the terms of the treaty of the Peace of Prague was the vulnerable position that the protestant princes that would have supported the terms of the treaty found themselves in. They were to be committed "either to a fruitless and ultimately unwinnable war of attrition against Swedes or to buying them off by making major financial and territorial concessions."[268] Such a position was not a peace enabling position that could have ended a war that had gone on for seventeen years as at the time. The Protestant Princes were major stakeholders for peace and leaving them in a vulnerable position was clearly an act of punctuating the prospects of peace in the terms of the treaty.

Whatever good the Peace of Prague 1635 might have achieved, the real truth was that it failed its ultimate purpose of ending the war and so the war carried on to the detriment of European nationals and European peace for a further thirteen years as religious wars as opposed to it been named a war of human cravings for power and authority as Ferdinand II and Pope Urban VIII clearly exemplified.

---

[267]   Ibid.

[268]   Ibid. p.116.

The forces of the Catholic armies and those of the Protestant states carried on fighting even after the death of Ferdinand II in 1637, although he was replaced by his son Ferdinand III. However, by 1648 all the European nation states involved in the Thirty Years War knew they could only resolve their religious and political difference by peaceful agreements and they accordingly entered various treaties embodied in the Peace of Westphalia.

7.3 The Peace of Westphalia 1648

The wars were finally ended basically by two settlements' treaties between the Empire and France at Münster; and between the Empire and Sweden at Osnabrück in November 1648. Although a third treaty which is also embodied in the Peace of Westphalia was actually agreed by Spain and the United Provinces of the Netherlands on 30th January 1648. It is well summed up by the international law scholar, Bardo Fassbender, which has already been quoted nonetheless his summation gives a helpful elucidation of the discussion:

> The Peace of Westphalia formally ended the Thirty Years War (1618 – 1648), a prolonged struggle over religion and power in which most European powers had been involved. The Thirty Years War was a religious conflict, the height of the struggle between Catholics and Protestants which had begun with the Reformation of the 16th Century. It was also a fight for the supremacy over Europe, with France and Sweden opposing the German Emperor who belonged to the house of Habsburg. Lastly, it was a conflict between the Emperor and the larger German territories which sought to throw off their constitutional commitments to the Emperor and to establish a sort of semi-independence.[269]

However, the treaties that ended the war called the Peace of Westphalia (1648), were extended to other European countries such as England, Poland, and the Principalities and Republics of Italy, Netherlands and the Swiss Cities because of the effect of the implications of the equality of

---

[269]   Ibid. Footnote 199 Fassbender at para 3

states and territorial controls in the treaties.[270] The Peace of Westphalia did not only achieve the religious freedom for the rulers of nation-states in Europe which wanted to profess the Christian faith as Protestants belonging to the Lutherans or Anabaptists or Calvinists, but it also achieved territorial boundaries for each of those nation states thus giving absolute control of territory to rulers and princes of the realms that made up Europe. The importance that international law has ascribed to the Peace of Westphalia has often been pointed out to how it defined and shaped the principle of state independence and territorial control in international law.[271]

7.4. Why Religious Freedom Has Remained An Issue in Europe and Beyond

As far as the actual reason for which the Thirty Years War was fought in Europe between 1618 and 1648 as discussed above by the Catholics and Protestant states respectively, the religious freedom that was achieved in the Peace of Westphalia was still the same cuius regio eius religio and not really the religious freedom of the individual person to hold his own free religious beliefs. It was rather the religious freedom of the various Protestant evangelical denominational churches such as Lutherans, Calvinists, Anabaptists etc. to exist alongside the Roman Catholic Church. In essence, it was only the rulers and princes that had religious freedom to decree which Christian denomination they wanted to believe in and which their subjects mustfollow in their lands.

The fact that the individual was not granted express liberty to his own freedom of religion in the Peace of Westphalia as to whether to be a catholic or protestant meant that from 1648 when European nations ended its wars of religious conflicts, the individual had been at war to emancipate himself from the religious dictates of princes and rulers in the nations of Europe and beyond until this day.

---

[270]   Ibid. Fassbender at para 5.

[271]   Brownlie, Ian, Principles of Public International Law Sixth Edition © 2003 Oxford University Press. pp.105-106 See the discussion on Sovereignty and Jurisdiction. Although no mention is made about the Peace of Westphalia, discussion therein has bearings.

Added to that is the fact that the inter-Christian denominational conflicts and wars prior to the Westphalian Treaty dealt irreparable damage to Christian heritage. For instance, the City of Constantinople which historically was where the books of the Holy Bible were compiled was lost to the Ottoman Tucks under Mehmed 11 the conqueror, who conquered it in 1453 and renamed it Istanbul (the City of Islam). That might not have occurred if not that there were divisions and internal fighting among believers in the Christian faith that weakened the Roman Empire. It was also the case that the Roman Emperor and his military were engaged in defending the Roman Catholic Church against the early skirmishes of Protestants as far as the fifteen century and prior to the thirty years (1618 – 1648) war between the Roman Catholic Church and the Roman Empire on one side and the Protestant denominations and their allied forces on the other side in the seventeenth century already discussed.

7.5 Evaluation and Summary

Arguably, if European nations had peace following the Peace of Westphalia (1648), it was probably because their attention was shifted from the continent of Europe to the nations of Africa and Asian where they embarked on imperialists missions and in the commercialisation of drugs such as opium as they did in China and in slave trade as they did to most people from the West African states between the fifteen and the nineteenth century. This view can be supported by the fact that as soon as slave trade was abolished in the early nineteenth century following the Toussaint Louverture led Haitian Revolution between 1793 and 1803, following the initial uprising in 1791,[272] and the British abolition of Slave Trade by the Slave Trade Act of 1807, the European nations' imperialists and colonisation of African nations started in a very organised way with the Berlin Conference of 1884/85 in which European nations agreed that African nations would be divided among the nations of Europe and the United States of America. European nationalists struggle with each other at the turn of the nineteenth century resulted in the First World War (WW1) between 1914 and 1918.[273]

---

[272]   Popkin, Jeremy D., You Are All Free The Haitian Revolution And The Abolition of Slavery © 2010 Cambridge University Press. pp. 1-4.

[273]   I. Bantekas and L. Ouette, International Human Rights Law and Practice (Cambridge University Press, 2016), 12-14

As if no lessons were learnt from the millions of lives lost in the four years of the WW1, rather than respect for the sanctity of human life, the Second World War (WW2) followed barely two decades after the WW1. The Second World War became inevitable as Germany under the leadership of Adolf Hilter and the Nazi Party, framed a nationalist policy of total elimination of the Jews and people with disabilities and others for which death was directed at because of their nationality such as the Roma and Sinti. The nations of the world still divided under imperialists powers fought along the lines of their alliances and a wholly and totally waste of millions of human lives was yet again wasted.

However, out of these unfortunate circumstances and extreme display of man's inhumanity to man came the eventual birth of human rights with the right to individual freedom to religious belief and freedom of conscience.

Nonetheless, we shall see in the subsequent chapters of this book how Christians in particular have remained the victims of restrain, persecution and in some cases have died in the course of exercising or practicing their Christian religious beliefs. But the paradox of it all, perhaps, are the cases about Christian leaders indulging in serious criminal acts in violation of those they were expected to give spiritual and moral guidance to. This is happening as we shall see even in the face of international human rights laws ascribing the right to freedom of conscience, belief and religion under the auspices of the United Nations Organization and in various continental regional human rights conventions signed by states with legal obligations to protect their citizens and ensure the enjoyments of these rights or redress for violations.

8

THE PEACE OF WESTPHALIA 1648 AND THE ABSENCE OF THE RIGHT TO THE INDIVIDUAL FREEDOM OF CONSCIENCE, RELIGION AND BELIEF

"You may judge us now, but God will judge you later."[274]

The Holy Bible and the ethics of the Christian religion place obligation on the individual person who have come to the profession of the faith to exercise and live the Christian faith in his individual capacity and not to profess or pretend to be a believer in the faith because of his ruler or priest. Jesus' places the emphasis on salvation on the one who believes and not on the state or nation that believe. Although the kings and rulers compelled their subjects to believe in their religions, it is the individual that will be judged on his individual standing and so the king or ruler cannot exercise his faith on behalf of the people in his land or region.

---

[274] Perpetua's remark at the Roman authorities that condemned her and her fellow converts to death, because of their refusal to recant her Christian faith and religion so that their lives could be spared in third century AD Rome. See: Perpetua in The Oxford Dictionary of the Christian Church © 1958, 1974 Oxford University Press. pp. 1064-1065. "The Martyrdom of Perpetua" http://www.jaysromanhistory.com/romeweb/christns/perpetua.htm

Jesus Christ said:

> For God so loved the world, that he gave his one and only
> son, so that everyone who believes in him will not perish
> but have eternal life.[275]

8.1. The Persecution of Christians by Kings and Rulers:

It did not take long after the Peace of Westphalia 1648 that ended the
Thirty Years' War in Europe with princes and rulers of the various
nations of Europe deciding whether those in their realms would profess
the faith of the Roman Catholic Church or Protestantism such as
Lutherans, Calvinists, Anabaptists and Anglicans, before the persecution
for the suppression of freedom of conscience and religious freedom of the
individual believers in various nation states of Europe became a thing
that led to new arguments and demands for the individual freedom of
conscience and religious freedom as opposed to simply conforming with
that of the ruler.

It has to be said that the divinity and spirituality of the Christian faith
were simultaneously elevated and marred at the conversion of Emperor
Constantine the Great who might have thought well in his proclamation
that the Roman Empire under him would be a Christian world. Because
Christianity is an individual thing that proclamation simply diluted the
spirituality and divinity of the religion to the extent that political almost
overtook the fear of God and the essence of the faith which is to proclaim
the love of God through his Son Jesus Christ. The opportunity to right
this wrong which came with the reformation in the sixteenth century
under Martin Luther who stood the test of his faith and refused to recant
his 95 Theses[276] was altered by the powers given to the princes and rulers
to choose the religion for their lands instead of giving the individual the
freedom of conscience and religious belief in the Peace of Westphalia
1648. At his trial in which Charles V, the Holy Roman Emperor, had
asked Luther, to recant his 95 Theses, he unequivocally, stated:

---

[275]   Holy Bible, John 3:16 (English Standard Version): https://biblehub.com/esv/john/3.htm

[276]   Luther, Martin, 95 Theses, Translated by Adolph Spaeth. First Rate Publishers.

> "Unless, I can be instructed and convinced with evidence
> from the Holy Scriptures or with open, clear, and distinct
> grounds of reasoning...then I cannot and will not
> recant, because it is neither safe nor wise to act against
> conscience."[277]

Luther's theses[278] for the reform of the Church that led to Protestantism were clearly based on the conviction that faith in God and Christian religious beliefs as in the Holy Bible just as was seen from the statement Jesus made in John 3:16, quoted early, is about the individual salvation and practice of Christian beliefs irrespective of how his ruler or prince chooses to practice his own faith.

The conflicts between ungodly rulers, albeit professing the Christian faith, who want to have their way and the Christians who want to stay true to their Christian faith and religious beliefs as admonished in the Holy Bible have brought deaths to some and torture to others at various times since after the Peace of Westphalia. The clear implication of this is that the Peace of Westphalia did not offer the individual Christian believer any religious freedom to exercise his faith and practice the Christian religion but it simply offered kings and rulers religious concessions to determine the religion they will have in their realm. The terms of the treaty insofar as religion was concerned ascribed freedom or the right to religious freedom to what the strong and powerful prince or ruler approves, making sense of the rather controversial definition of justice that we read in the dialogue of the sophists where Thrasymachus told Socrates that:

> "Justice or right is simply what is in the interest of the
> stronger party."[279]

This was quite obvious in various European nations in the seventeenth and eighteenth centuries where rulers denied their citizens or subjects' religious freedom wherever it was not in conformity with their own traditions and practices. In England for example, in the seventeenth century, following the Peace of Westphalia (1648), King Charles II of

---

[277] Galli, Mark and Oslen, Ted, 131 Christians Everyone Should Know © 2000 Christianity Today, Inc. Martin Luther, p.35.

[278] Martin Luther, 95 Theses, First Rate Publishers. Translated by Adolp Spaeth.

[279] Plato, The Republic with an introduction by Melissa Lane. Penguin Classics 2007. p. 18.

England, wanted everyone in England to profess the Christian faith in conformity with the Church of England. When evangelicals such as John Bunyan, the tinker who got converted by the Separatist Church where he became a Lay Minister and later a Congregational Minister[280] refused to comply with the King's order to belong to the Church of England, he was arrested and jailed for 12 years for the crime of not complying with the King's order. It was not important to king Charles II that Bunyan was entitled to hold his own religious beliefs and act according to his conscience and thoughts; it was more important to the king that Bunyan expresses his Christian faith and religious beliefs by belonging to the Church of England, in which he was the head. After all, the king was entitled to this stance under the terms of the Peace of Westphalia in which "cuius regio, eius religio" was the basis for religious freedom and the king was the ruler of the land. Although some say that Bunyan's years in prison led to his writing one of the most famous Christian books The Pilgrim's Progress, which brought him great fame and honour[281], the point of relevance here is that Bunyan was denied his freedom of religious beliefs and freedom of conscience after the peace of Westphalia (1648).

8.2 Christianity and Mandatory Education

The tendency of kings and rulers, sometimes in conjunction with some unholy and immoral members of the priesthood to subject people within their realms to do their biddings in the guise of doing the will of God as "cuius regio, euis religio" dictated led to disagreements between some of the pure Christians and the rulers and ungodly priests who were deceiving the people by imposing ungodly rules on the people. In England, a group of Christians who were determined to do the will of God based on the word of God as contained in the Holy Bible, decided to disassociate themselves from the practices of the Roman Catholic Church and the Church of England. These group of Christians became known as the Puritans in 16th and 17th Century England.

A good number of these English people moved to America in the 16th and 17th Centuries with a desire to establish a Christian community that will

---

[280] See Galli, M., and Olsen, T., 131 Christians Everyone Should Know, John Bunyan, pp. 116.

[281] Galli, M., and Olsten, T. Ibid. p.117

be pure and free from the influence of the Roman Catholic Church and the Church of England.

Their determination to ensure that their children knew God by being able to read the word of God in the Holy Bible for themselves and therefore protected from deception as to what the will of God is led them to make education mandatory. In Massachusetts they passed a law that predated the independence of the United States of America. The "Old Deluder Satan Act of 1647 (1647)"[282] was passed to make schooling mandatory so that people could be able to read the Holy Bible for themselves.[283]

This was how free and compulsory education started with all the benefits that comes with education besides the ability to read the Holy Bible, which paradoxically today, has now been removed from the curriculum of many State Schools, especially in the United States and European countries.

8.3 Evaluation and Summary

The oppression of individual religious freedom and freedom of conscience was so severe and so widespread in England and indeed in other European nations in the sixteenth, seventeenth and eighteenth centuries that leading philosophers and scholars wrote about it. In England for instance, one of the most influential thinkers of the time, John Locke, in his write up pointed out that:

> For whatsoever some people boast ...of the pomp of their outward worship; others, of the reformation of their discipline; all, of the orthodoxy of their faith...... and all others of this nature, are much rather marks of men striving for power and empire over one another, than of the Church of Christ.[284]

---

[282] See "Old Deluder Satan Act of 1647 (1647) by David Carleton, published on January 1, 2009, last updated on July 2, 2o24, Free Speech Center, At Middle Tennessee State University: https://firstamendment.mtsu.edu/article/old-deluder-satan-act-of-1647/

[283] Ibid.

[284] Locke, John, The Second Treatise of Government And A Letter Concerning Toleration, Dover Thrift Editions, © 2002 by Dover Publications Inc., p. 115

As if to remind kings, rulers and in some cases others who were in authority in the Church as leaders as seen in previous discussions, but were void of the love Jesus Christ exemplified, by the acts of cruelty and barbarism they showed their fellow men, Locke quoted the admonition of Jesus Christ whom every Christian should emulate thus:

> "The Kings of the Gentiles exercise lordship over them" said our Saviour to his disciples, "but ye shall not be so."[285]

He went on to make plain the basis for which the Christian religion is an individual thing before it can be a community thing in his "Letter Concerning Toleration" by saying:

> The business of true religion is quite another thing. It is not instituted in order to the erecting of an external pomp, nor to the obtaining of ecclesiastical dominion, nor to the exercising of compulsive force, but to the regulating of men's lives, according to the rules of virtue and piety.[286]

However, some of what we know today as human rights was civil liberties in England before the end of the seventeenth century. For example, the Habeas Corpus Act 1679 gave citizens the right to freedom from unlawful detention or arbitrary imprisonment. And the Toleration Act 1689 allowed those who were nonconformist Christians, such as non-members of the Church of England, like the Baptists and Congregationalists, the right to their own religious worship without the fear of arrest and imprisonment that people such as John Bunyan were made to undergo just because of their refusal to belong to the Church of England.

---

[285] Ibid. An apparent paraphrase of Luke 22:25-26

[286] Ibid. Footnote 205.

9

THE BASIS OF THE DECLARATION OF UNIVERSAL HUMAN RIGHTS AND THE MAKING OF HUMAN RIGHTS' LAWS

Rulers have few incentives to enact laws to protect their subjects from them. That is, of course, precisely why such constraints must ultimately be imposed on the state at some level superior (or at least external) to itself – and the only such level that we have is that of the international community.[287]

9.1 The Practice of States on Individual Rights and Liberties

In the course of human civilisation and development over the centuries, every nation state or kingdom in the case of monarchies, have granted a number of liberties and privileges to citizens of the state or subjects of the kingdom. But these rights and privileges were universally at variance. The rights of a person in China are not the same as the rights of a person in Brazil. And the rights of a person in the United Kingdom of Great Britain and Northern Ireland are not the same as the rights of a person in the kingdom of Saudi Arabia.

---

[287] The above remarks were made by Paul Sieghart justifying the basis for international human rights law. See Sieghart, Paul, The Lawful Rights of Mankind © 1985 Oxford University Press. p.44.

In the United Kingdom for example, individual rights and liberties trickled down from the Magna Carta 1215[288] in which King John of England faced with the rebellion of his barons agreed to be bound by law and ceded some rights and privileges to individual subjects of his kingdom. Although, at the time, it was only limited more or less to the aristocrats/barons, until when the Habeas Corpus Act 1679, was passed to protect the individual subject from unfair arrest and imprisonment, citizens were vulnerable to arbitrary arrest and detention. In 1689, parliament passed two laws that had bearings on people's civil liberties and which has bearings today on human rights. The Toleration Act[289] which allowed for freedom of worship by nonconformists and members of the Church of England, such as the Congregationalists and Baptists was passed in May 1689. In December of that same year, the English Bill of Rights 1689 was passed by Parliament prohibiting the individual subjects of the monarchy from cruel treatment and torture. From thereon citizens acquired more civil liberties and indeed the present human rights, such as the rights enacted by parliament in the Human Rights Act 1998. However, in most other places in the world, the treatments of citizens depending on the form of government, whether military regimes such as it was in Uganda under Idi Amin's government[290], where Amin was reputed to have said: "There is freedom of speech, but I cannot guarantee freedom after speech" or in Chile under the government of Augusto Pinochet[291], where people were brutalised and killed at the behest of the head of government without resort to legal remedies at the time, which was as recent as the last quarter of the twentieth century.

---

[288]   Magna Carta With a new commentary by David Carpenter © 2015 Penguin Classics.

[289]   While the Toleration Act 1689 allowed the freedom of worship of nonconformists such as Baptists and Congregationalists, it said that Roman Catholics and disbelievers did not benefit from the act. See the discuss on The Toleration Act 1689 in F.L Cross and E.A. Livingstone, The Oxford Christian Dictionary © 1974 at p. 1384.

[290]   A summation of Idi Amin's terror and the alleged 300,000 he killed while he was head of State of Uganda is captured in Michael T Kaufman's article about his death published in the New York Times of August 17, 2003, under the title: "Idi Amin, Murderous and Erratic Ruler of Uganda in the 70's Dies in Exile." https://www.nytimes.com/2003/08/17/world/idi-amin-murderous-and-erratic-ruler-of-uganda-in-the-70-s-dies-in-exile.html

[291]   General Augusto Pinochet Ugarte was widely known across the globe as the head of state of Chile whose reign of terror saw people disappear or executed while thousands of others were detained or tortured. The story about his death by Jonathan Kandell in the New York Times under the title: "Augusto Pinochet, Dictator Who Ruled by Terror in Chile, Dies at 91", sums up what the world knew about Pinochet and human rights violations of his countrymen and countrywomen. https://www.nytimes.com/2006/12/11/world/americas/11pinochet.html

9.2 The Christian Influence in Ascribing Rights to the Individual under International Law

Against the backdrop of the different forms of cruel and degrading treatments that many individuals have had to undergo amidst various other forms of unfair treatments such as trials experienced by people in different nations of the world under cruel and tyrannical rulers, even where democracy was supposedly practiced as a form of government in some cases, the United Nations initiative to define and protect individual human rights from the time of its inception became a noble and welcome development for the good of humanity.

In his account of the development of human rights law, Paul Sieghart in his book, The Lawful Rights of Mankind, states that:

> But the events preceding and precipitating the second world war made it plain that the international community constituted by all those states could not afford to continue to leave it to each of them to choose alone, in the exercise of its unfettered sovereignty, between the absolutist strand and the strand of constraints: a superior and external set of constraints had to be imposed on each of them, in the interests of all. And so, from 1945 onwards, that community installed an overriding code of international human rights law...The code does not depend on any prior theory of 'divine', 'moral', 'natural', or any other kind of rights. Instead, just as scientists and engineers have got together to agree on international standards such as the metre and the gram in order to avoid disputes about miles, leagues, ells, pounds, ounces, and grains, so the nations have now simply agreed on international legal standards of human rights, thereby creating positive law among themselves.[292]

The importance that the State-Parties of the United Nations Organization (UN) as the body representing the international community gave to human rights took prime place by what is stated in the preamble of the Charter and in the very first article of the Charter:

---

[292]   Sieghart, Paul, The Lawful Rights of Mankind, © 1985, Oxford University Press. Pp. 39-40

WE THE PEOPLE OF THE UNITED NATIONS DETERMINED to save succeeding generations from the scourge of war, which twice in our lifetime has brought untold sorrow to mankind, and reaffirm faith in fundamental human rights, in the dignity and worth of the human person, in the equal rights of men and women and of nations large and small, and to establish conditions under which justice and respect for the obligations arising from treaties and other sources of international law can be maintained....do hereby establish an international organization to be known as the United Nations.[293]

Article 1

The Purpose of the United Nations are:

1(1) To maintain international peace and security....

1(2) To develop friendly relations among nations based on respect for the principle of equal rights and self-determination of peoples....

1(3) To achieve international co-operation in solving international problems of economic, social, cultural or humanitarian character, and in promoting and encouraging respect for human rights and for fundamental freedoms for all without distinction as to race, sex, language, or religion;[294]

One other account that gives compelling grounds for the birth and development of human rights by the United Nations Organization at the time of its formation is given by Samuel Moyn in his book Christian Human Rights.[295] Moyn recounts that while the Second World War was on-going without certainty of what will become the outcome and with Christians fighting on either side, the Pontiff of the Roman Catholic

---

[293] See the full text of the preamble of the United Nations Charter 1945 at: https://www.un.org/en/sections/un-charter/preamble/index.html

[294] See the full text of Article 1 of the United Nations Charter 1945 at: https://www.un.org/en/sections/un-charter/chapter-i/index.html

[295] Moyn, Samuel, Christian Human Rights © 2015 University of Pennsylvania Press.

Church, Pope Pius XII delivered the following Christmas Day Message in 1942:

> Dignity of the Human Person. He who would have the Star of Peace shine out and stand over society should cooperate, for his part, in giving back to the human person the dignity given to it by God from the beginning...He should uphold respect for and the practical realization of .... fundamental personal rights... The cure of this situation becomes feasible when we awaken again the consciousness of a juridical order resting on the supreme dominion of God, and safeguarded from all human whims; a consciousness of an order which stretches forth its arm, in protection or punishment, over the unforgettable rights of man and protects them against the attacks of every human power.[296]

But the concern of Christians according to Moyn did not stop with the Christmas Day 1942 Message of Pope Pius XII. Moyn says:

> Around the same time, ecumenical formations of transatlantic Protestant elites proclaimed human rights to be key to future world order. The communion between human rights and Christianity was therefore a novel and fateful departure in the history of political discourse.[297]

From the statement in the preamble of the United Nations Charter to the statements in various articles of the Charter such as Articles 1, 55, and 56, the United Nations Commission for Human Rights set up by the Economic and Social Council (1946), and the United Nations Human Rights Committee which actually investigates individual complaints, the intention to protect individual human rights is clear. The United Nations demonstrated its commitments to human rights by further making the Universal Declaration of Human Rights (1948), and more legally binding treaties such as the International Covenant on Economic, Social and Cultural Rights (1966), International Covenant on Civil and Political Rights (1966); and subsequent other international human rights

---

[296] Ibid. p.2 As quoted by Moyn see Pius XII, "The Internal Order of States and People" (Christmas Day Message for 1942), in Vincent Yzermans, ed., Major Addresses, 2 vols. (St Paul, MN: North Central Publishing, 1961) 2:60.

[297] Ibid footnote 214 page 3

conventions such as the Convention on the Elimination of All Forms of Discrimination against Women, CEDAW, (1979), Convention on the Rights of the Child, CRC, (1989), and various other international human rights treaties including human rights treaties such as the European Convention on Human Rights and Fundamental Freedoms, ECHR, (1950), and the American Convention on Human Rights, ACHR, (1969), and the African Charter on Human and Peoples' Rights, ACHPR, (1981).

However, while the above accounts of Sieghart and Moyn are relevant to what has become of human rights law today, the concept of human rights and its development goes as far back as the development of human society. Bantekas and Oette recognised this when they stated in their book that:

> While the notion of human rights is arguably of more recent origin, it is part of a broader development that can be traced back to the earlier stages of human history.[298]

9.3 Evaluation and Summary

However, the essence of human rights today cannot be divorced from the over two thousand four hundred years old argument of 'a just man' and a 'just society' presented in The Republic[299] by Plato. The argument for justice and fairness as ingredients of happiness, were also at the centre of Aristotle's arguments in the Nicomachean Ethics[300] and these are the fabrics of human rights just as they have been the basis of moral and political philosophy and the defining principles of democratic societies.

---

[298] Bantekas, Ilias, and Oette, Lutz, International Human Rights Law And Practice, Second Edition, Cambridge University Press © 2016. P.6

[299] Plato, The Republic is still a current philosophy reading textbook for some undergraduate philosophy and political science degree students in Universities in Europe, America, Africa etc. universities because democracy is largely practiced in most, if not all nation-states of these continents; and Socrates explored the merits of democracy as well as oligarchy, timocracy and tyranny as forms of government in his dialogue about the just man and the just society in his discussion of unjust constitutions in book VIII of The Republic.

[300] Although Aristotle's Nicomachean Ethics might be easily summed up as a treatise on happiness, the fact that his discourse shows that happiness is not a feeling but a range of activities such as courage, generosity and justice that are demonstrably virtuous points to the fact that human rights can be best enjoyed in a society of well-educated people that are led by just leaders. Like Plato, and indeed Socrates who argued that only proper education can produce proper conduct in a just society, Aristotle argues in book V of his Nicomachean Ethics that proper education will produce justice and fairness in the society.

In both The Republic and the Nicomachean Ethics, the arguments for the proper education of the just man and the just ruler are strenuously emphasised. It is perhaps the reason why those who drafted the United Nations International Covenant on Economic, Social and Cultural Rights, (1966) stated in Article 13 of that covenant:

The States Parties to the present Covenant recognize the right of everyone to education. They agree that education shall be directed to the full development of the human personality and the sense of its dignity, and shall strengthen the respect for human rights and fundamental freedoms...[301]

To the extent that most of the laws of human rights as stated in various international articles are qualified rights because of some of the limitations placed on the individual person's enjoyment of the rights, it follows that the individual person intended to enjoy those rights is expected to have such virtue as to understand the boundaries of how his enjoyment of a right can cause harm to others or the society at large. For example, the "right to privacy and family life" ceases to be a right if in the exercise of that right the individual concerned engages in unlawful acts such as accumulation of weapons for the harm or destruction of other individuals in the society or even himself or members of his family:

No one shall be subjected to arbitrary or unlawful interference with his privacy, family, home or correspondence, nor to unlawful attacks on his honour and reputation.

- Article 17 (1), International Covenant on Civil and Political Rights, ICCPR.

and

Everyone has the right to respect for his private and family life, his home and his correspondence."

"There shall be no interference by a public authority with the exercise of this right except such as is in accordance

---

[301]   Article 13 (1), International Covenant on Economic, Social and Cultural Rights.

with the law and is necessary in a democratic society in the interests of national security, public safety or the economic well-being of the country, for the prevention of disorder or crime, for the protection of health or morals, or for the protection of the rights and freedoms of others.

- Article 8 (1), and 8(2), European Convention for the Protection of Human Rights and Fundamental Freedoms, ECHR.

These rights are qualified with the limitation that justifies interference by the State with respect to national security. If a person is suspected of theft or causing injury to another person then there would be lawful grounds for the police to even break into his house and arrest him, if they have obtained a court order to go to the extent of breaking into house to arrest him because they could not apprehend him in any other way.

Furthermore, insofar as the emergence of human rights law is concerned it can be said that because the Covenant of the League of Nations 1919 stated its duty to "guarantee freedom of conscience and religion, ..."[302],

...the Members of the League:

(a) Will endeavour to secure and maintain fair and humane conditions of labour for men, women, and children,"[303]

the legal basis for human rights goes back to the period of the League of Nations and not 1945. Along these lines, Brownlie stated in his book, Principles of Public International Law that:

The appearance of human rights in the sphere of international law and organizations is often traced to the era of the League Covenant 1919, and the Minorities Treaties and League of Nations mandated areas which were associated with Covenant.[304]

---

[302] Read through The Covenant of the League of Nations, Article 22: http://avalon.law.yale.edu/20th_century/leagcov.asp

[303] Ibid. Article 23

[304] Brownlie, Ian, Principles of Public International Law, Sixth Edition, Oxford University Press © 2003. p. 530.

As it were, the League of Nations metamorphosed into the United Nations Organization, so it was imperative that human rights had such prominence in the United Nations Charter that the contents of its preamble and its very first article bore emphasis on.

Now that the origin and the birth of the legal foundations for international human rights law have been established in the discussions above, it is paramount to focus the remaining chapters of this book specifically on the practise of States towards human rights law enforcement and protection.

10

INTERNATIONAL HUMAN RIGHTS LAWS ON INDIVIDUAL RIGHT TO FREEDOM OF CONSCIENCE, RELIGION AND BELIEF

> No way whatsoever that I shall walk in against the dictates of my conscience will ever bring me to the mansions of the blessed. I may grow rich by an art that I take not delight in, I may be cured of some disease by remedies that I have no faith in; but I cannot be saved by a religion that I distrust, and by a worship that I abhor. It is vain for an unbeliever to take up the outward show of another man's profession. Faith only, and inward sincerity, are the things that procure acceptance with God.[305]

The journey to what is today known as the right to freedom of thought, conscience, religion and belief has been a long one as it was once the sole prerogative of kings and rulers to determine what freedom of thought, conscience, religion and belief an individual could hold and maintain in their realm as the discussion in chapter 8 on The Peace of Westphalia 1648 and the Absence of the Right to Individual Freedom of Conscience, Religion and Belief shows.

---

[305] Locke, John, The Second Treatise of Government and A Letter of Toleration © 2002 Dover Publications, Inc. at p.131

10.1 From Advocacy to Reality

Although, a strong case for the individual right to freedom of conscience and to hold his own religious beliefs was made by great thinkers such as Locke as far back as the late seventeenth and early eighteenth centuries[306] just as the statement to this opening chapter reveals, not much happened to achieve this until the twentieth century; and this was after two world wars had been fought to the detriment of humanity.

Freedom of religion and freedom of conscience are today, at least, legalised as individual human right, but as the previous discussions on the freedom of religion has shown, there was a time in human history when thoughts and acts in accordance with one's conscience were not free, if you were not a king or ruler. The severity of this and how it affected people in the world in the past was so serious that Locke in his "A Letter Concerning Toleration" presented the argument for the individual to be free to exercise his right to freedom of conscience, thought, belief and religion thus:

> The one only narrow way which leads to heaven is not better known to the magistrate than to private persons, and therefore I cannot safely take him for my guide, who may probably be as ignorant of the way as myself, and who certainly is less concerned for my salvation than I myself am. Amongst so many kings of the Jews, how many of them were there whom any Israelite, thus blindly following, had not fallen into idolatry, and thereby into destruction? Yet nevertheless, you bid me be of good courage, and tell me that all is now safe and secure, because the magistrate does not now enjoin the observance of his own decrees in matters of religion…Would an Israelite, that had worshipped Baal upon the command of his king, have been in any better condition,..?[307]

By the end of the Second World War (WW2), it dawned on the victorious allied forces that it was not only the sanctity of human lives

---

[306]   Ibid. pp.115-153

[307]   Locke, John as in footnote 206 at p.130

that should be secured but also a list of human rights that give dignity to the life of every individual person in the world.

Whereas international law until after the Second World War was primarily concerned with the conduct and relationships between nation-states in their dealings with each other, and as such, states were mainly the subjects of international law; the international community through the Charter of the United Nations have ascribed and affirmed some human rights on the individual which has effectively raised the individual to the level of being subjects of international law since 1945, although it has taken decades for this to be apparent.

However, in respect of the right to freedom of conscience, thought, belief and religion, it has to be said that following the Peace of Westphalia 1648, as discussed in chapter 5, the recognition of the need for religious freedom and the initial effort to give legal validity to it was limited to kings and rulers under the doctrine of cuius regio euis religio – the religion of the ruler is the religion of the followers. This was opposed to the individual right to freedom of conscience, thought, belief and religion which Locke advocated for after the Peace of Westphalia.

Since the Peace of Westphalia ascribed the right to freedom of religion only to kings and rulers, many individuals who had contrary religious beliefs and convictions to that of their king or ruler paid with their lives for holding such contrary belief or where their lives were spared, they were subjected to some other forms of cruelty including years of imprisonment. In seventeenth century, England, for instance, the famous author John Bunyan, a protestant Christian who was a member of the Separatist Church, was arrested and tried under the orders of King Charles II and was imprisoned for 12 years[308] for merely exercising his freedom of conscience and right to religious beliefs different from how the King chose to exercise his. In actual fact, Bunyan's offence was not holding a different religious belief to the king as the Christian, but failure to attend the same Church such as the Church of England, which had the King as its head. It is important to note that that happened at a time when the treaty of the Peace of Westphalia had just come into

---

[308] John Bunyan is the author of one of the most famous Christian books - The Pilgrim's Progress. He wrote the book during his 12 years imprisonment. For a slightly more elaborate reading on him see: 131 Christians Everyone Should Know. Pp.115 – 117.

force in Europe, and those in every European nation or Kingdom were expected to follow the religion of their ruler and possibly attend the same church. But if John Bunyan's exercise of his freedom to hold religious belief was met with oppression and imprisonment then Archbishop Thomas Becket's exercise of his freedom of thought and conscience was more costly in twelfth century England. Becket who was appointed Archbishop of Canterbury by King Henry II of England in 1155 later fell out of favour with the King, in the exercise of his duty. Becket had sought to ensure that the discipline of erring clergy was a matter for the Church Council but the King wanted the State to be responsible for such discipline and possibly any trial. The difference in opinion led to the King getting Archbishop Becket to understand whose authority was superior and the chain of events that followed led to four of the King's knights confronting Becket in the Cathedral building and murdering him in 1170 on the allegation that he was a 'traitor.'[309] If the King had not ordered those knights to murder Becket then there would have been no basis for them not to have been arrested and subjected to criminal trial and sentencing at the time, but they weren't. However, by the eighteenth century the story was significantly different because of the Toleration Act (1689), which allowed for freedom of worship at least for the nonconformists such as Baptists and Congregationalists in England.

In France, freedom of religion was guaranteed following the revolution that produced the 1789 Declaration of the Rights of Man and of the Citizen. However, the historical evidence suggests that efforts were made by the state to suppress Christian religious practices which invariably would have affected individuals who held Christian religious beliefs.[310] Stories of cruel treatments meted out to priests even to the extent of execution is documented.[311]

However, it was against the numerous incidents of cruelty and killings across many nation states of the world that it became necessary for the right to the individual freedom of thought, conscience, and religious beliefs to be enshrined in the various United Nations international

---

[309]   Thomas Becket. Ibid. pp.367 -368.

[310]   See Christianity.com on French Revolution "Freedom", for a catalogue of incidents showing that France's Declaration of the Rights of Man merely tolerated religion and did not actually guarantee individual right to enjoy freedom of religion. https://www.christianity.com/church/church-history/timeline/1701-1800/french-revolutionary-freedom-11630320.html

[311]   Ibid.

human rights covenants and continental regional treaties of human rights. Nevertheless, it has to be said that a measure of religious freedom which was void of the cruelty that has been exposed in the discussions above about the United Kingdom and France, was enjoyed by citizens of the United States because the First Amendment to the Constitution adopted on December 15, 1791, allowed religious freedom for the citizens without the state's or government's interference. But the cases that will be examined in the next chapter will show how the courts in the United States introduced some restrictions to individual rights to religious freedom which arguably were well intended for a democratic society.

But from international law stand point the individual right to freedom of conscience, thought, and religion is the first individual human right that the international community sought to protect because it was enshrined in the Covenant of the League of Nations (1919):

The Covenant of the League of Nations

THE CONTRACTING PARTIES,

In order to promote international co-operation and to achieve international peace and security by the acceptance of obligations not to resort to war, by the prescription of open, just and honourable relations between nations, by the firm establishment of the understanding of international law as the actual rule of conduct among Governments, and by the maintenance of justice and a scrupulous respect for all treaty obligations in the dealings of organised peoples with one another, Agree to this Covenant of the League of Nations.[312]

ARTICLE 22

To those colonies and territories......

Other peoples, especially those of Central Africa, are at such as stage that the Mandatory must be responsible for

---

[312] Preamble to the Covenant of the League of Nations 1919 (including Amendments adopted to December 1924). See Yale Law School, The Avalon Project Documents in Law, History and Diplomacy: https://avalon.law.yale.edu/20th_century/leagcov.asp

> the administration of the territory under conditions which guarantee freedom of conscience and religion, subject only to the maintenance of public order....[313]

The implication of this is that the international community from the time of the League of Nations to the present United Nations Organization, had recognised the fact that the right to freedom of thought, conscience and religion is fundamental to human liberty and freedom and its denial also pose a great threat to not only the security and peace of the individual person, but indeed to that of the nation state and the international community at large; therefore the protection of such a right was not just to secure the protection of the individual person but also communities and the state at large.

10.2 Concrete Foundations

It became therefore imperative that every regional and international governmental organisation on cooperation, and not just the United Nations and the Regional Continental treaties had to guarantee or encourage the protection of the right to freedom of thought, conscience, religion and belief. As already stated, the need to protect human rights, especially, the right to freedom of thought, conscience, religion and belief, is seen as what should be protected by every international governmental organisation and The Organisation for Security and Co-operation, (CSCE), in Europe which is made up of 35 Eastern and Western European states with United States and Canada also as participating members have in their conferences for security and co-operation in Europe signed agreements which has in this respect included the protection of such human rights as:

> Respect for the human rights and fundamental freedoms, including freedom of thought, conscience and religion and belief[314]

---

[313] Ibid. Article 22 of the Covenant of the League of Nations.

[314] See section 1 of the Final Act of The Organisation for Security and Co-operation in Europe signed on 1 August 1975 Principle No.7, "Respect for human rights and fundamental freedoms, including freedom of thought, conscience and religion and belief'; For a more detailed discussion on the CSCE and its human rights development with respect to the right to freedom of thought, conscience and religion and belief, see Robertson and Merrills, Human Rights in the World, An introduction to the study of the protection of human rights, chapter 5, pp.179 – 182.

Before examining the extent to which individual rights to freedom of thought, conscience, religion and belief is protected by State parties to the United Nations and regional continental treatises, as would be done in the next chapter, it is important to set out the articles guaranteeing these rights from the Universal Declaration of Human Rights, UDHR, to the various international covenant of the United Nations such as the International Covenant on Civil and Political Rights, ICCPR, (1966); to the various continental regional treaties such as the European Convention for the Protection of Human Rights and Fundamental Freedoms, ECHR, (1950), American Convention on Human Rights, ACHR, (1969) and the African Charter on Human and Peoples' Rights, ACHPR, (1981).

Historically, it was the Organisation of American States (OAS), in its American Declaration of the Rights and Duties of Man[315], adopted at Bogota Colombia, in May 1948 that first made declarations of some human rights including the individual "right to fully profess a religious faith, and manifest and practise it both in public and in private" in its article 3, but the Universal Declaration of Human Rights, UDHR, stated far more broad facts about individual human rights.

Beginning with the UDHR, the declaration for the right of freedom of thought, conscience and religion and belief says:

In this chapter the discussion will be specifically on the right to freedom of thought, conscience and religion which stated in Article 18 of the UDHR, (1948), and in Article 18 of ICCPR states inter alia:

Article 18

Everyone has the right to freedom of thought, conscience, and religion; this right includes freedom to change his religion or belief, and freedom, either alone or in community with others and in public or private, to

---

[315] See American Declaration of the Rights and Duties of Man, May 1948, which was 7 months before the Declaration of the Universal Declaration of Human Rights, 1948. https://www.oas. org/dil/access to information human right American Declaration of the Rights and Duties of Man.pdf

manifest his religion, or belief in teaching, practice, worship and observance.[316]

However, in order to ensure to give legal protection and effect to what was a mere declaration of a desire for everyone's right to freedom of thought, conscience, religion and belief, as stated in the UDHR, the United Nations proceeded to translate the same wordings of the UDHR into law for individual benefits in its international covenant on civil and political rights, ICCPR, (1966), which binds signatories among the state parties to it. The corresponding article to the right to freedom of thought and religion in the ICCPR, says:

Article 18

1. Everyone shall have the right to freedom of thought, conscience and religion. This right shall include the freedom of have or to adopt a religion or belief of his choice, and freedom, either individually or in community with others and in public or private, to manifest his religion or belief in worship, observance, practice and teaching.

2. No one shall be subject to coercion which would impair his freedom to have or to adopt a religion or belief of his choice.

3. Freedom to manifest one's religion or beliefs may be subject only to such limitations as are prescribed by law and are necessary to protect public safety, order health, or morals or fundamental rights and freedom of others.

4. The States Parties to the present Covenant undertake to have respect for the liberty of parents and, when applicable, legal guardians to ensure the religious and moral education of their children in conformity with their own convictions.[317]

As could be seen, the wordings of the UDHR Article 18 and the ICCPR Article 18 (1) are almost exactly the same, but in ICCPR Article 18 (3), limitations were introduced to the rights in article 18 (1) for the purpose of public safety, order, health, morals or fundamental rights and freedom of others, hence making the right to freedom of thought,

---

[316] Article 18 of the UDHR in Sieghart, P., The Lawful Rights of Mankind, Oxford University Press © 1985. p.175; Also at: https://www.un.org/en/universal-declaration-human-rights/

[317] Ibid footnote 241 Sieghart, p.184; ICCPR article 18. Also at: https://treaties.un.org/doc/publication/unts/volume%20999/volume-999-i-14668-english.pdf

conscience, religion and belief, a qualified individual human right which sometimes the state can deny instead of protect and guarantee the individual enjoyment. The merits and problems of this will be shown in the discussions of later chapters.

In ways similar to the United Nations international instrument for the protection of the right to freedom of thought, conscience, religion and belief, the continental regional instruments for the protection of this same right equally qualify it in ways that could rightly or wrongly limit the enjoyment by the very individual it seeks to offer the right. The wording of the relevant article in the European Convention for Human Rights in this respect says:

Article 9

1. Everyone has the right to freedom of thought, conscience and religion; this right includes freedom to change his religion or belief, and freedom, either alone or in community with others and in public or private, to manifest his religion or belief, in worship, teaching, practice and observance.
2. Freedom to manifest one's religion or beliefs shall be subject only to such limitations as are prescribed by law and are necessary in a democratic society in the interests of public safety, for the protection of public order, health or morals, or for protection of the rights and freedoms of others.[318]

The limitations that the European Convention for Human Rights places on the individual right to freedom of thought, conscience, religion and belief is the same as that which is seen in the United Nations instrument such as the International Covenant on Civil and Political Rights.

Although the wording of the equivalent article in the American Convention on Human Rights is moderately different, the restriction in effect if examined bears the same face. This is what it says:

Article 12 – Freedom of Conscience and Religion

1. Everyone has the right to freedom of conscience and of religion. This includes freedom to maintain or change one's religion or

---

[318]   Ibid. Footnote 241 ECHR article 9, Sieghart, p.198. Also at: https://www.echr.coe.int/Documents/Convention_ENG.pdf

beliefs, and freedom to profess or disseminate one's religion or beliefs either individually or together with others, in public or in private.

2. No one shall be subject to restrictions that might impair his freedom to maintain or change his religion or beliefs.

3. Freedom to manifest one's religion and beliefs may be subject only to the limitations prescribed by law that are necessary to protect public safety, order, health or morals, or the rights or freedoms of others.

4. Parents or guardians, as the case may be, have the right to provide for the religious and moral education of their children or wards that is in accord with their own convictions.[319]

The nearest to what seemed like an absolute guarantee of the individual right to freedom of conscience, religion and belief would have been found in the equivalent article of the African Charter on Human and Peoples' Rights but then States are wary of guaranteeing absolute liberties and so even in the African charter with near guarantee wording, the usual language of limitation was inserted. This is what is stated in the ACHPR:

ARTICLE 8

Freedom of conscience, the profession and free practice of religion, shall be guaranteed. No one may, subject to law and order, be submitted to measures restricting the exercise of these freedoms.[320]

10.3 Evaluation and Summary

The right to freedom of conscience, religion and belief remains a qualified human right which in many ways is justifiable but in someways calls for international concerns especially in some states as the discussions in the following chapters will show.

---

[319] Ibid. Footnote 241 ACHR article 12, Sieghart, p.224. Also at: https://www.cidh.oas.org/basicos/english/basic3.american%20convention.htm

[320] Ibid. Footnote 241. Sieghart, p233 ACHPR Article 8. See also at: https://au.int/sites/default/files/treaties/36390-treaty-0011 - african charter on human and peoples rights e.pdf

PART III

HUMAN RIGHTS AND THE
PROBLEM OF STATE PROTECTION
AND ENFORCEMENT OF THE
INDIVIDUAL HUMAN RIGHT TO
FREEDOM OF CONSCIENCE
AND RELIGIOUS FREEDOM

11

STATE RELIGION, RELIGIOUS PLURALISM AND THE PROBLEM OF INDIVIDUAL RIGHT TO FREEDOM OF RELIGIOUS BELIEF AND PRACTICE

You twist justice, making it a bitter pill for the oppressed.
You treat the righteous like dirt.

- Amos 5:7 (NLT).

11.1 Law and Semantics

The language of the Constitution is predicated in the belief that there will be tolerance in a religious pluralistic society without bias in a situation where the State has adopted a particular religion such as the Islamic Republic of Pakistan. So instances of violation of the individual rights to religious belief where the victims are in the minority that hold alternative religious beliefs in the state that has adopted a religion tend to sometimes pass without adequate address.

The International Covenant on Civil and Political Rights, ICCPR, (1966), Article 18 (1) (2):

> 18 (1) Everyone shall have the right to freedom of thought, conscience and religion. This right shall include freedom to have or to adopt a religion or belief of his choice, and

freedom, either individually or in community with others and in public or private, to manifest his religion or belief in worship, observance, practice and teaching.

18 (2) No one shall be subject to coercion which would impair his freedom to have or to adopt a religion or belief of his choice.

Although the United Nations has gone beyond drafting and enacting international treaties guaranteeing the right to freedom of religion and practice to ensuring the liberty of the individual to enjoy such rights through its monitoring bodies such as the United Nations Human Rights Committee, however, the lack of absolute commitment of state parties to ensure the implementation and enforcement of the individual rights as enshrined in the covenants and conventions have left a lot to be desired in practice. The role of the UN Human Rights Committee[321] is to ensure that:

...individuals should not suffer disadvantages in their enjoyment of religion or belief rights...[322]

However, this is especially more problematic in cases where a "State identifies itself with a particular religion or belief."[323]

11.2 The Evidence of Bias from the Islamic State of Pakistan

The evidence from cases where a state has adopted a particular religion such as Islam and some citizens in minority hold some alternative religiously beliefs have showed that judges in such cases are often inclined to produce a bias decision in favour of their own religious inclinations.

---

[321] McGoldrick, Dominic, The Human Rights Committee Its Role in the Development of the International Covenant on Civil and Political Rights © 1994, 1996 Clarendon Press Oxford.

[322] Ghanea, Nazila, Religion, Equality, and Non-Discrimination in Religion & Human Rights An Introduction, Edited by John Witte, Jr. & M. Christian Green © Oxford University Press, Inc. p. 212

[323] Ibid. p.211

For example, some of the cases that have raised international concern about the treatment of religious minorities such as Christians in the Islamic Republic of Pakistan might not have come to international awareness but for the fact that Pakistan besides being an Islamic State has as per section 295 of the Pakistan Penal Code enacted a blasphemy law which several cases decided by the Supreme Court of Pakistan show that some religious bigots and mischief makers have continuously exploited blasphemy law to the detriment and in some cases destruction of the lives of non-Muslims in Pakistan. The contrast in the Islamic Republic of Pakistan State laws when viewed with some scrutiny shows that while on the one hand, the Constitution of the State as per article 4 guarantees 'protection' of the 'life', 'liberty', 'body', 'reputation' or 'property', "of any person" in Pakistan; on the other hand, the mere allegation by any individual Muslim against a non-Muslim in Pakistan that the non-Muslim has used derogatory language to blaspheme the founder of the Islamic faith and the Holy Quran in contravention of section 295 of the Pakistan Penal Code, automatically makes such an unfortunate person vulnerable to suffer loss of protection of the rights guaranteed under the constitution. Unless such a person in the event that he is not instantly extra-judicially murdered by a mob of Islamic religion adherents, who might swiftly carry out such execution in the belief that the accused actually committed the act is acquitted of the charges in a Court of law. The most recent victim of this sort of occurrence is Asia Bibi[324] whose case raised international concern and clearly shows that in cases where a state identifies with a particular religion the protection of the minorities and the rights of such minorities to freedom of religion and belief and practice are often far more uncertain.

The rigorous examination of facts and evidence which made the Supreme Court of Pakistan to acquit Asia Bibi of the sentence to death passed on her by the Trial Court and the High Court of Appeal, respectively, did not only reveal that she did not commit the offence of blaspheming the founder of the Islamic faith and the Holy Quran, but that Christians and religious minority people in Pakistan are at the mercy of Muslim majority who could easily make frivolous accusations about blasphemy and subject them to the cruelty and possibly death in the hands of bigots.

---

[324]   See Asia Bibi Vs. The State, In the Supreme Court of Pakistan, Criminal Appeal N0.39 – L of 2015. http://www.supremecourt.gov.pk/web/user_files/File/Crl.A._39_L_2015.pdf

The facts of Asia Bibi's case were that she was a Christian woman who was working with Muslim women in a field plucking falsa. On the 14.06.2009 while she was in the field plucking falsa she had gone to fetch drinking water and had offered the water to her falsa plucking colleagues in the field. She was unfortunately told by two of the Muslim Women namely Mafia Bibi and Asma Bibi, who incidentally are sisters, that they would not drink water fetched by her since she was not a Muslim. An altercation thereby followed and in a bid to harm Asia Bibi, the two Muslim women conspired and concocted a story that she had blasphemed the founder of the Islamic faith and the Holy Quran by making derogatory statements.

They told the story to their local mosque priest (Imam) Qari Muhammad Salaam, whose wife was also their Islamic religious teacher. According to the account of the Qari Muhammad Salaam, Asia Bibi made a public confession before him and several other people on the 19.06. 2009, to the effect that she did commit the act of blasphemy in breach of section 295-C of the Pakistan Penal Code. And on the 19.06.2009, he reported her to the Local Police for the offence she committed. She was allegedly investigated by the Police and was found to have committed the Offence and was charged in Court.

Asia Bibi who was fortunate to have escaped extra-judicial execution in the hands of Islamic bigots ended up in prison for about 10 years for the offence of blasphemy which she had not committed but for the fact that her right as a Christian could not be guaranteed and protected by the Islamic State of Pakistan. This was because the State has identified herself with a particular religion and has extended that identification with an instrument of protection of that religion in ways that did not only pose a threat to the breach of her obligations to protect the right to religious freedom and beliefs and practice of all and sundry in her territory under the international human rights law, that she is a party to, but more seriously, opens herself up to violation of such rights by her citizens who may be given to bigotry.

Nevertheless, it is clear from the decisions of the Supreme Court of Pakistan that the judiciary at the Supreme Court are careful to ensure that justice is done to the cases it decides. In the Asia Bibi's case for instance, the complainant was duly reminded by the Court of the seriousness of making false allegations of blasphemy as per the case of

Malik Muhammad Mumtaz Qadri Vs. the State (PLD 2016 SC17) when it cited a portion of that saying thus:

> Commission of blasphemy is abhorrent and immoral besides being a manifestation of intolerance but at the same time a false allegation regarding commission of such as offence is equally detestable besides being culpable. If our religion of Islam comes heavily upon commission of blasphemy then Islam is also very tough against those who level false allegations of a crime. It is, therefore, for the State of the Islamic Republic of Pakistan to ensure that no innocent person is compelled or constrained to face an investigation or trial on the basis of false or trumped-up allegations regarding the Commission of such an offence.[325]

However, the Trial Court that first heard Asia Bibi's blasphemy case convicted her of committing the offence and sentenced her to death. She appealed against that conviction but the High Court of Appeal that heard it dismissed her appeal and upheld her conviction and death sentence. She appealed subsequently to the Supreme Court of Pakistan.

At the Supreme Court, when her appeal was examined in the light of the evidence and the facts of her case, the following conclusion was reached:

> The entirety of the prosecution case resolved around the Statement of two ladies, namely, Mafia Bibi (PW.2) and Asma Bibi (PW.3) and the extra-judicial confession of the appellant. The said (PW's) stated that the appellant, in the presence of other Muslim ladies passed derogatory remarks against the Prophet Muhammad. It is pertinent to mention here that admittedly, as is evident from the FIR and also the statements of the witnesses, there were 25-30 ladies present at the spot when the appellant allegedly passed the blasphemous remarks against the Prophet Muhammad, however, none of the other ladies except Mafia Bibi (PW.2) and Asma Bibi (PW.3) reported the matter to anyone."[326]

---

[325] Asia Bibi Vs. The State, In the Supreme Court of Pakistan, Criminal Appeal No. 39 – L of 2015. At paragraph
h 15

[326] Ibid Asia Bibi Vs. The State, Judgement of the Supreme Court of Pakistan at paragraph 28.

The Supreme court in the examination of facts and evidence stated that:

> ...material contradictions and inconsistent statements of
> the witnesses are tantamount to cast further doubts on the
> coherence of the evidence pertaining to the questions set
> below;
>
> a. Who informed the Complainant about the occurrence of such;
> b. Who was present at the time of disclosure regarding the
>   allegation made by the appellant;
> c. How many people were present at the time of the public
>   gathering;
> d. Where the public gathering took place;
> e. What was the distance between the place
> f. of the public gathering and the house of the appellant; and
> g. How and who brought the appellant to the public gathering;[327]

Upon establishing the inconsistencies of material facts and testimonies of
the prosecution witnesses, the Supreme Court decided thus:

> In the eventuality, the said PWs could not be termed as
> truthful witnesses and the death sentence could not be
> inflicted on the testimony of such eye witnesses, which
> even otherwise are interested witnesses.[328]

It is a well settled principle of law that one who makes an assertion has
to prove it.........If the presumption of innocence is a golden thread to
criminal jurisprudence, then proof beyond reasonable doubt is silver, and
these two threads are forever intertwined in the fabric of criminal justice
system.[329]

For the foregoing reasons, this appeal is allowed. The judgment of the
High Court as well as the Trial Court are reversed. Consequently, the
conviction as also the sentence to death awarded to the appellant is set
aside and she is acquitted of the charge.[330]

---

[327] Ibid. At paragraph 31.

[328] Ibid. At paragraph 40.

[329] Ibid. At paragraph 48.

[330] Ibid. At paragraph 50

Unlike those who seek to demonstrate bigotry towards non-Muslims and even go to the extreme of seeking to kill or actually killing non-Muslims in the name of the Islamic religion, the judges of the Supreme Court of Pakistan in the Asia Bibi case went at lengths not only in applying the Constitution and the laws of the Islamic Republic of Pakistan in deciding the case but also in citing the Islamic religion Holy Quran on several occasions in their judgment.

In fact, even the concurring opinion of Asif Saeed Khan Khosa, J., one of the Supreme Court judges that took part in hearing Asia Bibi's Appeal case and judgment, bore some riveting insights both on the substance of the case and its religious bearings on Muslims treatment of Christian minorities in Pakistan. He remarked thus in his concurring opinion:

> The glaring and stark contradictions in the evidence produced by the prosecution in respect of every factual aspect of this case, noticed by me above, lead to an irresistible and unfortunate impression that all those concerned in the case with providing evidence and conducting investigation had taken upon themselves not to speak the truth or at least not to divulge the whole truth. It is equally disturbing to note that the courts below had also, conveniently or otherwise, failed to advert to such contradictions and some downright falsehood. All concerned would have certainly done better if they had paid heed to what Almighty Allah has ordained in the Qu'ran:

> O you who have believed, be persistently standing firm for Allah, witnesses I justice, and do not let the hatred of a people prevent you from being just. Be just, that is nearer to righteousness. And fear Allah; indeed, Allah is acquainted with what you do.[331]

> (Surah Al-Ma'idah: verse 8)

---

[331]   Ibid. At paragraph 20 of the Concurring Opinion of Asif Saeed Khan Khosa, J.;

Manifestly evident from the testimonies of Mafia Bibi and Asma Bibi are incongruent facts that in a fair and impartial judicial trial should have led to the acquittal of Asia Bibi right at the Pakistan Court of Sessions where she was first tried and sentenced to death. But paradoxically it seemed pious to people who want to be seen as honouring God to conspire against the facts and truth to subject another human being to barbaric and degrading treatment just because she professes another religious belief to theirs.

The fact that another Christian and a religious minority citizen of Pakistan was experiencing these same despicable humiliations after the sensational case of Ayub Masih which decided by the Supreme Court in 2002 suggests that Pakistan like most other states indeed, need to do something about educating her citizens in understanding that even by the Islamic religion as the Supreme Court judges stated in the Asia Bibi judgment, nefarious designs such as fabrications about acts of blasphemy that would lead to the death of innocent persons cannot attract blessings of God and it is a crime as it perverts the course of justice. If perpetrators of such evil acts are made to understand that their acts are not acceptable to God and they are not acceptable to State and her Government then there would be less appeal for it to continue.

While it becomes obvious that the Asia Bibi's 10 years predicament 'through the valley of shadow of death' in the bid to free herself from death sentence passed on for blasphemy was as a result of the nefarious act of malice visited upon her by Mafia Bibi and Asma Bibi with whom she had had an altercation on the 14.06.2009 while at work plucking falsa, the most serious point is that such is the fate that befalls people who are in minority in their religious beliefs and practice in various states of the world especially where the State has identified herself with a particular religion.

However, if Asia Bibi's false accusation of blasphemy as a result of malice from her Muslim work colleagues as has been established by the Supreme Court is abhorrent to any decent person then the case of Ayub Masih which had to do with an allegation of him committing blasphemy by a neighbour who wanted to have him executed for blasphemy so that he could take ownership of his land and possessions is mildly speaking obnoxious.

Mr. Ayub Masih, a citizen of Pakistan who professes the Christian faith and religion, was arrested and detained by the Police on 14 October 1996, following a complaint to the Police by one of his neighbour Mr Muhammad Akram, who said Mr Masih had offended him by committing blasphemy in contravention of section 295-C of the Pakistan Penal Code.[332] Although, Mr Masih denied the allegation of blasphemy levelled against him, his denial was disregarded and the testimony of the complainant, Mr Akram, was believed without further evidence while Mr Masih was left in detention. But it was not only Mr Masih that was visited with injustice and indignity that day, 14 October 1996 following the allegation of blasphemy made against him and his arrest. The entire population of Christians in his village which comprised of 14 families were also forced to flee, abandoning their homes and belongings that day because of attack from other villagers who were Muslims.[333]

While Mr Masih was facing charges in court for blasphemy the complainant, Mr Akram injured and shot him on 6 November 1997, in the halls of the Court and he was not arrested or prosecuted.[334]

Mr Masih was tried between 8th January and 20th April 1998 and was convicted for blasphemy and sentenced to death and a fine of 100,000 Rupees. However, he lodged an appeal against his conviction with the High Court. After over 3 years of delay in hearing the appeal, the High Court heard his appeal on 24 July 2001 and affirmed Mr Masih's conviction and death sentence under the blasphemy law.[335]

Following the dismissal of Ayub Masih's appeal and the affirmation of his death sentence by the High Court, in Lahore Pakistan, Freedom Now, the United States, Washington based non-profit, non-governmental and non-partisan organization that works to free individuals who are prisoners of conscience mounted an intense campaign to secure the

---

[332] Ayub Masih Vs. The State (PLD 2002 SC 1048); See also Freedom Network: http://www.freedom-now.org/campaign/ayub-masih/, See attached Freedom Now petition to the U.N. Working Group on Arbitrary Detention and U.N. Working Group communication with the Government of Pakistan on Ayub Masih attached to the Freedom Now story and as well as the United State Senate whose 12 Distinguished Senators signed a letter to the then President of Pakistan, His Excellency Pervez Musharat asking for the release or presidential pardon for Ayub Masih

[333] Ibid

[334] Ibid. See especially Freedom Now petition to the U.N. Working Group on Arbitrary Detention.

[335] Ibid. See also Ayub Masih Vs The State (PLD 2002 SC1048).

release and freedom of Mr Ayub Masih. Freedom Now on October 8, 2001, petitioned the U.N. Working Group on Arbitrary Detention on behalf of Ayub Masih and requested it to exercise its power under Resolution 1997/50 of the Commission on Human Rights as reconfirmed by Resolution 2000/36 and consider the petition in pursuant to the Working Group "Urgent Action" procedure and give an opinion. Acting on that petition, the Working Group contacted the Government of Pakistan, and requested information about Ayub Masih. The Pakistan Government duly responded with the requested information and upon further communication with Freedom Now, the Working Group, on 30 November 2001, adopted an opinion and requested the Government of Pakistan inter alia saying:

> The Working Group finds that the procedure conducted against Ayub Masih did not respect the fundamental rights of a person charged. He was not provided with documentary or other evidence against him. This prevented him to properly prepare his defence; he was not informed of his rights as an accused. The verdict against him was based on the testimony of a single, biased witness. The threats by extremists against him and his defence lawyer during trial and appeal, and the hostile atmosphere – characterised inter alia by the fact that the complainant shot on him in the court without apparently being sanctioned by the court – intimidated accused and counsel alike, thereby restricting the effectiveness of the defence. All this was coupled with the fact that under Pakistan law blasphemy cases insulting the Muslim religion are compulsorily heard by Muslim judges, which undermines the credibility that a fair and impartial trial is being conducted. These serious deficiencies in proceedings where capital punishment is not only provided by law as an alternative penalty, but compulsory, if the accused is found guilty, basically deprives the procedure of its requisite fair character.[336]

The U.N. Working Group further concluded its findings after due consideration of the petition of Freedom Now and the response of the Government of Pakistan that:

---

[336]   U.N. Working Group on Arbitrary Detention, Opinion No. 25/2001 (Pakistan). Concerning Ayub Masih, At paragraph 15.

> The deprivation of liberty of Ayub Masih is arbitrary, being in contravention of Articles 9 and 10 of the Universal Declaration of Human Rights and falls within category III of the categories applicable to the consideration of cases submitted to the Working Group.[337]

It requested that Government of Pakistan "take the necessary steps to the remedy the situation of Mr. Ayub Masih" either by a "retrial, or granting pardon or commutation would be an appropriate remedy."[338]

The pressure on the Government of Pakistan was not let off following the opinion of the U.N. Working Group on Arbitrary Detention criticising the manner in which Ayub Masih was haphazardly tried and convicted in court without due process and procedures and requesting for remedies for the unfair treatment he had had, but it was rather heightened as a number of Senators of the United States Senate signed a letter dated July 2, 2002 and sent it to His Excellency, Pervez Musharraf, the then President of the Islamic Republic of Pakistan, pointing out to him that they have concerns for Mr Ayub Masih, who was arrested since 1996 and sentenced to death for violating blasphemy laws. They pointed out that:

> The international community has also recognised that serious irregularities occurred in the proceedings.[339]

They cited the opinion of the United Nations Working Group on Arbitrary Detention whose opinion says:

> Mr Masih was deprived of his liberty in contravention [of] the Universal Declaration of Human Rights and the Government of Pakistan to take steps to remedy his situation....

> We urge you to use the pardon powers granted to you under the Constitution of Pakistan to release Mr. Masih. We also respectfully request that you provide

---

[337]   Ibid. At para. 16

[338]   Ibid. At para.17

[339]   United States Senate Letter to His Excellency, Pervez Musharraf, President of the Islamic Republic of Pakistan asking for the release of Mr Ayub Masih. Copy of Letter attached to Freedom Now story on Ayub Masih. See: http://www.freedom-now.org/campaign/ayub-masih/

any information that the Government of Pakistan has concerning the health and welfare of Mr. Masih to the United States Charge d'Affaires in Islamabad.

In a manner rather dramatic but equally welcoming, the Supreme Court of Pakistan heard the appeal of Mr Ayub Masih on 15 August 2002, less than two months from the date when a number of Senators of the US Senate wrote the President of Pakistan about their concerns for Mr Masih's and asking for his release, his appeal was heard and upheld by the Supreme Court of Pakistan. He was acquitted of the charges of blasphemy and was free from the death sentence that hung over his existence over the years he was first convicted of blasphemy in January 1998.

The Supreme Court of Pakistan observed in their hearing of Mr Masih's appeal that:

> "the Complainant wanted to grab the plot on which Ayub Masih and his father were residing and after implicating him in the said case, he managed to grab the seven-marla plot. The appeal was accepted by this court and the conviction was set aside.[340]

The question arises as to what the text of the Pakistan Blasphemy Law otherwise section 295 – of Pakistan Penal Code says that makes it so easy for non-Muslims such as Ayub Masih and Asia Bibi to be easily accused and convicted of blasphemy? Well, here is what it says:

> Whoever by words, either spoken or written, or by visible representation, or by any imputation, innuendo, or insinuation, directly or indirectly defiles the sacred name of the Holy Prophet (PBUH)...shall be punished with death, or imprisonment for life, and shall be also liable to fine.[341]

The text of the blasphemy law is so loose that it is easy for any Muslim in Pakistan to frame a non-Muslim of committing blasphemy without realising that he is acting in an ungodly and cruel way that is offensive

---

[340] Ayub Masih Vs. The State (PLD 2002 SC 1048); cited by the Supreme Court of Pakistan in Asia Bibi Vs. The State, Criminal Appeal No.39 – L of 2015 at paragraph 13.

[341] Text of Section 295 – C, of the Pakistan Penal Code otherwise known as the Blasphemy Law.

to God and humanity in every sense. However, it cannot be said the person making the allegation is acting unlawfully because alleging that someone has made a hint or insinuation about a person is a matter of individual perception and inference which could be based on false premise or genuine belief even if wrong. For an offence that attracts such grievous penalty as the death penalty the offence should be anything but a suggestion that someone has made an 'innuendo' or 'insinuation.' It is very important that religious leaders and founders are accorded high respect and honour but killing innocent people for alleged disrespectful insinuation or innuendo is actually in the mind and judgment of every reasonable an act of dishonour and disrespect to the religious founders and leaders that should be honoured.

What can be inferred from the Supreme Court of Pakistan's cases in Asia Bibi vs the State (2018), Malik Muhammad Mumtaz Qadri vs the State (PLD 2016 SC 17), and Ayub Masih vs. the State (PLD 2002 SC 1048), is that Christians and other religious minorities are targets of persecutions in the Islamic Republic of Pakistan because the wording of the blasphemy law gives them legal grounds to do so. There is a contrast between the right that the Constitution of the Islamic Republic of Pakistan confers on citizens' freedom of religion and the broad interpretation that can be given to the language of the blasphemy law, in section 295 – C of the Pakistan Penal Code. It is so loose that it gives liberty to Muslim citizens of the State with malicious and nefarious intents to misuse the law by making frivolous allegations against other citizens who are people with other religious beliefs in Pakistan. Most unfortunately as the cases discussed have shown, the Islamic State of Pakistan continues to fail in her duty to protect non-Muslims. Both the State of Pakistan and the international community under the umbrella of the United Nations need to do more towards the protection of the right to religious freedom and beliefs and practice. It is disconcerting that in the case of Asia Bibi, the Supreme Court recognised that there are people murdered in Pakistan on the allegations of blasphemy which have not even been charged and tried in Court:

> ...Stately, since 1990, 62 people have been murdered as a result of blasphemy allegations, even before their trial could be conducted in accordance with the law. Even prominent figures, who stressed the fact that the blasphemy laws

have been misused by some individuals, met with serious repercussions. A latest example of misuse of this law was the murder of Mashal Khan, a student of Abdul Wali Khan University, Mardan, who in April 2017 was killed by a mob in the premises of the University merely due to an allegation that he posted blasphemous contents online.[342]

There is no doubt about the fact that abusive comments and any form of disrespect and dishonour to religious founders and leaders should not be encouraged or tolerated because such acts of impropriety are immoral and sacrilegious and capable of precipitating civil unrest and total anarchy. However, any law that enables any people of one religion to kill and maim others on unproven accusations of blasphemy fabricated by those who harbour malice against their neighbours threatens not just one nation state with violations of human rights but the entire world with disharmony and religious war. It is important that the Islamic Republic of Pakistan and indeed other nations with similar constitutional and legal frameworks abrogate any blasphemy law that gives room to false accusations of blasphemy that will lead to unjust execution and killings of innocent citizens and persons in the territory of such a state.

It is particularly interesting that the nearest the Courts in Pakistan have come to asking the state to abrogate the Blasphemy Law in Pakistan which is section 295 – S of the Pakistan Penal Code was in the case of Muhammad Ismail Qureshi Vs. Pakistan through Secretary, Law and Parliamentary Affairs (PLD 1991 FSC 10), in which the Federal Shariat Court ruled that:

> … Section 295 – C was repugnant to the fundamental principles of Islam to the extent that it provided for the punishment of life imprisonment which acted as an alternative to a death sentence.[343]

While perhaps the emphasis of eliminating the alternative sentence of life imprisonment so as to have only a penalty of death sentence may probably go some way in acting as a deterrent from blaspheming the

---

[342] Asia Bibi Vs the State, in the Supreme Court of Pakistan, Criminal Appeal No. 39 – L of 2015, decided on the 08.10.2018 at para.12.

[343] Cited at Para 10 of the Asia Bibi Vs. the State judgment of the Supreme Court.

Holy Prophet [PBUH] and founder of Islam, the Federal Shariat Court does not appear to have considered the incidents of false allegations of blasphemy directed at innocent citizens that had led to the death of many of which the Supreme Court of Pakistan acknowledged that as many as 62 persons have been murdered.

More fundamentally, every law in any nation state must be fair and just for all the citizens of the State. What makes the blasphemy law in Pakistan, to be quite unfair to non-Muslims is the fact that it leaves a lacuna in the protection of founders and leaders of other religious such as Christianity, Buddhism etc. from being blasphemed against and provides only protection against blasphemy for the founder of the Islamic religion. The problem with such a law is that it simply makes a lot of room to those Muslim citizens of the State who may be given to mischief and nefarious acts the license to either provoke other religious persons by insulting their leaders and religious founders and thus cause them to fall into the trap of making what may later be interpreted as blasphemy against the Holy Prophet [PBUH] of Islam. It is to avoid such lopsided protection of one religion over the order and more serious making room for injustice to thrive that the present blasphemy law should be abrogated.

The judgment of the Supreme Court in the Asia Bibi case supports the need for the Islamic Republic of Pakistan to abrogate the blasphemy law in Section 295 – C of the Pakistan Penal Code. The blasphemy law has clearly become a means by which some of her Islamic citizens are contravening some of the teachings of the Holy Quran which the Supreme Court judgement quoted

The Holy Quran has mentioned in clear terms that:

"...he who slays a soul unless it be (in punishment) for murder or for spreading mischief on earth shall be as if he had slain all mankind; and he who saves a life shall be as if he had given life to all mankind.

[Al-Ma'idah (5:32)]

To this end it may also be essential that more Islamic education on this verse of the Quran should be taught more widely to enable the citizens in Islamic Republics understand their duties to maintain peace and to be tolerant of others, so that those who may be inclined to carrying out such nefarious intentions of framing up people with false accusations of blasphemy and those who will rush to maim and kill such accused persons will realise that they will not be honouring God by such acts of cruelty and refrain themselves and allow the Court to decide each case and determine the right penalty. This applies not just for the Islamic Republic of Pakistan but to all other states where the State has identified itself with one religion and the citizens think it is their rights to persecute and kill those who do not share the same religious beliefs as them.

It has to be said that the judgments of the Supreme Court of Pakistan in the cases examined and discussed here are demonstrably indicative of intent of the court to ensure that justice is done for those who are falsely accused of blasphemy and had survived the persecution and threats to their lives that usually followed such accusation before court trial. This would be appreciated when cases of other nations where no form of justice at all has been done to those who have suffered persecution or unlawful killings because of their religious beliefs is discussed.

11.3 Conflicts in Religious Pluralistic States Such as Nigeria

In the case of countries such as Nigeria, in addition to the obligation to ensure 'the right to freedom of thought, conscience and religion' under the International Covenant on Civil and Political Rights is also the obligation to guarantee such right under the African Charter on Human and Peoples' Right.

African Charter on Human and Peoples' Rights (1981) Article 8:

> Freedom of conscience, the profession and free practice of religion shall be guaranteed. No one may, subject to law and order, be submitted to measures restricting the exercise of these freedoms.

As far as the individual citizen's right to freedom of conscience and freedom of religion is concerned, only the African Charter on Human and Peoples' Rights expressly says such freedom shall be guaranteed.

However, besides the beauty of the wordings of Article 8 of the African Charter, what is being witnessed in the continent of Africa are a number of State parties of the Charter facilitating or tolerating the outright violations of the right enshrined in article 8 on freedom of conscience and practice of religion.

In Nigeria where in actual fact the population of Christians according to the 2010 survey conducted by the Pew Forum, which has been accepted to be reliable statistics, is 49.3% of the population, followed by Islam with 48.8% while the remaining 1.9% of the population are said to be practitioners of indigenous religion or affiliations[344], there has always been harmony and deep friendships between Christians and Muslims until very recent.

Since 29 May 2015, when Muhammadu Buhari became President of the country, there has been an alarming rate of violations of Article 8 of the African Charter, with regards to the killings of Christians' mostly in the northern part of Nigeria while they are exercising their religious rites and beliefs. Much cannot be done in this chapter to render justice to this grave issue by way of academic discourse and examination of the numerous incidents that call for international investigation of human rights violations with specific regard to the incidents of killings of Christians in the act of exercising their rights to freedom of religion and practice between 2015 and 2019. But the examples that would be cited and discussed here are a reflection of the many that are not discussed as the few cited are intended to crystallise the problem and point to the need for the matter to be addressed by the mechanisms available within the United Nations systems to deal with mass violations of human rights and crimes against humanity.

There were a number of instances of killings of Christians that were reported to be targeted killings as opposed to some occasions of unfortunate instances in which both Christians and Muslims have fallen victims to terrorist attacks by Boko Haram terrorists in the Northern part of Nigeria. In some cases, the silence of President Muhammadu Buhari has made some wonder whether he was complicit. One such instance was

---

[344] See "Religious Beliefs in Nigeria" in: https://www.worldatlas.com/articles/religious-beliefs-in-nigeria.html

the beheadings of some Christians on a Christian Day 2019, by Islamist terrorists.[345]

Reputable news outlets in Nigeria such as the "Morning Star News" and the "World Watch Monitor" which monitors the reports of Christians under pressure in various countries around the world in their investigations of the Nigeria situation gave the following grave account of human rights abuses and killings:

> Muslim Fulani herdsmen with machetes killed the Rev. Zakariya Joseph Kurah of the Evangelical Church Winning All (ECWA) on Thursday (June 30) while he was working at his farm, sources said......The Rev. Silas Thomas, former secretary of the ECWA's Lafia District Church Council, confirmed that the pastor was murdered by Muslim Fulani herdsmen while working at his farm, and that his funeral took place in Zonkwa, Kaduna State today [5 July 2016].[346]

While the Federal Government of Nigeria was yet to give explanation as to how they will deal with this ugly trend of religious murder, within a week of Joseph Kurah's internment, between 5:00 a.m. and 5:30 a.m. in the early morning hours of Saturday, 9 July 2016, another Christian pastor was killed in a similar way. Mrs Eunice Elisha, a 42 years old mother of seven who was also a pastor of the Redeemed Christian Church of God, RCCG, probably the most popular evangelical and Pentecostal church in Nigeria, was stabbed and hacked to death while she was evangelising on the street in the Gbazango area of Kubwa which is a suburb of Abuja the Capital of Nigeria.

According to a report by a major Nigerian Newspaper the Punch, Mrs Eunice Elisha:

> ...was stabbed in the stomach and also had a cut in her neck.

---

[345] Morley, Nathan, "I S militants behead 11 Christians in Nigeria on Christmas Day." Vatican News, 27 December, 2019: https://www.vaticannews.va/en/world/news/2019-12/islamic-state-nigeria-christians-killed-on-christmas.html

[346] "Muslim Fulani Herdsmen Kill Pastor in Nasarawa State, Nigeria." Morning Star News, July 5, 2016: https://morningstarnews.org/2016/07/muslim-fulani-herdsmen-kill-pastor-in-nasarawa-state-nigeria/

The 42-year-old woman was a deaconess at the Divine Touch Parish of the RCCG, Old NEPA Road, Phase 4, Kubwa. The RCCG preacher was found dead in a pool of her blood with a copy of the Bible, a megaphone and a mobile phone. She was found dead by residents who alerted policemen who came to evacuate her remains to the police station where her husband went to identify the body......

The FCT Police Command told the News Agency of Nigeria that it had arrested some suspects in connection with the killing of the RCCG preacher.[347]

Even though this dastardly act took place in Abuja the capital of the Federal Republic of Nigeria, and not in some remote village far away from the presence of security personnel, no one has been prosecuted for the murder of Mrs Eunice Elisha whose manner of death clearly depict religious hatred as she was killed while evangelising openly in the street of Kubwa in Abuja.

The killings of Joseph Kurah and Mrs Eunice Elisha in broad daylight and the religious implication of the violations of the right to the freedom of these Christians to practice their religious beliefs have made some people in Nigeria to cast aspersions on president Muhammadu Buhari of Nigeria, who is a Muslim, for not publicly condemning the killings. It has left many wondering how the right to freedom of religious belief and practice for Christians especially in northern Nigeria are protected and guaranteed with respect to Nigeria's commitment to carrying out her international obligations following her signing of the United Nations International Covenant on Civil and Political Rights in 1976, thereby according her citizens the right to freedom of religious belief and practice as per article 18 of the ICCPR.[348]

The unimaginable pains and hardships that the families bereaved of their fathers and mothers in the unfortunate circumstances resulting from the

---

[347]   "How Female Redeemed preacher was killed during morning evangelism." Adelani Adepegba, The Punch, July 10, 2016: https://punchng.com/female-redeemed-preacher-killed-morning-evangelism/

[348]   It can be seen under the "Status of ratification" of the International Covenant on Civil and Political Rights that Nigeria ratified it and in fact its first optional protocol in 1976: https://www.ohchr.org/EN/ProfessionalInterest/Pages/CCPR.aspx

murder of people such as Joseph Kurah and Eunice Elisha would be inexplicable but a report from a media organisation called "Christian Today" about what was reported as remarks from the nephew of the murdered Rev Joseph Kurah sum up some aspects of it:

> A man who identified himself as Kurah's nephew posted graphic photos on twitter, saying: "They attacked him on his farm, cut off his arms and legs; then they chopped his head with a machete. I received a call on Thursday evening that my uncle, a pastor with ECWA was killed by Fulani herdsmen." He called on the authorities to find the killers: "All I want is justice to be done. Nasarawa State and the Federal Government must find the killers of my Uncle. Whoever is close to Governor Al-Makura of Nasarawa state should please inform him that we demand the perpetrators should be brought to book....We have become preys that are hunted by marauding beasts in our land. For how long will we suffer? He has left a very young family; three children are currently in the university. No one is saying anything about the clandestine killings by Fulani herdsmen happening almost every day.[349]

Crime can take place in any society, however, lawful a society might be. however, what is expected is that the perpetrators of such crimes must be pursued, tracked down, arrested and dealt with according to law to discourage others from perpetrating similar acts. A society becomes lawless and risk slipping into anarchy, if criminals can commit grievous crimes such as killing innocent individual members of the society and walk away without been apprehended for their crimes. The reason why Nigeria presently poses a threat to her own peace and that of the international community is the severity of the crimes committed in breach of international human rights law especially on the right to freedom of religion and practice and the failure of government to stop the continuation of such crimes as well as going after those who have perpetrated such acts.

---

[349] "Evangelical Pastor 'hacked to death' in Nigeria. By James Macintyre, Christian Today, Wed 6 July 2016: https://www.christiantoday.com/article/evangelical-pastor-hacked-to-death-in-nigeria/89953.htm

In a report by the World Watch Monitor, dated December 20, 2016, in which they discussed the killings of Joseph Kurah and Eunice Elisha, in which they stated that:

> five months after her brutal murder…the police are yet to name the perpetrators.[350]

World Watch Monitor, Nigeria, went on to say in the same report that:

> In June, at least 81 people were killed in recent attacks by ethnic Fulani in Logo and Ukum areas of Benue state in central Nigeria. An undetermined number of Churches were ransacked and burned a local source told World Watch Monitor. Benue State has been wracked with deadly violence. More than 500 people were killed in February in the mainly Christian area of Agatu. About 20,000 people are thought to have fled the wave of attacks.[351]

While all the above killings of Christians for which no arrest and prosecution has yet been made, well over three years today since the killings of Kurah and Elisha, another dimension of criminal conducts had been taking place again against Christians in northern Nigeria. It is increasingly becoming obvious that a war against Christians may actually be going on in Northern Nigeria, besides the violation of various human rights laws, such as the right to freedom from torture, degrading and inhuman treatment etc. On the 19 February 2018, over 100 Christian girls who were students of the Government Girls Science and Technical Secondary School in Dapchi, Yobe State, North East Nigeria, were abducted by Boko Haram, the Nigerian terrorist organisation, which now also goes by the name of Islamic State in West Africa Province (ISWAP). Among the over 100 Christian girls that were abducted from Dapchi is a teenage girl called Leah Sharibu.[352]

---

[350] "UPDATE: Five months after killing of female Nigerian preacher suspects yet to be named." World Watch Monitor Nigeria, December 20, 2016. See https://www.worldwatchmonitor. org/2016/12/update-five-months-after-killing-of-female-nigerian-preacher-suspects-yet-to-be-named/

[351] Ibid.

[352] See "Nigeria Says Leah Sharibu Is Alive; Herdsmen Attacks Continue" Morning Star News, September 1, 2019: https://morningstarnews.org/2019/09/ nigeria-says-leah-sharibu-is-alive-herdsmen-attacks-continue/

As a result of negotiations between the Federal Government of Nigeria and the representatives of the kidnappers (ISWAP), on the 21st March 2018, barely a month after they were abducted all the other girls except Leah Sharibu were released because they had renounced their faith as Christians and become Muslims. Sharibu had refused to renounce her faith as a Christian so the Islamic terrorists refused to release her. To this day, Leah Sharibu remains in the hands of her abductors without anyone being certain as to whether she has been killed or whether she is still alive.[353] But Sharibu's continuous stay with her abductors makes every reasonable person wonder whether the government of president Muhammadu Buhari in Nigeria is sympathetic to the terrorist group? Otherwise, what other satisfactory explanation can be given for the Nigerian government's meeting the conditions of the terrorists for the release of all other girls who were kidnapped with Leah that have converted to Islam while Leah remained captive? Surely, it cannot be said that it was the negotiation of the Federal Government of Nigeria that freed the other girls who, as a result of their renouncing their faith and converting to Islam, were in one faith and religion with their Islamic abductors and therefore could not be morally and religiously held further in captivity under the Islamic faith. A government that realises her obligations and is sensitive to what is expected of it, would have made it known to the terrorist group that the only person the terrorists needed to release to give the government some sense of responsibility is Leah Sharibu. The Government should have realised through their negotiators or mediators that the real deal they needed to settle for was asking the terrorists to release Leah Sharibu in exchange for the terms that they asked the government to meet which is what happens in such negotiations. The government negotiator(s) or mediator(s) could have told the representative(s) of the terrorist that all the girls that converted to Islam were their sisters and therefore before the God that they claim to have faith in they would be committing an unpardonable crime to keep those girls who had become Muslims, therefore Leah Sharibu was the only one for which the government would exchange in meeting their demands. Such a stance would have seen Leah Sharibu released. Leah Sharibu remains continuously in the hands of the terrorists and no one knows for sure if she has been killed or if she is still alive but the Muhammadu Buhari government claims she is alive. Whether Leah Sharibu is alive or dead, she

---

[353] "Leah Sharibu Inspires Nigeria's Christians, Faces Execution by Boko Haram." – Sunday Oguntola, Christianity Today, October 15, 2018: https://www.christianitytoday.com/news/2018/october/free-leah-sharibu-boko-haram-execution-dapchi-nigeria.html

is a clear case of a Nigerian whose right to freedom of religion and practice was clearly trampled upon to the extent that she was not released by her abductors simply because she refused to renounce the Christian faith and become a Muslim. But there are Nigerian Muslims sympathetic to her. As the report of Christianity Today says:

> Incidentally, even Muslims have expressed displeasure with her captivity, saying there's no compulsion in Islam[354]

In other words, keeping Leah Sharibu in captivity because she refused to renounce her faith was even by Islamic religious teachings ungodly and immoral, just as the Supreme Court of Pakistan's judgment in the Asia Bibi's case also says when it talked about Islam being opposed to oppression and injustice. However, the negotiating agent that represented the Federal Government of Nigeria and negotiated with the terrorists failed in telling the terrorists about the unreasonableness of their decision in holding continually Leah Sharibu captive when the other girls were to be released. It is hard to fathom how the not so well-educated terrorists' agents of the then Boko Haram could so easily outsmart the kind of mediators and negotiators that the Federal Government of Nigeria would have engaged in such a sensitive task of negotiating the release of Leah Sharibu and those that were held captive with her. As at the time of writing on 28 September 2019, well over a year and half since those who were held captive with Leah Sharibu were released because they converted to Islam, Sharibu remains in captivity.

While Nigeria has been known to be generally peaceful without major religious conflicts between the Christians and Muslims since independence, it is now argued by some that there is a case of general insecurity in Nigeria between 2015 and 2020, mainly bordering on some Islamic extremist elements inciting religious hatred and conflicts because of the numerous reports of killings of innocent Nigerians, as discussed in this chapter. This can be deciphered from the reaction of the leader of the Christian Association of Nigeria (CAN) who visited president Muhammadu Buhari on 10 November 2017, following an incident in which five Christians were sentenced to death by a High Court judge in Yola, the capital of the North Eastern of Adamawa. A report by the World Watch Monitor in Nigeria in respect of this incident reads thus:

---

[354] Ibid.

The Christian Association of Nigeria (CAN) has called on President Muhammadu Buhari to intervene after five Christian youths were sentenced to death in the North-eastern State of Adamawa, warning of a "miscarriage of justice" and bemoaning a lack of consistency in bringing killers to justice.

On 11 June, a judge at the High Court in Yola, the capital of Adamawa, found Alex Amos, Alheri Phanuel, Holy Boniface, Jerry Gideon and Jari Sabagi, all from Demsa Local Government Area (LGA), guilty of 'criminal conspiracy and culpable homicide.

The youths were found to have "wilfully and intentionally conspired and attacked" three herdsmen rearing cattle, killing one of them, Adamu Buba, and throwing his body into a river, and also maiming several cows in Kodumun village, part of Demsa LGA, on 1 June, 2017.

However, Nigeria's Independent news site reported that the victim fell into the river and drowned, while being chased by the five youths.

The victim was said to have been the ringleader of an attack that claimed 48 lives in Kodamun, a predominantly Christian village, in 2016.

In a statement published on Tuesday, 19 June, CAN said that it did not support "jungle justice or any criminality." However, the Church body called for consistency, noting "with regret how hundreds of our members in Southern Kaduna, Benue, Taraba, [and] Plateau States in the north – central geo-political zones, and a state like Enugu in the south, have been killed and are still being killed on a daily basis by some criminals parading themselves as Fulani herdsmen, but are yet to be apprehended....[355]

That after three years following the murders of Rev. Joseph Kurah and Pastor Eunice Elisha, no culprit has been arrested and prosecuted for those murders should be matters of international concern about the abuse of human rights in Nigeria and the threat to peace and security in Nigeria, especially as those who are killed are mostly Christians; and the

---

[355] "Why have killers of Christians been set free? – Christian Association of Nigeria. June 25, 2018 By World Watch Monitor Nigeria: https://www.worldwatchmonitor.org/coe/why-have-killers-of-christians-been-set-free-christian-association-of-nigeria/

manner in which they were killed cannot be separated from their choice of religious belief and practice. So, the challenge is upon the United Nations to re-examine its instrument of implementing human rights enforcement by state parties to its covenant and conventions.

According to reports just months after Muhammadu Buhari was sworn in for a second term of office as President of Nigeria in May 2019, there has been manifest renewed bouts of killings of Christians, climaxed perhaps by the Boko Haram killings of 9 Christians and 2 others that they held in captivity on Christmas Day 2019.[356]

While Nigerian Christians were still in shock at the provocation of the Boko Haram terrorists who also bear the name of Islamic State's West Africa Province (ISWAP), by their choice of Christmas Day for the killing of the Christians they were holding captive, they have gone on to perpetrate yet another provocative act of the beheading of other Christians. The reports of the killings of various Christians are said to have been carried out by the terrorist group in January 2020. In one instance they killed the Chairman of the Christian Association of Nigeria (CAN) in Michika Local Government Area of Adamawa State, the Reverend Lawan Andimi whom Boko Haram reportedly beheaded on 20 January 2020.[357] What is even more disheartening about the beheading of Rev Andimi is the fact that during negotiations for his release between 2 January 2020 when he was abducted by the terrorists and 20 January State Religion, Religious Pluralism and the Problem of Individual Right 2020 when he was beheaded, an offer of payment of a ransom in the sum of fifty million Nigerian Naira (N50million) was made to the terrorists but they rejected it and proceeded to kill him because he would not convert to Islam. It is clear that these terrorists have an agenda to possibly Islamise Nigeria which has peacefully existed as a State with about fifty per cent Christians and fifty per cent Muslims since the colonial era to the post-independence. Even though their prospect of achieving such in the twenty-first century is zero, they are nonetheless stoking a religious war between Nigerian Christians

---

[356]   "Nigeria terror group kills nine Christians and two Muslims in Christian Day horror." Anglican Communion News Service, ACNS. Posted on: January 7, 2020: https://www.anglicannews.org/news/2020/01/nigerian-terror-group-kills-nine-christians-and-two-muslims-in-christmas-day-horror.aspx ; see also "Islamic State in Nigeria 'beheads Christian hostages'. BBC News World Africa, 27th December 2019: https://www.bbc.co.uk/news/world-africa-50924266

[357]   "Christian Pastor Beheaded in Adamawa by Boko Haram" Churchleaders.com by Megan Briggs. January 21, 2020:https://churchleaders.com/news/369399-adamawa-can-leader-rev-andimi-beheaded-by-boko-haram.html

and Nigerian Muslims, and it is taking place in flagrant disregard to Nigerian Government's obligation to guarantee the right to freedom of religion under their African Charter as well as under the ICCPR. The reaction of the President of the Christian Association of Nigeria (CAN), His Eminence Dr Samson Ayokunle speaks of the increasing frustration of the Christians in Nigeria under the Buhari presidency.[358]

11.4 Burkina Faso and Its Own Dimension of Religious Violations of the Right to Individual Freedom of Religion

The government in Burkina Faso is reported to be clearly standing aloof oblivious of her responsibility to protect her citizens and respect their rights to their freedom of religion and practice under international human rights law. As if it is helpless, the Government watches people who profess to be Muslims forcibly driving out Christians from their homelands and sending them fleeing as refugees. The matter is no longer a secret as "Christian Today" quoted the United Nations in their recent report about the Islamic extremist ultimatum for Christians to convert to Islam or leave Burkina Faso:

> Since the violence began escalating in the once seemingly peaceful country in 2015, the U.N. reported this month that nearly 300,000 people have fled from their homes and over 500 have been killed....

The U.N. notes that there has been an average of 30,000 people displaced from their homes each month since the beginning of 2019.[359]

In the face of such human rights violations and gross abuse of Christians for nothing other than the profession of their religious beliefs and practice as Christians in Burkina Faso, it is rather surprising that both the Government of Burkina Faso and the United Nations seem to be helpless in addressing the attacks and killings of Christians and in putting a stop to the somewhat threat to international peace and security.

---

[358] "CAN Condemns FG Over Rev Andimi's Beheading": https://aljazirahnews. com/can-condemns-fg-over-rev-andimis-beheading/

[359] "Islamic extremists tell Christians to convert or leave." Samuel Smith, Sunday 22 Sep 2019: https://www.christiantoday.com/article/extremists-in-burkina-faso-tell-christians-to-convert-or-leave/133278.htm

11.5 Evaluation and Summary

What can be seen in the examination of the protection of the right to freedom of conscience, religious beliefs, and practice and indeed the respect for international human rights is that the good faith with which States enter into international treaties does not often translate into effective execution of their legal obligations to implement the protection of such when it comes to performance. This has been especially more prevalent in the manner in which states carry out their international obligations in the implementation and enforcement of individual human rights under the international covenant on civil and political rights (ICCPR).

When it comes to the individual right to freedom of religion and belief, it becomes even more glaring that states are having difficulties balancing the conflicting interests that stand on the way of their guaranteeing the individual right to freedom of religion, conscience, belief and practice and their obligations to the wider public insofar as winning the support of the citizenry who maybe averse to their religious beliefs is concerned.

Some of the recent events that have attracted global outcry in recent years with respect to the individual right to freedom of religion and practice shows that in some cases States' heads of Governments are more interested in winning public support than in ensuring that individual right to freedom of religion and belief and practice are duly respected. This becomes more serious when "the State identifies itself with a particular religion or belief"[360] and consequently, individuals who hold religious beliefs contrary to that which the state has as state religion had to "suffer disadvantages in their enjoyment of religion or belief rights..."[361] There are several examples of such cases across the globe but some of the examples of cases decided by the Supreme Court of Pakistan is examined here to crystallise the point.

---

[360] Nazila Ghanea, "Religion, Equality, and Non-Discrimination" in Religion and Human Rights An Introduction, Edited by John Witte, Jr. & M. Christian Green, Oxford University Press © 2012. p.211

[361] Ibid. p. 212

12

THE UNITED KINGDOM AND THE EMERGING PATTERN OF LIMITING THE INDIVIDUAL RIGHT TO FREEDOM OF CONSCIENCE, RELIGIOUS BELIEF AND PRACTICE BY HER COURTS AND THE EUROPEAN COURT OF HUMAN RIGHTS

The law has become paralyzed, and there is no justice in the Courts.[362]

European Convention on Human Rights and Fundamental Freedoms, (1950) Article 9 (1):

Everyone has the right to freedom of thought, conscience and religion; this right includes freedom to change

---

[362] This is stated in the Holy Bible, Habukkuk 1:4a. To the extent that those who will be discussed in this chapter in the case of Eweida and others v the United Kingdom lost their cases in the United Kingdom courts not because they were not Christians or they were not practicing their faith and religious belief in accordance with what the Holy Bible admonishes them to do but because their rights to freedom of conscience, religious belief and practice as stated in international human rights laws both in Article 18 of the United Nations International Covenant on Civil and Political Rights, ICCPR, 1966; and in Article 9 (1) of the European Convention on Human Rights, ECHR, (1950), is superseded by domestic law in line with for example the provisions of Article 9 (2) of the ECHR, it can be said that the law given them the right to freedom of conscience and religious belief and practice has been paralyzed.

his religion or belief and freedom, either alone or in community with others and in public or private, to manifest his religion or belief, in worship, teaching, practice and observance.

12.1 The Law and the Interpretation of the Court

In the United Kingdom and most of the European states where human rights could be easily assumed to be taken seriously and respected because of the legal instruments and mechanisms for the protection and enforcement of human rights such as the European Convention of Human Rights and the European Court of Human Rights, the truth is that people are just as much suffering from inability to enjoy these rights in some cases because the price for actualisation or enjoyment of such rights is often unaffordable to most citizens. Ordinarily, most people live with injustice because of inability or lack of resources to pursue the actualisation of their legal rights or to obtain justice. However, in the case of human rights the cost is far more too high to meet because of the general requirement of the applicant exhausting domestic remedies in other words, pursuing his claim through the domestic courts before resorting to going to the international or continental regional court to obtain justice that was denied in the domestic courts. The financial discouragement of pursuing the actualisation of such rights and the uncertainty of the outcome is so daunting that most applicants could easily opt for living with injustice than embark on it. This fact is more obvious when a critical look and examination is given to some of the decisions of the European Court of Human Rights on cases based on the right to freedom of religion, conscience, belief and practice. For instance, the decision of the European Court of Human Rights in Eweida and Others v the United Kingdom[363] clearly demonstrates this fact.

In Eweida and Others v the United Kingdom, four nationals of the United Kingdom made four applications (nos. 48420/10, 59842/10, 51671/10 and 36516/10) against the United Kingdom under Article 34 of the Convention for the Protection of Human Rights and

---

[363] Eweida and Others v. The United Kingdom, nos. 48420/10, 59842/10, 51671/10 and 36516/10, 27 May 2013.

Fundamental Freedoms to the European Court of Human Rights complaining that their domestic law has failed to offer them protection to manifest their human rights to freedom of conscience, religious beliefs and practice. The four applicants were Ms Nadia Eweida[364], Ms Shirley Chaplin[365], Ms Lillian Ladele[366] and Mr Gary McFarlane[367] and they were represented by different solicitors except for Ms Chaplin and Mr McFarlane who were represented by the same person, Mr Paul Diamond. Ms Eweida and Ms Chaplin, both were complaining about the restrictions their respective employers had placed upon them restricting them from wearing such Christian religious symbols as the cross visibly around their necks. While Ms Ladele and Mr McFarlane complained about the sanctions their respective employers had imposed on them because of their refusal to perform duties which condone homosexual relationships.

Ms Eweida, Ms Chaplin and Mr McFarlane invoked Article 9 of the Convention – "the right to freedom of thought, conscience and religion" – taken alone and in conjunction with Article 14 – "protection from discrimination. Discrimination occurs when you are treated less favourably than another person in a similar situation and this treatment cannot be objectively and reasonably justified" – while Ms Ladele complained only under Article 14 taken in conjunctions with Article 9. The Court joined all the applications by the date of judgment. The first applicant Ms Eweida has been in the employment of British Airways which is a private company, since 1999. However, in 2004, British Airways introduced a new uniform policy which included an open-necked blouse for women, to be worn with a cravat that could be tucked in or tied loosely at the neck.[368] The rules for female wearing the uniform clearly stated that:

---

[364] For a background to Eweida's case see: Eweida v British Airways [2010] EWCA Civ 80.

[365] For a background understanding of see Chaplin v Royal Devon and Exeter NHS Foundation ET/1702886/2009. See also Chaplin v Royal Devon and Exeter Hospital NHS Foundation Trust: Exeter Employment Tribunal, April 2010 Religious Symbol – uniform policy – Employment Equality by Frank Cranmer and Russell Sandberg in Ecclesiastical Law Journal, Cambridge University Press, Volume 13 Issue 2 May 2011.

[366] See Ladele v London Borough of Islington [2009] EWCA Civ 1357.

[367] See McFarlane v Relate Avon Ltd [2010] EWCA Civ 771.

[368] See Eweida and Others v the United Kingdom at paras 9-10.

Any accessories or clothing item that the employee is required to have for mandatory religious reasons should at all times be covered by the uniform.[369]

Although Ms Eweida was not pleased with the uniform rules requiring her to conceal her cross which she wore in expression of her religious belief, she complied with it until on 20 May 2006. On that day she went to work wearing her cross openly until her manager asked her to remove the chain and the cross or conceal them under the cravat and she eventually complied with the order following the intervention of another senior manager. However, she attended work on 7 August 2006 wearing her cross visibly again until she was warned and threatened to be sent home without pay before she complied with the uniform code of concealing her cross. But on 20 September she went to work and refused to conceal her cross and was consequently sent home without pay pending her willingness to return to work in compliance with the company uniform rules. Nonetheless, on 23 October 2006, she was offered administrative work which did not require contact with customers. But she declined the offer.[370]

By a twist in the cause of events in October 2006, some articles appeared in a number of newspapers critical of British Airways handling of Ms Eweida's case. British Airways consequently responded on 24 November 2006 by announcing a review of its uniform policy with respect to wearing of religious and charity symbols. At the end of its consultation on 19 January 2007, it adopted a new policy which took effect from 1 February 2007, allowing people to wear religious symbols such as the cross and charity badges. As a result of the new policy allowing her to wear a cross and manifest her religious belief, Ms Eweida went back to work on 3 February 2007. However, British Airways refused to pay her for the period between 20 September 2006 and 2 February 2007, on the grounds that Ms Eweida chose not to work during the time.

Ms Eweida who prior to all this had lodged a claim with the Employment Tribunal on 15 December 2006, claiming among other things damages for indirect discrimination contrary to regulation 3 of the Employment Equality (Religion and Belief) Regulations 2003 and also complaining

---

[369]   Ibid.

[370]   Ibid. At para 12.

of breach of her right to manifest her religion contrary to Article 9 of the Convention. However, the Employment Tribunal rejected Ms Eweida's claim on the grounds that:

> ...the visible wearing of a cross was not a mandatory requirement of the Christian Faith but Ms Eweida's personal choice. There was no evidence that any other employee, in a uniformed workforce numbering some 30000 had ever made such a request or demand, much less refused to work if it was not met. It followed that the applicant had failed to establish that the uniform policy had put Christianity generally at a disadvantage, as was necessary in order to establish a claim of indirect discrimination.[371]

Ms Eweida appealed to the Employment Appeal Tribunal and her appeal was dismissed by the Appeal Tribunal on the thrust that:

> ...the concept of indirect discrimination implied discrimination against a defined group and that the applicant had not established evidence of group disadvantage.[372]

In pursuit of justice, she approached the Court of Appeal with an appeal against the decision of the Employment Appeal Tribunal but had her appeal yet again dismissed by the Court on 12 February 2010. Although she argued that the Employment Tribunal and Employment Appeal Tribunal erred in law by how they dismissed her claim because "evidence of disadvantage to a single individual should suffice in establishing indirect discrimination" the Court of Appeal rejected this argument and instead endorsed the approach of the Employment Appeal Tribunal by holding that:

> ...in order for indirect discrimination to be established, it must be possible to make some general statements which would be true about a religious group such that an employer ought reasonably to be able to appreciate that any

---

[371] Ibid At para 14.

[372] Ibid. Para 15

particular provision may have a desperate impact on the group.[373]

The Court of Appeal went on to say:

> ...even if Ms Eweida's legal argument were correct, and indirect discrimination could be equated with disadvantage to a single individual arising out of her wish to manifest her faith in a particular way, the Employment Tribunal's findings of fact showed the rule to have been a proportionate means of achieving a legitimate aim. For some seven years no one, including Ms Eweida, had complained about the rule and once the issue was raised it was conscientiously addressed. In the interim, British Airways had offered to move the applicant without loss of pay to work involving no public contact, but the applicant had chosen to reject this offer and instead to stay away from work and claim pay as compensation.[374]

The European Court of Human Rights (ECHR) noted that the Court of Appeal viewed it as a Court that would not entertain Ms Eweida's application because the Appeal Court rested its grounds not to uphold Ms Eweida's case on the basis of the judgment of the House of Lords in R(SB) v Governors of Denbigh High School [2006] UKHL 15, where Lord Bingham analysed the case-law of the Court and Commission and concluded that:

> The Strasbourg institutions have not been at all ready to find an interface with the right to manifest religious belief in practice or observation where a person has voluntarily accepted an employment or role which does not accommodate that practice or observance and there are other means open to the person to practise or observe his or her religion without undue hardship or inconvenience.[375]

It is rather interesting that the highly esteemed Court of Appeal premised its decision on the wrong perception of what the ECHR might do in Ms

---

[373]   Ibid. Para 16

[374]   Ibid.

[375]   Ibid

Eweida's application to the court. There clearly also was an oversight in the way Ms Eweida's case was handled by the domestic court because in considering her rights under Article 9, which gives her right to freedom of conscience, religious belief and practice besides indirect discrimination, consideration was not given to the fact that she was exercising her freedom of conscience when eventually she refused to compromise with the restriction of her wearing the cross openly in expression of her Christian religious beliefs. It was rather excessively subjective of the Court of Appeal judges to have held that "visible wearing of the cross was not a mandatory requirement of the Christian faith but Ms Eweida's personal choice."[376] There are Christians, indeed, some denominations of the Christian faith that see the wearing of the cross as a far deeper expression and display of their Christian religious belief than a mere personal choice to wear it. It should also be noted that British Airways introduced a new uniform policy in 2004 which required Ms Eweida who was before then wearing her cross openly to begin to conceal the cross she wore under her new uniform cravat and that led to her problems with British Airways; and so the highly esteemed Court of Appeal judges conclusion that she was concealing her cross for 7 years or from the day she was employed with British Airways was wrong. In actual fact, the new uniform and the rules of concealing religious symbols were new terms of working conditions that were imposed on Ms Eweida as a variation of her employment contract and working conditions and the Court ought to have seen that as a breach of her employment contract as well as a violation of her Article 9 right under the Convention, and indeed indirect discrimination insofar as any Christian of her denominational background whose wearing of the cross is a fundamental expression of her faith would have behaved as she did. It follows that the case of R (SB) v Governors of Denbigh High Street [2006] that the Court of Appeal depended on was not the right authority because in 1999 when Ms Eweida took up employment with British Airways there was no rule prohibiting her from wearing the cross openly until 2004, which was 5 years into her employment with British Airways. It should be expected that a good employer should consult and agree with its employees before changing their terms of working condition after confirmation of an employee's employment which for most employers and employees is usually between the period of '3 and 6 months' time. For Ms Eweida, who had worked for British Airways for 5 years at the time of the change

---

[376]   Ibid. Para 14

of uniform and code of dressing, British Airways was unfair to her. It was rather disappointing that the Supreme Court refused Ms Eweida leave to appeal on 26 May 2010 and consequently by this case exposed the United Kingdom as a state party that cannot adequately guarantee the right to freedom of conscience, religious beliefs and practice for her nationals.

The extent to which the European Court of Human Rights succeeded in righting the wrongs Ms Eweida suffered would be discussed later in this chapter. For now it is vital to examine how the domestic courts handled the case of another Christian who also had a problem at work because of her determination to wear the cross openly in expression of her faith as a Christian and the United Kingdom courts ruled against her doing so.

The second applicant, Ms Chaplin was a qualified nurse. At the time of the issue of her wearing a cross at work, she was a practising Christian who had worn the cross as demonstration of her Christian faith since 1971. She was employed as a nurse by the Royal Devon and Exeter NHS Foundation Trust, which is a state hospital. She was credited with an exemplary record of work from April 1989 to July 2010. And for that entire period of 11 years, she wore a cross openly while she performed her duties excellently. However, in the process of the hospital implementing a uniform policy based on guidance from the Department of Health, the hospital stated in paragraph 5.1.5 that

> If worn, jewellery must be discreet

> 5.3.6 To minimise the risk of cross infection will be [sic] keep jewellery to a minimum (see 5.1.11). That is:

> One plain smooth ring which will not hinder hand hygiene,

> One pair of plain discreet earrings.

> No necklaces will be worn to reduce the risk of injury when handling patients.

> Facial piercing if present should be removed or covered."

Paragraph 5.1.11 provided:

> Any member of staff who wishes to wear any particular types of clothes or jewellery for religious or cultural reasons must raise this with their line manager who will not unreasonably withhold approval.[377]

Following this policy was the introduction of new uniforms at the hospital which "included a V-necked tunic for nurses in June 2007." Ms Chaplin's manager requested her in June 2009 to "remove her necklace but she insisted that the cross was a religious symbol and sought approval to wear it." [378] However, her request was turned down on the ground that "the chain and the cross might cause injury if an elderly patient pulled on it." Ms Chaplin then:

> proposed wearing the cross on a chain secured with magnetic catches, which would immediately break apart if pulled by a patient.[379]

The health authority rejected her proposal on the basis that the cross itself was a "risk to health and safety if it were able to swing free" and come into contact with open wounds.[380] The hospital eventually moved Ms Chaplin in November 2009 to a non-nursing temporary position which ended in July 2010.

In the midst of her disagreements with the hospital, Ms Chaplin applied to the Employment Tribunal in November 2009, complaining of both direct and indirect discrimination on religious grounds. However, the Employment Tribunal held that:

> there was no direct discrimination since the hospital's stance was based on health and safety rather than religious grounds.[381]

It further stated in respect of her complaint about indirect discrimination that:

---

[377]   Ibid. Para 19.

[378]   Ibid. Para 20.

[379]   Ibid.

[380]   Ibid

[381]   Ibid. Para 21

...there was no evidence that "persons", other than the applicant had been put at a particular disadvantage.[382]

At the time Ms Chaplin was also advised that:

> ...in the light of the case of Court of Appeal's judgment in the Eweida's case, an appeal on points of law to the Employment Appeal Tribunal would have no prospect of success.[383]

Thus Ms Chaplin, a nurse with an unblemished record of over ten years' service was dispensed with to the detriment of patients care for holding on to her own religious belief and practice because both the hospital and the Employment Tribunal were acting in compliance with a policy which though good on the surface insofar as it seeks to advance health and safety does not take into consideration the conscientious work of a nurse such as Ms Chaplin who had ensured that she attended patients with care and diligence without causing health and safety hazards to them for over ten years. Were the Employment Tribunal not too much in a hurry to dispense of her case in favour of the hospital who was the stronger party in the case, it should have given due consideration to the fact that Ms Chaplin had an unblemished record of service and posed no risk to patient safety by wearing a cross. The tribunal should have indeed examined the nature of the cross and necklace that Ms Chaplin wore such as its weight and length to consider the potential injury it could cause, if at all it posed a risk, before reaching the decision they reached. But the tribunal like the hospital management simply took what might have been the convenient but possibly unfair decision of simply forbidding her from wearing a symbol of her religious belief in disregard to her preferred form of religious belief and practice.

While the extent to which the European Court of Human Rights judgment on Ms Chaplin case will be examined later in this chapter to see how it strengthens the enforcement of the rights to freedom of conscience, religious belief and practice, the need to examine the domestic courts judgments of the cases of the third and fourth applicant is of immediate relevance.

---

[382] Ibid. Para 21

[383] Ibid. Para 22

The third applicant Ms Ladele is a Christian who by virtue of her Christian religious beliefs opines that marriage should only be a union between a man and a woman. She was employed by the London Borough of Islington, a local government public authority council, from 1992. In 2002, Ms Ladele became a registrar of births, deaths and marriages. At the time, the Civil Partnership Act 2004 which came into force in December 2005 was not in force so Ms Ladele had no problems with her duties. However, when the Civil Partnership Act 2004 came into force and those in the position of Ms Ladele's position as registrars were required to register same-sex union, she found problems exercising her right to freedom of conscience and practising her Christian religious beliefs and registering same-sex civil partnerships. Ms Ladele's challenges were compounded by two additional issues within the Islington Borough procedures of effecting the enforcement of the Civil Partnership Act 2004. The first issue, was that unlike some other London Boroughs who consulted with their employers who were registrars like Ms Ladele before the Civil Partnership Act 2004 came into force to establish those who were willing to carry out duties involving registering of same-sex partnerships, Islington Borough simply imposed the duty on those who were registrars such as Ms Ladele to carry on their work with the additional responsibility of conducting ceremonies and registration of same-sex partnerships. The second issue, was that Islington Borough had a "Dignity for All" equality and diversity policy, which by the Borough's interpretation whether intentionally or unintentionally overrode Ms Ladele's right to freedom of conscience and religious belief and practice. The policy read thus:

> Islington is proud of its diversity and the council will challenge discrimination in all its forms. 'Dignity for all' should be the experience of Islington staff, residents and service users, regardless of the age, gender, disability, faith, race, sexuality, nationality, income or health status...

> The council will promote community cohesion and equality for all groups but will especially target discrimination based on age, disability, gender, race, religion and sexuality...

> In general, Islington will:

(a) Promote Community cohesion by promoting shared community values and understanding, underpinned by equality, respect and dignity for all ....

It is the council's policy that everyone should be treated fairly and without discrimination.

Islington aims to ensure that:

- Staff experience fairness and equity of treatment in the workplace
- Customers receive fair and equal access to council's services
- Staff and customers are treated with dignity and respect

The Council will actively remove discriminatory barriers that can prevent people from obtaining the employment opportunities and services to which they are entitled. The council will not tolerate processes, attitudes and behaviour that amount to discrimination, including harassment, victimisation and bullying through prejudice, ignorance, thoughtfulness and stereotyping... All employees are expected to promote these values at all times and to work within the policy. Employees found to be in breach of this policy may face disciplinary action."[384]

In December 2005 Islington decided to designate all existing registrars of births, deaths and marriages as civil partnership registrars. It was not required to do this, the legislation simply required to ensure that there was a sufficient number of civil partnership registrars for the area to carry out that function. Some other United Kingdom local authorities took a different approach, and allowed registrars with a sincerely held religious objection to the formation of civil partnership to opt out of designation as civil partnership registrars.[385]

When the Civil Partnership Act 2004 came into force in December 2005, Ms Ladele did not flagrantly breach the Act and Islington Council

---

[384] Ibid. Para 24.

[385] Ibid. Para 25

code of conduct and equality policy, in spite of the Council's failure to consult with registrars who may object such as Ms Ladele. She made informal arrangements with her colleagues who performed same-sex civil partnership union ceremonies and registration while she conducted marriage ceremonies and registrations of heterosexual couples.

However, in a manner that seemed as if Ms Ladele was targeted even though no member of the public had raised any complaint about her:

> In March 2006, two colleagues complained that her refusal to carry out such duties was discriminatory. In a letter dated 1 April 2006 Ms Ladele was informed that, in the view of the local authority, refusing to conduct civil partnership could put her in breach of the Code of Conduct and the equality policy. She was requested to confirm in writing that she would henceforth officiate at civil partnership ceremonies.[386]

The April 1, 2006, letter directed Ms Ladele to conduct civil partnership ceremonies or face charges of breach of code of conduct and equality can on balance of consideration of the Islington Council's failure to consult Ms Ladele prior to the Act coming into force and the refusal of the Council to acknowledge and respect her right to freedom of conscience and religious belief and practice be deemed bullying with intent to get her to act against her conscience and religious belief and practice. Quite predictably like those with strong Christian religious belief and practice before her who would rather be killed than compromise their faith as discussed, Ms Ladele refused to confirm in writing that she would comply with the council's directive. She rather requested the Council to accommodate her beliefs.

With Ms Ladele's refusal to carry out duties of civil partnership ceremonies of same-sex union, her homosexual colleagues argued that they felt victimised because of the rota difficulties and the burden it places on them. As a consequence, in May 2007, Islington Council conducted a preliminary investigation which concluded in July 2007:

---

[386] Ibid. Para 26.

with a recommendation that a formal disciplinary complaint be brought against Ms Ladele that, by refusing to carry out civil partnerships on grounds of sexual orientation of the parties, she had failed to comply with the local authority's code of conduct and equality and diversity. A disciplinary hearing took place on 16 August 2007. Following the hearing, Ms Ladele was asked to sign a new job description requiring her to carry out straightforward signings of the civil partnership register and administrative work in connection with civil partnerships, but with no requirement to conduct ceremonies.[387]

Faced with an impending dismissal and left with no other option to assert her own right to freedom of conscience and religious belief and practice as a legal right which is not stripped off from her by virtue of her work which at the time she was employed had nothing to do with conducting same-sex partnership, Ms Ladele went to the Employment Tribunal to seek redress.

Ms Ladele made an application to the Employment Tribunal on grounds of religion or belief and harassment. On 1 December 2007 the Statistics and Registration Act 2007 came into force and, instead of remaining an office employed by the Registrar General, Ms Ladele became an employee of the local authority, which now had the power to dismiss her.

On 3 July 2008, the Tribunal upheld the complaints of direct and indirect religious discrimination, and harassment, holding that the local authority had "placed a greater value on the rights of the lesbian, gay, bisexual and transsexual community than it placed on the rights of [Ms Ladele] as one holding an orthodox Christian belief.[388]

Islington Council appealed to the Employment Appeal Tribunal against the decision of the Employment Tribunal ruling in favour of Ms Ladele. In its ruling on 19 December 2008 the Employment Appeal Tribunal reversed the decision of the Employment Tribunal. "It held that the local

---

[387] Ibid.

[388] Ibid. Para 27-28.

authority's treatment of Ms Ladele had been a proportionate means of achieving a legitimate aim, namely providing the registrar service on non-discriminatory basis.[389]

In the belief that she would get justice Ms Ladele appealed the decision of the Employment Tribunal to the Court of Appeal but the Court ruled against her on 15 December saying:

> ...the fact that Ms Ladele's refusal to perform civil partnerships was based on her religious view of marriage could not justify the conclusion that Islington should not be allowed to implement its aim to the full, namely that all registrars should perform civil partnerships as part of its Dignity for All policy. Ms Ladele was employed in a public job and was working for a public authority; she was being required to perform a purely secular task, which was being treated as part of her job; Ms Ladele's refusal to perform the task involved discriminating against gay people in the course of that job; she was being asked to perform the task because of Islington's Dignity for All policy, whose laudable aim was to avoid, or at least minimise, discrimination both among Islington's employees, and between Islington (and its employees) and those in the community they served; Ms Ladele's refusal was causing offence to at least two of her gay colleagues; Ms Ladele's objection was based on her view of marriage, which was not core part of her religion; and Islington's requirement in no way prevented her from worshipping as she wished.[390]

When due consideration is given to the fact that as at when Ms Ladele was employed in 1992 and when she became a registrar of births, deaths and marriages in 2002, it was not part of her duty, and indeed it was not in her job description to conduct ceremonies for civil partnership; otherwise same-sex union, because the Civil Partnership Act 2004 was passed by the United Kingdom Parliament two years later, and indeed it did not come into force until December 2005; it becomes pertinent to ask why the Employment Appeal Tribunal failed to uphold Ms Ladele's

---

[389]   Ibid. Para 27-28

[390]   Ibid. Para 29

victory at the Employment Tribunal? And perhaps more disconcerting is the decision of the Court of Appeal to uphold the Employment Appeal Tribunal's judgment, inter alia that:

> Ms Ladele's objection was based on her view of marriage, which was not a core part of religion[391]

The fact about Ms Ladele's refusal to conduct same-sex civil partnership ceremonies says:

> She holds the view that marriage is the union of one man and one woman for life, and sincerely believes that same-sex civil partnerships are contrary to God's law.[392]

God's law which Ms Ladele premised her belief and view as a Christian speaking of God's decision at the time of creation says:

> Then God said, "Let us make man in Our image, according to Our likeness; and let them rule over the fish of the sea and over the birds of the sky and over the cattle and over all the earth." God created man in His own image, in the image of He created him; male and female He created them. God blessed them; and God said to them, "Be fruitful and multiply, and fill the earth, and subdue it, and rule over the fish of the sea and over the birds of the sky and over every living thing that moves on earth."[393]

Following creation, we read God's order on man and woman union in marriage as follows:

> Then the LORD God said, "It is not good for the man to be alone. I will make a helper who is just right for him."

> So the LORD God caused the man to fall into deep sleep. While the man slept, the LORD God took out one of the man's ribs and closed up the opening. Then the LORD

---

[391] Ibid. Para 29 quoting paragraph 52 of the Court of Appeal judgment.

[392] Ibid. At para 23

[393] The Creation. Genesis 1:26-28. (Translation: New American Standards Bible)

God made a woman from the rib, and he brought her to the man.

"At last!" the man exclaimed.

"This one is bone from my bone, and flesh from my flesh!

She will be called 'woman,' because she was taken from 'man.'"

This explains why a man leaves his father and mother and is joined to his wife, and the two are united into one."[394]

On the laws of God saying marriage must only be between man and woman and that other forms of sexual intercourse save that between a man and a woman or male and female of other living things among God's creatures are acts of abomination, the Holy Bible has this to say:

Do not practice homosexuality, having sex with another man as with a woman. It is a detestable sin.

A man must not defile himself by having sex with an animal. And a woman must not offer herself to a male animal to have intercourse with it. This is a perverse act.[395]

There is no doubt about the fact that the highly esteemed judges of the Employment Appeal Tribunal and justices of the Court of Appeal erred when they stated in their judgments that Ms Ladele's objection to same-sex union "was based on her view of marriage, which was not a core part of her religion." These are some verses from the

Holy Bible that clearly condemns homosexuality, lesbianism, and gay sexual lifestyles. It even makes clear that negative consequences will follow those who live such lifestyle:

They traded the truth about God for a lie. So they worshipped and served the things God created instead

---

[394]   Genesis 2:18, 21-24 (New Living Translation of the Holy Bible).

[395]   Forbidden Sexual Practices. Leviticus 18:22 23.
(New Living Translation of the Holy Bible)

of the Creator himself, who is worthy of eternal praise! Amen. That is why God abandoned them to their shameful desires. Even the women turned against the natural way to have sex and indulged in sex with each other. And the men, instead of having normal sexual relations with women, burned with lust for each other. Men did shameful things with other men, and as a result of this sin, they suffered within themselves the penalty they deserved.[396]

One of the most common expressions following Christian Church weddings which some people probably treat as a cliché is "what God has joined together let no man put it asunder" extrapolated from a statement Jesus Christ made while teaching on the sanctity of a man and a woman marriage, when he was questioned about justifications for divorce. Here is the story:

> Some Pharisees came to Jesus, testing Him and asking, "Is it lawful for a man to divorce his wife for any reason at all?" And He answered and said, "Have you not read that He who created them from the beginning MADE THEM MALE AND FEMALE, and said, 'FOR THIS REASON A MAN SHALL LEAVE HIS FATHER AND MOTHER AND BE JOINED TO HIS WIFE, AND THE TWO SHALL BECOME ONE FLESH'? So they are no longer two, but one flesh. What therefore God has joined together let no man separate.[397]

Against the backdrop of the position of the laws and precepts of God in the Christian Holy Bible as stated above, it is difficult to understand why the judges in the Employment Appeal Tribunal would consider the position of Ms Ladele on marriage as "her view of marriage, which was not a core part of her religion". If there are judges who do not know what the Christian religion teaches on marriage and would act on a premise that a Christian's Biblical view of the marriage as in the Holy Bible is not a core part of her religion then the risk of unjust decisions being made in judgments against Christians such as Ms Ladele will remain high and possibly strip such of their right to freedom of religious belief

---

[396]   Romans 1:25-27 (New living Translation of the Bible).

[397]   Jesus Christ on marriage and divorce. Matthew 19:3-6 (New American Standard Bible).

and practice. If Islington Council could not be seen to have breached her contract of employment by frustrating her as an employee who took up employment as a registrar before the Civil Partnership Act 2004 came into force and therefore quite entitled to opt out then there is no protection for Christians who want to hold on to human rights to freedom of conscience and religious belief and practice as per Article 9 of the European Convention on Human Rights.

Insofar as the decisions of the Employment Appeal Tribunal and the Court of Appeal decisions go in the Ms Ladele's case, what is obvious is that those who want to exercise their human right to freedom of conscience, religious belief and practice in the face of a contradicting law such as the Civil Partnership Act; and a policy such as the Islington's Policy on Equality which though fair could be said to have been applied in a rather heavy-handedly way against Ms Ladele, stand to suffer detriment in the enjoyment of their right to freedom of conscience and religious belief and practice.

Before looking at the decision of the European Court of Human Rights on Ms Ladele's application, an examination of how the United Kingdom courts decided the case of McFarlane before he took his case to the European Court of Human Rights needs to be similarly discussed just like the other three candidates.

Mr McFarlane is described as a practising Christian who at one time had held some pastoral responsibility as an elder of his former church which was a multicultural church in Bristol. Based on his Christian religious beliefs founded on the teachings of the Holy Bible he believes that homosexual activity is sinful. Therefore, he decided that he would not have anything to do with endorsing it by way of advising homosexuals about their relationships. However, he took employment with Relate, which is a national private organisation which provides a confidential sex therapy and relationship counselling service. Both Relate as an organisation and its individual counsellors are members of the British Association for Sexual and Relationship Therapy (BASRT).[398] The Association in its Code of Ethics and Principles of Good Practice which Relate and its counsellors abide by states at paragraphs 18 and 19 thus:

---

[398]   Eweida and Others v United Kingdom at paragraphs 31-32.

Recognising the right to self-determination, for example:

18. Respecting the autonomy and ultimate right to self-determination of clients and others with whom clients may be involved. It is not appropriate for therapist to impose a particular set of standards, values or ideals upon clients. The therapists must recognise and work in ways that respect the value and dignity of clients (and colleagues) with due regard to issues such as religion, race, gender, age, beliefs, sexual orientation and disability.

Awareness of one's own prejudices, for example:

19. The therapist must be aware of his or her own prejudices and avoid discrimination, for example on grounds of religion, race, gender, age, beliefs, sexual orientation, disability. The therapist has a responsibility to be aware of his or her own issues of prejudice and stereotyping and particularly to consider ways in which this may be affecting the therapeutic relationship.[399]

Relate Avon, Bristol, which employed McFarlane in addition to the BASRT code of conduct for good practice also have the following Equal Opportunities Policy which Mr McFarlane was expected to comply with. Part of it reads as follows:

Relate Avon is committed to ensuring that no person – trustees, staff, volunteers, counsellors and clients, receive less favourable treatment on the basis of personal or group characteristics, such as race, colour, sexual orientation, marital status, disability [or] socio-economic grouping. Relate Avon is not only committed to the letter of the law, but also to a positive policy that will achieve the objective of ensuring equality of opportunity for all those who work at the centre (whatever their capacities), and all our clients.[400]

---

[399] Ibid. At paragraph 32 of the judgment paragraphs 18 and 19 of the British Association for Sexual and Relationship Therapy is quoted.

[400] Ibid.

Mr McFarlane's initial hesitation in counselling homosexual couples subsided when he was told by his supervisor that simply counselling homosexual couples did not amount to "endorsement of such relationship."[401] He went on to provide counselling services to some lesbian couples. However, in spite of Mr McFarlane commencing Relate's post-graduate Diploma in psycho-sexual therapy, in 2007, he still found a conflict in his duty of advising couples on same-sex relationships at work and his Christian religious responsibility of teaching the Bible in his Church. Since it was rather not practicable to skip Relate's policies and BASRT code of conduct for good practice to let him advise only heterosexual couples, Mr McFarlane was eventually subjected to disciplinary action in March 2008 for non-compliance with Relate's policies and BASRT code of conduct for good practice. He was dismissed for gross misconduct.

Mr McFarlane took his case to the Employment Tribunal where he made a claim for direct discrimination and indirect discrimination as well as unfair dismissal and wrongful dismissal. The Tribunal in its judgment on 5 January 2009 found that Mr McFarlane "had not suffered direct discrimination contrary to Regulation 3 (1)

(a) of the 2003 Regulations."[402] It further found that:

> He had not been dismissed because of his faith, but because it was believed that he would not comply with the policies which reflected Relate's ethos.[403]

However, it noted that:

> With regard to the claim of indirect discrimination under Regulation 3 (1) (b),…that Relate's requirement that its counsellors comply with its Equal Opportunities Policy would put an individual who shared Mr McFarlane's religious beliefs at a disadvantage.[404]

---

[401]   Ibid. Para 33.

[402]   Ibid. Para 38.

[403]   Ibid.

[404]   Ibid.

But it went further to say:

> ...the aim of the requirement was the provision of a
> full range of counselling services to all sections of the
> community, regardless of sexual orientation, which was
> legitimate.[405]

Upon all considerations of Mr McFarlane's claim, the Tribunal decided
that "his dismissal had been a proportionate means of achieving a
legitimate aim.[406]

Mr McFarlane appealed to the Employment Appeal Tribunal against the
findings of the Employment Tribunal in respect of his claim but in its
ruling on 30 November 2009, it decided that the decision of the Tribunal
was correct:

> It rejected Mr McFarlane's argument that it was not
> legitimate to distinguish between objecting to a religious
> belief and objecting to a particular act which manifested
> that belief, and held that such an approach was compatible
> with Article 9 of the Convention. It noted Relate's
> arguments that the compromise proposed by Mr McFarlane
> would be unacceptable as a matter of principle because it
> ran "entirely contrary to the ethos of the organisation to
> accept a situation in which a counsellor could decline to
> deal with particular clients because he disapproved of their
> conduct", and that it was not practicable to operate a system
> under which a counsellor could withdraw from counselling
> same-sex couples if circumstances arose where he believed
> that he would be endorsing sexual activity on their part.
> Relate was entitled to refuse to accommodate views which
> contradicted it fundamental declared principles. In such
> circumstances, arguments concerning the practicability of
> accommodating the applicant's views were out of place.[407]

In pursuit of his right to freedom of conscience, religious belief and
practice as in Article 9 (1) of the Convention, Mr McFarlane decided to

---

[405]   Ibid

[406]   Ibid.

[407]   Ibid. Para 39.

appeal to the Court of Appeal against the decision of the Employment Appeal Tribunal ruling but in a manner far from giving relevance to the right to freedom of conscience and religious belief and practice as contained in Article 9 (1) of the Convention, the Court of Appeal:

> on 20 January 2010, refused the application on the basis that there was realistic prospect of the appeal succeeding in the light of the Court of Appeal judgment of December 2009 in Ladele.

> Following the refusal by the Supreme Court to allow leave to appeal in Ladele, Mr McFarlane renewed his application for permission to appeal. After a hearing, that was again refused on 29 April 2010 on the basis that the present case could not seriously be distinguished from Ladele.[408]

12.2 Superimposing one law over another

Generally speaking, what is manifestly obvious in the outcome of the cases of these four applicants Ms Eweida, Ms Chaplin, Ms Ladele and Mr McFarlane based on the decisions of the English Courts is that it superimposed some other domestic laws such as the equality and anti-discrimination laws over these individuals' right to religion and belief in a manner that actually left these applicants that were asserting their exercise of the right to manifest their religious belief deprived of the very equality and fair treatment including the right not to be discriminated against that they were held in some instances to have breached and the European Court of Human Rights did not quite do justice in each case in making the interpretation of what it means to manifest the right to religion and belief in practice. Mr McFarlane argued, "it was not legitimate to distinguish between objecting to a religious belief and objecting to a particular act which manifested that belief", the limitations imposed by Article 9 (2) of the Convention allows for the interpretation of Regulation 3 of the Employment Equality (Religion or Belief) 2003 to supersede the rights that should be enjoyed under Article 9 (1) on freedom of conscience, religious belief and practice" and the courts appear to unwittingly side-track the right to religious belief and practice in such a

---

[408] Ibid. Para. 40

way that as per these decisions the idea of practicing your religious belief as a Christian cannot be sustained at work in most cases depending on the individual nature of employment.

12.3 Evaluation and Summary

It now remains to examine the extent to which the European Court of Human Rights interpretation of Article 9 (1) "the right to freedom of conscience, religious belief and practice" in respect of each of these four applicants' cases elucidates understanding on how those who hold Christian religious belief and practice and find themselves in the positions Ms Eweida, Ms Chaplin, Ms Ladele, and Mr McFarlane, can best comport themselves at their places of work, and if they can still enjoy their right to freedom of conscience, religious belief and practice at work.

Beginning with the first applicant, Ms Eweida, the European Court of Human Rights "found a violation" of Eweida's right to freedom of conscience, religious belief and practice by the United Kingdom because "the domestic law, as applied to her case, did not strike the right balance between the protection of her right to manifest her religion and the rights and interests of others."[409] However, it did not accept Ms Eweida's evidence of financial losses suffered.[410] Consequently, it did not rule in her favour for the United Kingdom to compensate her for loss of earnings. But it did consider the fact:

> that violation of her right to manifest her religious belief must have caused Ms Eweida considerable anxiety, frustration, and distress. It therefore awards her EUR 2,000 in respect of non-pecuniary damage.

With respect to Ms Eweida's claim for costs and expenses incurred before the court which was put at "approximately EUR 37,000 (inclusive of the value added tax) including GBP 9,218, in Solicitors' and GBP 15,000 in counsel's fees"[411], she ended up bearing the liability of some of the costs. Nonetheless, following the court's "case-law, an applicant is entitled to the

---

[409]   Ibid. Para 114.

[410]   Ibid.

[411]   Ibid. Para 115.

reimbursement of costs and expenses ...the court considers it reasonable to award EUR 30,000 for the proceedings before the court, together with any tax that may be chargeable to Ms Eweida."[412]

While Ms Eweida might be said to have gotten the justice she sought for, the process was rather at a cost that most people cannot afford and that is what makes the right to freedom of conscience, religious belief and practice too costly to enjoy, where a state party to the treaty guaranteeing the right chooses not to enforce the right within its domestic system.

In fact, rather discouraging insofar as the enjoyment of the right to freedom of conscience, religious belief and practice is concerned are the decisions of the European Court of Human Rights in respects of the cases of the other three applicants, namely: Ms Chaplin, Ms Ladele and Mr McFarlane.

Upon examination of the case of the second applicant Ms Chaplin, the European Court of Human Rights, stated:

> As with Ms Eweida....the Court considers that the second applicant's determination to wear the cross and chain at work was a manifestation of her religious belief and that the refusal by the health authority to allow her to remain in the nursing post while wearing the cross was an interference with her freedom to manifest her religion.[413]

However, in a rather unusual twist in reasoning the Court went on say:

> In this case, there does not appear to be a dispute that the reason for the restriction on jewellery, including religious symbols, was to protect the health and safety of nurses and patients.[414]

The Court's inference that "there does not appear to be a dispute that the reason for the restriction on jewellery, including religious symbols, was to

---

[412]   Ibid. Para 117.

[413]   Ibid. Para 97

[414]   Ibid. Para 98

protect the health and safety of nurses and patients"[415] is not absolutely
right because Ms Chaplin's submission was that:

> no evidence was adduced before the Employment Tribunal
> to demonstrate that the wearing of the cross caused health
> and safety problems.[416]

In what seems like an act of attribution bias, the European Court of
Human Rights ruled against Ms Chaplin by saying:

> The Court considers that, as in Ms Eweida's case, the
> importance for the second applicant of being permitted
> to manifest her religion by wearing the cross visibly must
> weigh heavily in the balance. However, the reason for
> asking her to remove the cross, namely the protection
> of health and safety on a hospital ward, was inherently
> of a greater magnitude than that which applied in
> respect of Ms Eweida. Moreover, this is a field where
> the domestic authorities must be allowed a wide margin
> of Appreciation...It follows that the court is unable
> to conclude that the measures of which Ms Chaplain
> complains were disproportionate. It follows that
> interference with her freedom to manifest her religion was
> necessary in a democratic society and that there was no
> violation of Article 9....and that there is no basis on which
> it can find violation of Article 14 either in this case.[417]

By acknowledging that Ms Chaplin's wearing of the cross at work was a
manifestation of her religion and that the refusal of the health authorities
to allow her remain at work while wearing the cross was an interference
to her right to exercise her right to religious belief, and then ruling against
her application by ascribing undefined 'wide margin of appreciation' to
the State, in this case the United Kingdom, to carry out the interference,
the European Court of Human Rights, stopped short of declaring the
international human rights law on the individual right to freedom of
conscience, religious belief and practice paralysed or limited to what a

---

[415]   Ibid.

[416]   Ibid. Para 69

[417]   Ibid. Paras 99-101.

state party to the international human rights treaties makes of it in the domestic jurisdiction.

In the case of the third applicant Ms Ladele, the jurisprudence of the European Court of Human Rights bear layers of opacity that does not help towards the understanding of the interpretation of law concerning the State's responsibility in ensuring that human rights such as the individual right to freedom of conscience, religious belief and practice in a democratic society is a right that should be enjoyed by individual members of a State Party to any of its treaties such as the ICCPR or ECHR. The joint dissenting opinion of Judges Vucinic and De Gaetano adduces to this while crystallising issues in the case insofar Ms Ladele's right to freedom of conscience and religious belief and practice is concerned. For instance, the Court upon examination of Ms Ladele's case acknowledged that:

For the Court, it is clear that the applicant's objection to participating in the creation of same-sex marriage civil partnership was directly motivated by her religious beliefs. The events in question fell within the ambit of Article 9 and Article 14 is applicable.[418]

However, just after acknowledging this fact in the Ms Ladele case, the European Court of Human Rights went on to rather strangely conclude in their ruling that:

> The Court generally allows the national authorities a wide margin of appreciation when it comes to striking a balance between competing convention rights...It cannot, therefore be said that there has been a violation of Article 14 taken in conjunction with Article 9 in respect of the third applicant.[419]

With that ruling it can be said that the outcome of Ms Ladele's pursuit to secure her right to freedom of conscience and religious belief and practice from the United Kingdom's courts through to the European Court of Human Rights was a costly and pathetic exercise that left a lot to be desired, insofar as the Court accepts that the events for which she sought

---

[418]   Ibid. Para 103

[419]   Ibid. Para 106

relief fell within the ambit of her rights under Article 9 and Article 14 of the Convention, but went on to say the United Kingdom had a 'wide margin of appreciation' with which to more or less deprive her of the enjoyment of such rights.

With the outcomes of the cases of Ms Eweida, Ms Chaplin and Ms Ladele as discussed, the prospect of what would become the outcome of the case of the fourth applicant Mr McFarlane is one of a simple conjecture. However, it is vital to consider the reasoning and ruling of the European Court of Human Rights in the case.

The European Court of Human Rights, upon considering the facts of Mr Farlane's application and the response of the United Kingdom, made the following opposing remarks and conclusions in the case ruling. The Court stated thus:

> The Court accepts that Mr McFarlane's objection was directly motivated by his orthodox Christian beliefs about marriage and sexual relationships, and holds that his refusal to undertake to counsel homosexual couples constituted a manifestation of his religion and belief. The State's positive obligation under Article 9 required it to secure his rights under Article 9.[420]

However, in a way that is sharply contradictory to what it has acknowledged, it ruled that:

> ...the Court does not consider that the refusal by the domestic courts to uphold Mr McFarlane's complaint gave rise to a violation of Article 9, taken alone or in conjunction with Article 14.[421]

While the ruling of the Employment Tribunal and position of the United Kingdom Government has been that the dismissal of the second, and especially, third and fourth applicants took place in order to achieve "proportionate and legitimate aim"[422] the question is should a 'legitimate

---

[420]   Ibid. Para 108.

[421]   Ibid. Para 110

[422]   Ibid. Paras 62-63

aim' defined by the domestic court in any given case supersede the obligation of the State party to an international human rights law treaty to comply with its duty to keep to the terms of the treaty, it has ratified? The rulings of the Court are expected to help with the understanding of the interpretation of the law but in these cases, it remains unclear. However, the joint partly dissenting opinion of Judges Vucinic and De Gaetano crystallises some of the issues. They opined:

> We are unable to share the majority's opinion that there has been no violation of the Convention in respect of the third applicant (Ms Ladele)....no one should be forced to act against one's conscience or be penalised for refusing to act against one's conscience...the State is obliged to respect the individual's freedom of conscience...

> In the third applicant's case, however, a combination of back-stabbing by her colleagues and blinkered political correctness of the Borough of Islington (which has clearly favoured "gay rights" over fundamental human rights) eventually led to her dismissal." We underscore these facts because the third applicant's situation is substantially different from the situation in which the fourth applicant found himself, or, more precisely placed himself. When Mr McFarlane joined Relate he must have known that he might be called upon to counsel same-sex couples. Therefore his position is, for the purposes of the instant case, not unlike that of a person who volunteers to join the army as a soldier and subsequently expects to be exempted from lawful combat duties on grounds of conscientious objection.[423]

It is noteworthy that in their dissenting opinion the two judges went on to express a view on what certainly would remain an issue in understanding the European Court of Human Rights' ruling in the Eweida and Others v The United Kingdom case. And that is the question of "wide margin of appreciation" that the State, in this instance, the United Kingdom, is given by the Court in the ruling. They stated in their dissenting opinion:

---

[423] Joint Partly Dissenting Opinion of Judges Vucinic and De Gaetano in Eweida v the United Kingdom (Applications nos. 4842/10/, 5984/10, 51671/10 and 36516/10).

...we do not fully subscribe to the reasoning ...that "the
State authorities ...benefitted from a wide margin of
appreciation in deciding where to strike the balance
between the applicant's right to manifest his religious
belief and the employer's interest in securing the right of
others......

For the above reasons, our conclusion is that there was a
violation of Article 14 taken in conjunction with Article 9
in respect of the third applicant.[424]

The outcome of the European Court of Human Rights in these four
cases referred to as Eweida and Others v The United Kingdom point
to the political and technical considerations that stand in the way of
substantive justice in international human rights law, especially, in
the individual enjoyment of the universal declaration to freedom
of conscience, and the right to religious belief and practice, that
are enshrined in the various international human rights covenants,
conventions, and charters that has been ratified by States such as the
United Kingdom.

While the Eweida and others v The United Kingdom cases clearly
demonstrate the limitations to the right to freedom of conscience,
religious belief and practice that Christians have at the work place and
in the businesses under the United Kingdom domestic legislation and
policies as decided by the domestic courts in the UK and confirmed by
the European Court of Human Rights in some cases, the recent decision
of

the United Kingdom Supreme Court in the Lee v Ashers Bakery [2018]
case[425] brought a glimmer of hope to the Christian community in the
United Kingdom insofar as the enjoyment of the right to freedom of
conscience and religious belief and practice is concerned. This is
because prior to the UK Supreme Court ruling in favour of Mr and Mrs

---

[424] Ibid.

[425] Lee (Respondent) v Ashers Baking Company Ltd and others (Appellants) (Northern Ireland
Reference by the Attorney General for Northern Ireland of devolution issues to the Supreme
Court pursuit to paragraph 34 of Schedule 10 to the Northern Ireland Act 1998 Reference by the
Attorney General for Northern Ireland of devolution issues to the Supreme Court pursuant to
paragraph 34 of Schedule 10 to the Northern Ireland Act (No 2) [2018] UKSC 49.

McArthur, owners of the Ashers Baking Company Ltd, a number of cases involving Christians at the work place and in businesses offering goods and services that went to the Courts in the UK, from the lowest courts to the Supreme Court met with unfavourable rulings against the Christians concerned. For instance, following the cases of Eweida, Chaplin, Ladele and McFarlane, was another case involving a Christian couple that went to court and the Christian couple Mr and Mrs Bull also lost against the claimant Mr Hall and Mr Preddy, who were same sex civil partners.

In Bull v Hall [2013] UKSC 73 [426] a devout Christian couple Mr and Mrs Bull who had a hotel business and clearly stated in their online booking policy that they let double room in their hotel only to a heterosexual married couple, took a double room booking by telephone without realising that Mr Hall and Mr Preddy who had booked the double room where same sex partners. When Mr Hall and Mr Preddy arrived at the hotel, and it was discovered that they were a same sex couple, the hotel policy was explained to them and they were turned away. Mr Hall and Mr Preddy with the support of the UK Equality and Human Rights Commission took Mr and Mrs Bull, proprietors of the hotel, to Court claiming discrimination. Mr and Mrs Bull in their defence argued in court that the UK's discrimination law must be applied so as to be compatible with their right to manifest their religion under the European Convention on Human Rights and Fundamental Freedom, (ECHR).[427] But at the Bristol County Court, the case was decided against Mr and Mrs Bull and an award of £1,800 each was awarded to Mr Preddy and Mr Hall for injury to their feelings. When Mr and Mrs Bull appealed to the Court of Appeal, interestingly, it was "acknowledged that the hotel policy was a manifestation of Mr and Mrs Bulls' religious beliefs within the meaning of their right under the ECHR."[428] However, the Court of Appeal judges went on to agree with the lower court's decision that Mr and Mrs Bulls' treatment of Mr Hall and Mr Preddy amounted to direct discrimination and that the rights of the Bulls under the ECHR "was justifiably limited by the laws relating to

---

[426]   Bull and another (Appellants) v Hall and another (Respondents) [2013] UKSC 73

[427]   See Case Summary of Bull and another v Hall and another [UKSC] 73 by Equal Rights Trust at https://www.equalrightstrust.org/ertdocumentbank/case%20summary%20preddy%20v%20bull.pdf

[428]   Ibid.

non-discrimination on grounds of sexual orientation, for the protection of the rights of homosexuals."[429]

When they appealed to the UK Supreme Court, the Law Lords "unanimously agreed Individual Right to Freedom of Conscience, Religion and Belief in the United Kingdom that the Appellants had unlawfully discriminated against the Respondents and dismissed the appeal.[430]

Against the backdrop of the above discussed cases, the victory of Mr and Mrs McArthur, and Ashers Baking Company Ltd against the claimant Mr Lee which will be discussed here sent an air of euphoria about the Supreme Court's appreciation of Christians' right to freedom of conscience and religious belief and practice in ways which the reasoning and the jurisprudence of the Supreme Court ruling in the Lee v Ashers Baking Company Ltd.'s decision does not give support to. Ashers Baking Company was owned by Mr and Mrs McArthur who were devout Christians and based in Northern Ireland. They had been running a bakery business since 1992 but in 2004 decided to run the bakery business under the name of Ashers Baking Company Ltd. The extent to which they were running the bakery business in line with their Christian faith can be deduced from the fact that they took the business name Asher from a verse in the Holy Bible:

> Bread from Asher shall be rich and he shall yield royal dainties.
>
> – Genesis 49:20

With a determination to run their business on the foundations of Christian ethics and precepts, Mr and Mrs McArthur, met with an unusual request from one of their customers. Mr Lee, a gay man, who was to attend a private event organised by Queerspace, a Lesbian, Gay, Bisexual and Transgender (LGBT) organisation at Bangor Castle on the 17 May 2014, decided to take a cake to the party. He was a customer of Ashers Bakery who had bought cakes there in the past but for the

---

[429]   Ibid.

[430]   Ibid.

occasion he ordered a cake with a request that it be designed with "the Queerspace logo" and the headline message Support Gay Marriage."[431]

When Mrs McArthur took the order from Mr Lee she raised no objection about his request at the time because she wanted to avoid causing any form of embarrassment to him. Mr Lee paid for the order. However:

> Over the following weekend, the McArthurs decided that they could not in conscience produce a cake with that slogan and so should not fulfil the order. On Monday 12 May 2014, Mrs McArthur telephoned Mr Lee and explained that his order could not be fulfilled because there were a Christian business and could not print the slogan requested. She apologised to Mr Lee and he was later given a full refund...[432]

Although Mr Lee was able to arrange for another bakery to provide the cake he needed to enable him take it to the event he was to attend, he went on to lodge a complaint against Ashers Baking Company Ltd and invariably the Mr and Mrs McArthur to the Equality Commission for Northern Ireland ("the ECNI") about the cancellation of his order. The ECNI consequently assisted him with a claim against Ashers Baking Company Ltd for direct and indirect discrimination on grounds of sexual orientation, religious belief or political opinion.

The district judge found that, when they (Ashers Bakery) refused to carry out the order, the defendants did perceive that Mr Lee was gay and/ or associated with others who were gay.[433]

However, Mr and Mrs McArthur acting as Ashers Baking Company Ltd and in their capacities as business owners appealed to the Court of Appeal, in Northern Ireland, it was found that the district judge:

> had made no finding that the order was cancelled because Mr Lee was perceived as being gay.[434]

---

[431] Lee v Ashers Baking Company Ltd [2018] UKSC 49 para 12.

[432] Ibid.

[433] Ibid. Para 13.

[434] Ibid.

In her decision the presiding district judge ruled against Ashers Baking Company Ltd saying:

> refusing to complete the order was direct discrimination on all three grounds.[435]

In their ruling on 24 October 2014, the Court of Appeal dismissed the appeal:

> It held that it was a case of associative direct discrimination on grounds of sexual orientation…and it was not necessary …to take account of the McArthurs' Convention rights[436]

When the McArthurs appealed to the UK Supreme Court, reference to some of the Court of Appeal findings such as:

> The District Judge did not find that the bakery refused to fulfil the order because of Mr Lee's actual or perceived sexual orientation. She found that they "cancelled this order because they oppose same sex marriage for the reason that they regard it as sinful and contrary to their genuinely held religious beliefs"…As the Court of Appeal pointed out, she did not take issue with the submission that the bakery would have supplied Mr. Lee with a cake without the message "Support Gay Marriage" and that they would also have refused to supply a cake with the message requested to a hetero-sexual customer …The objection was to the message, not the messenger.[437]

The reasoning of Supreme Court in pointing out that "the objection was to the message, not the messenger" is worthy of note because it alters the entire argument of the claim that the McArthurs' and Ashers Baking Company Ltd discriminated against Mr Lee on grounds of sexual orientation as a gay man as the judgment of the District Judge says; or associative direct discrimination on grounds of sexual orientation as the Northern Ireland Court of Appeal judgment says. It is also noteworthy because the Supreme Court did not accord recognition to the validity

---

[435] Ibid. Para 15.

[436] Ibid. Para 16

[437] Ibid. Para 22.

of the McArthurs' action by cancelling the cake order because of their right to freedom of conscience, religious belief and practice under Article 9 (1) of the European Convention of Human Rights and Fundamental Freedom.

The Supreme Court took time to examine the two issues upon which the claim of Mr Lee against the McArthurs and Ashers Bakery revolves around: direct discrimination and equalities within the UK domestic law.

In examining the issue of direct discrimination insofar as it relates to the case the Court looked at the definition of direct discrimination from Article 3(1) of the Fair Employment and Treatment Order (FETO) (Amendment) Regulations (Northern Ireland) 2003, where it states:

> (a) discrimination on the ground of religious belief or political opinion." By article 28 (1),, "It is unlawful for any person concerned with the provision (for payment or not) of goods, facilities or services to the public or a section of the public to discriminate against a person who seeks to obtain or use those goods, facilities or services – (a) by refusing or deliberating omitting to provide him with any of them:[438]

The Court looked at the case of Coleman v Attride (Case C-303/06) [2008] ICR 1128, which has remained a classic case of associative discrimination since it was decided by the European Court of Justice, ECJ. The claimant in the case made a claim of less favourable treatment meted out to his disabled son. He claimed that the son is less favourably treated because of his disability and the ECJ ruled that the disabled son was indeed less favourably treated because of his disability.

On the issue of equality law and discrimination in the United Kingdom the Supreme Court made reference to the argument the Counsel David Scoffield QC to the Ashers Baking Company Ltd has presented in the case and stated thus:

> Not surprisingly, Mr Scoffield, for the bakery, argues that this cannot be right. The purpose of discrimination law is to protect a person (or person or persons with whom

---

[438]   Ibid. Para 39

he is associated) who has a protected characteristic from being treated less favourably because of that characteristic. The purpose is not to protect people without such a characteristic of the alleged discriminator. This was reflected, for example, in section 45 (1) of the Equality Act 2006 which made it clear that the discrimination has to be on ground of the religion or belief of someone other than the alleged discriminator.

It is also a well –established principle of equality law that the motive of the alleged discriminator is relevant: see R (E) v Germany Body of JFS [2009] UKSC 15; [2010] 2 AC 278, e.g. at paras 13-20, citing R v Birmingham City Council, Ex p Equal Opportunities Commission [1989] AC 1155 and James v Eastleigh Borough Council [1990] 2 AC 751."[439]

After addressing the issues about direct discrimination and equality law, the Court proceeded to stress the fact that the McArthurs' right under Article 9 of the ECHR is a qualified right which does not allow a business offering services to the public to discriminate on certain grounds:

> The bakery could not refuse to provide a cake – or any other of their products – to Mr Lee because he was a gay man or because he supported gay marriage. But that important fact does not amount to a justification for something completely different – obliging them to supply a cake iced with a message with which they profoundly disagreed.[440]

However, after pointing out that Article 9 of the ECHR is a qualified right, the Supreme Court also went on to point that:

> "Under section 3 (1) of the Human Rights Act 1998, all legislation is, so far as it is possible to do so, to be read and given effect in a way which is compatible with the Convention rights."[441]

---

[439] Ibid. Para 43.

[440] Ibid. Para 55

[441] Ibid. Para 56

It is hard to say whether in the cases that preceded this case the UK judges have made efforts to give prominent to the Convention rights especially Article 9 - right to freedom of conscience, religious belief and practice – but it is remarkable that the Law Lords in the Supreme Court in this case of Ashers Bakery have painstakingly brought out this obvious important fact in the consideration of the appeal of the McArthurs and Ashers Baking Company Limited.

In conclusion, in upholding the McArthurs appeal, the Supreme Court decided that:

> they did not have to consider the position of the company separately from that of Mr and Mrs McArthur.[442]

They referred to a number of decisions made by the European Court of Human Rights such as:

> X v Switzerland (Application No 7865/77), Decision of 27 February 1979, and in Kustannus oy Vapaa Ajattelija Ab v Finland (Application No 20471/92), Decision of 15 April 1996, the European Commission held that limited companies could not rely upon article 9 (1) to resist paying taxes. In this case, however, to hold the company liable when the McArthurs are not would effectively negate their convention rights.[443]

Although the United Kingdom Supreme Court did not base its decision to uphold Mr and Mrs McArthur and indeed Ashers Baking Company Ltd appeal on their right to freedom of conscience, religious belief and practice as a justification for either the McArthurs or Ashers Bakery to act in a discriminated way by how they sell or offer their products and services, they have by their reasoning in the case also shown that any spurious claim of discrimination against Christians who exercise their freedom of conscience, religious belief and practice is likely to fail. What remains a matter of concern is the cost involved for those who want to assert their rights to freedom of conscience, religious belief and practice

---

[442]   Ibid. Para 57

[443]   Ibid.

in cases where they believe they are being unduly accused or deprived of their right to freedom of conscience and religious belief and practice.

But this problem is not just a problem for Christians in the United Kingdom. For instance, after the UK Supreme Court hearing of the case of Lee V Ashers Baking Company as it prepared to deliver its judgment a case in the United States of America involving a Christian bakery and a gay couple was also decided by the United States Supreme Court. In the case known as Masterpiece Cakeshop Ltd v Colorado Civil Rights Commission, the facts are as follows:

> A Christian baker refused to create a wedding cake for a gay couple because of his opposition to same sex marriage. There is nothing in the reported facts to suggest that the couple wanted a particular message or decoration on their cake.[444]

The case was first heard by the Colorado Civil Rights Commission who ruled against Masterpiece Cakeshop Ltd. It then went to the Colorado courts which also ruled against the baker:

> they held that the baker had violated the Colorado law prohibiting business which offered sales or services to the public from discrimination based on sexual orientation.[445]

The baker then complained that the decision of the Colorado Civil Rights Commission and the Colorado courts in the case violated his First Amendment rights under the US Constitution which protects his freedom of religion.[446]

When the United States Supreme Court heard the case and handed down a judgment (unreported) on 4 June 2018:

> The majority held that

---

[444] Ibid. Para 59.

[445] Ibid.

[446] The First Amendment Rights under the US Constitution protects the freedom of speech, religion, and the press. The Amendment and the rights therein was adopted in 1791. See https://www. law.cornell.edu/constitution/first_amendment and also see https://www.history.com/topics/ united-states-constitution/first-amendment

the delicate question of when the free exercise of his religion must yield to an otherwise valid exercise of State power needed to be determined in an adjudication in which religious hostility on the part of the state itself would not be a factor in the balance the state sought to reach...When the Colorado Civil Rights Commission considered this case, it did not do so with the religious neutrality that the constitution requires.[447]

The United Kingdom Supreme Court went on to differentiate between the case of Lee v Ashers Baking Company Ltd and Masterpiece Cakeshop Ltd v Colorado Civil Rights Commission by pointing out the element of vital difference thus:

> The important message from Masterpiece Bakery case is that there is a clear distinction between refusing to produce a cake conveying a particular message, for any customer who wants such a cake, and refusing to produce a cake for particular customer who wants it because of that customer's characteristics. One can debate which side of the line particular factual scenarios fall. But in our case there can be no doubt. The bakery would have refused to supply this particular cake to anyone, whatever their personal characteristics. So there was no discrimination on grounds of sexual orientation. If and to the extent that there was discrimination on grounds of political opinion, no justification has been shown for the compelled speech which would be entailed for imposing civil liability for refusing to fulfil the order.[448]

Based on the cases discussed in this chapter, several issues arise from the United Kingdom judicial approach to individual Christian's right to freedom of conscience, religious belief and practice. The first issue is expressed in the opinion of the dissenting two judges of the European Court of Human Rights in the Ms Ladele case where they said:

> What is in issue is the discriminatory treatment of the third applicant at the hands of the Borough, in respect of which

---

[447] Lee V Ashers Baking Company Ltd [2018] at para 60.

[448] Ibid. Para 62

treatment she did not obtain redress at the domestic level (except before the first instance Employment Tribunal). Given the cogency, seriousness, cohesion and importance of her conscientious objection (which, as noted earlier, was also a manifestation of her deep religious convictions) it was incumbent upon the local authority to treat her differently from those registrars, who had no conscientious objection to officiating at same-sex unions – something which clearly could have been achieved without detriment to the overall services provided by the Borough including those services provided by registrars, as evidenced by the experience of other Local authorities. Instead of practising the tolerance and the "dignity for all" it preached, the Borough of Islington "pursued the doctrinaire line, the road of obsessive political correctness. It effectively sought to force the applicant to act against her conscience or face the extreme penalty of dismissal – something which, even assuming that the limitations of Article 9 (2) apply to prescriptions of conscience, cannot be deemed necessary in a democratic society. Ms Ladele did not fail in her duty of discretion: she did not publicly express her beliefs to service users. Her beliefs had no impact on the content of her job. She never attempted to impose her beliefs on others, nor was she in anyway engaged, openly or surreptitiously in subverting the rights of others.[449]

Increasingly as the UK courts judgments in the cases of Eweida, Ladele and to an extent Bull and another v Hall and another, show, there is a tendency by the UK domestic courts to treat Christians who want to uphold the tenets of their religious beliefs in a discriminatory way while addressing the issues of their perceived acts of discrimination in the practice of their Christian religious beliefs based on the teaching of the Holy Bible which defines the conduct that should mark a Christian's behaviour at all times. Ms Ladele as the European Court of Human Rights dissenting judges observed is a classic example of how Christians sometimes suffer such discriminatory treatments in ways that are psychologically torturous and painful as physical harm.

---

[449] See paragraph 7 of the joint dissenting opinion of judges Vucinic and De Gaetano in Eweida and Others v The United Kingdom [2013].

The second issue arises from the recognition that the president of the United Kingdom Supreme Court Lady Hale (with whom Lord Mance, Lord Kerr, Lord Hodge, and Lady Black) agreed in the Lee v Ashers Baking Company Ltd judgment when she stated inter alia:

> Under section 3 (1) of the Human Rights Act 1998, all legislation is, so far as it is possible to do so, to be read and given effect in a way which is compatible with the Convention rights.[450]

There does not appear to be a manifest demonstration in most of cases decided by the UK domestic courts as discussed here to show that the interpret of the domestic law was done in a way that it is compatible with the Convention right of the individual concern whether it was Ms Eweida or Ms Ladele. As already stated above, there is rather a manifest tendency to make the domestic supersede the Convention right in ways that seem as if the State is simply emasculating the convention rights such as the right to freedom of conscience, religious belief and practice. And finally the third issue is the point made by majority of justices in the United States Supreme Court when they remarked that in the Masterpiece Cakeshop Ltd v Colorado Civil Rights Commission case that:

> When the Colorado Civil Rights Commission considered this case, it did not do so with the religious neutrality that the constitution requires.[451]

It has to be said that the European Court of Human Rights in the cases that have to do with the Convention right such as Article 9 have not maintained a consistent jurisprudence that helps the understanding of how it interprets Article 9 (1). This can be seen simply by the variations in its decisions from its first decision on the issue in the case known as Kokkinakis v Greece (Application No. 14307/88) [1993] ECHR20 (25 May 1993) to recent judgments such as Eweida and others. Whereas Kokkinakis was a classic decision on the right to manifest freedom of religion, the decision of Ms Ladele as has been stated simply avoids what would have been a right decision by ascribing a wide margin of appreciation to the State to do as it wants without a defined limit.

---

[450]   Ibid. Para 56

[451]   Ibid. para 60

While the discussions on the need for States to guarantee the individual right to freedom of thought, conscience and religion under Article 9 (1) of the Convention has been made in this chapter and the prior, in the next chapter the need for the State to also use its power to intervene to save gullible men and women who could be misled to suffer material loss and even self-destruction by cultists and criminals disguising as religious leaders will also be discussed under Article 9 (2) of Convention, inter alia.

13

CRIMES AGAINST HUMANITY BY RELIGIOUS LEADERS AND JUSTIFIABLE GROUNDS FOR STATE INTERVENTION INTO ILL-MANIFESTATION OF THE RIGHT TO FREEDOM OF CONSCIENCE, RELIGIOUS BELIEF AND PRACTICE

A low standard of Christianity is responsible for all the shame and sin and wickedness in the world.[452]

Guard your heart above all else, for it determines the course of your life.[453]

By their nature rights can either be absolute or subject to limitations or qualifications.[454]

European Convention on Human Rights and Fundamental Freedoms (1950) Article 9 (2):

---

[452] Lake, John G; His Life, His Sermons, His Boldness of Faith © 1994 Kenneth Copeland Publications. P. 7.

[453] Ibid. Proverbs 4:23

[454] Bantekas, Ilias and Oette, Lutz, International Human Rights Law and Practice, 2nd Edition © 2016 Cambridge University Press. p.75

Freedom to manifest one's religion or beliefs shall be subject only to such limitations as are prescribed by law and are necessary in a democratic society in the interests of public order, health or morals, or for the protection of the rights and freedom of others.

13.1 Between Licence and Abuse

The right to freedom of conscience, religious belief and practice is a limited and qualified right for the reasons embedded in the wordings of article 9(2) which on the surface is apparent just and fair. However, the application of article 9 (2) by the State seems often to strip off the right enshrined in article 9 (1) and the courts as shown in the case of Ms Ladele had not helped matters by the nature of the wide margin of appreciation it ascribed to the State in the interpretation of article 9 (2) in limiting the right to freedom of conscience and religion where the individual does not pose a risk to the public or others but only wants to exercise her right in sticking to her faith and religious beliefs such as in the case Ms Ladele.

There is no argument about the validity of article 9 (2) when one looks at the wickedness some popes and some other religious leaders have caused their fellow men and humanity in general, in the past and to some extent up to the present time. One thing that is evident from the cases that will be discussed here especially regarding Christians shows that often those who profess a religious belief do not necessarily respect every aspect of the precepts of the religious faith they profess. For instance, two categorical imperatives define the Christian faith following the confession of Jesus Christ as Lord and Saviour (John 3:16). These two categorical imperatives are:

(1) Jesus replied, "You must love the LORD your God with all your heart, all your soul, and all your mind. This is the first and greatest commandment. A second is equally important: 'Love your neighbour as yourself.'"[455]

---

[455] Holy Bible, Matthew 22:37-39 (NLT)

(2) Then Peter came to him and asked, "Lord, how often should I forgive someone who sins against me? Seven times?" "No, not seven times," Jesus replied, "but seventy times seven."[456]

Those who profess Christianity as their religious belief and faith are expected to live their lives daily on the basis of those two categorical imperatives. In fact, the importance of the 'forgiveness' as an essential element of the Christian faith was emphasised in the only prayer that the Lord Jesus Christ taught his disciples and in essence everyone who has become a Christian:

Pray then like this:

Our Father in heaven, hallowed be your name.

Your kingdom come, your will be done, on earth as it is in heaven. Give us this day our daily bread, and forgive us our debts, as we also have forgiven our debtors. And lead us not into temptation, but deliver us from evil.[457]

To point out the categorical importance of forgiveness for the Christian, Jesus specifically emphasised the essence of it by saying:

For if you forgive others their trespasses, your heavenly father will also forgive you, but if you do not forgive others their trespasses, neither will your heavenly Father forgive your trespasses.[458]

Against that background of Jesus Christ's teachings and commands, it defies human comprehension to believe that any Christian religious leader who had attained the height of a representative of Jesus Christ on earth such as the Pope of the Roman Catholic Church would display a degree and height of un-forgiveness that extends vindictiveness to a person that had been long dead. Even pagans and atheists who had no fear of God have never been heard to take vengeance on anyone who is dead and buried but such was the wickedness of Pope Martin V of the Roman Catholic Church

---

[456]   Holy Bible, Matthew 18:21-22 (NLT)

[457]   This9-13. is the prayer Jesus taught his disciples and subsequent generations of Christians to pray. Holy Bible, Matthew 6:9-13 (ESV).

[458]   Ibid. Matthew 6:14-15.

that in 1427, he ordered that the bones of John Wycliffe, who had died in 1384, well over 40 years by 1427, should be exhumed from the grave and burned to ashes and the ashes cast into the river Swift.[459]

What was John Wycliffe's offence at the time? Wycliffe had simply argued in a pamphlet he published that the Church which was then the Roman Catholic Church should not 'pursue wealth and power' but should rather have the 'poor at heart'.[460] Wycliffe wanted everyone to be able to read the Holy Bible and understand the word of God for themselves and so he translated the Bible into the English language and Pope Martin in 1427 felt that those were 'sins in his own theology' that did not deserve forgiveness even after Wycliffe had died and was buried over forty years before the time of his order for his bones to be exhumed.[461]

Besides the case of Pope Martin, there had been a catalogue of a number of religious abuses that amounts to crimes against humanity in some cases and most of these will not be discussed here as it is not necessary to draw a chronicle of such abuses and crimes in order to make the point.

However, the cases discussed in this chapter are intended to make the case for state intervention when there are legitimate grounds to do so.

13.2 The Roman Catholic Church and 21st Century Cases of Sexual Abuses and Injustices

For a church that has ordered those who feel called into the priesthood to live a life of celibacy, the avalanche of allegations of rape and sexual abuses in the Roman Catholic Church has raised huge concerns about the sanity and sanctity of some of those who have enlisted into the priesthood. A matter that for many decades and possibly centuries had been an internal secret of the Roman Catholic Church world-wide in spite of increasing loud voices of accusations by victims was eventually brought to the public

---

[459] See "The Murderous History of Bible Translations in History Extra, The Official Website of BBC History Magazine, May 2, 2019: https://www.historyextra.com/period/medieval/murderous-history-bible-translations-catholic-murder-version-who-wrote-when/ See also John Wycliffe: Did you know? https://christianhistoryinstitute.org/magazine/article/john-wycliffe-did-you-know

[460] Ibid.

[461] Ibid.

domain in an e-mail by Pope John Paul II, who is held as one of the most respected Popes of the late twentieth and earlier twenty-first centuries because of his piety. The pope had good reasons to make a public apology and went on to do so by sending e-mail in November 2001 in which he apologised "for a string of injustices, including sexual abuse, committed by Roman Catholic clergy in the pacific nations.[462]

The BBC News report on the Pope's apology cited the pope's reference to "a report on a Synod meeting held in 1998" in which "the pope wrote that bishops from the region "apologised unreservedly" for the "shameful injustices done to indigenous people" in Australia, New Zealand and the islands of the South Pacific."[463] The pope went on to say that:

> In certain parts of Oceania, sexual abuse by some clergy has caused great suffering and spiritual harm to the victims.[464]

While the Pope's blanket apology revealed an acknowledgment of the incidents of offences and crimes of sexual abuses in the Roman Catholic Church by its clergy in the Australian continent, the matter had not gone away. In various other parts of the world victims are seeking for justice to be done from specific offenders within the clergy of the Roman Catholic Church.

In the United States of America for instance, in one of the most notorious cases of paedophilia in a series of many committed by Roman Catholic priests in different parts of the world, Reverend Father Oliver Francis O'Grady, who served as a Catholic priest in California in the 1970s and 1980s confessed to have repeatedly raped and sexually abused boys and girls, some as young as 5 years old and in fact, even a 9 months' old. [465]

---

[462] Pope Sends first e-mail apology. BBC NEWS Friday 23 November 2001 09:03 GMT: http://news.bbc.co.uk/1/hi/world/europe/1671540.stm

[463] Ibid.

[464] Ibid.

[465] See "The Lives of Priest and Victims in the Silence After the Anguish" by A.O. Scott, in New York Times, October 13, 2006. (This was actually a review of a movie titled "Deliver Us From Evil" written and directed by Amy Berg about Oliver O'Grady.): https://www.nytimes.com/2006/10/13/movies/13evil.html ; See also "Priest makes 'Most honest confessions' of his life" by Drew Griffin and Kathleen Johnston, CNN, Wednesday, June 28, 2006 (This is also a review of the documentary movie about the defrocked Reverend Father Oliver O'Grady by Amy Berg): http://edition.cnn.com/2006/LAW/06/27/griffin.priestabuse/

O'Grady was defrocked and convicted in 1993 on four counts of lewd and lascivious acts on minors, and was sentenced to jail. He spent 7 years in jail before he was released on parole in 2000 and was deported from the United States to his home country of Ireland. In a 'honest confession' he made about his crimes after his return to his native country of Ireland, he stated that officials of the Roman Catholic Diocese of Stockton, California, USA, under which he served as a Roman Catholic priest knew about his abuses of children for two decades but failed to remove him from ministry.[466] The veracity of his claim that Church Officials of the Diocese knew about his abuse but failed to remove him from ministry was eventually proved right in a subsequent case made against the Roman Catholic Diocese of Stockton, California, by two brothers, Jon and James Howard, who were his victims. They argued that the Diocese allowed O'Grady to abuse them by not removing him when they knew that he was abusing children. The two brothers, Jon and James Howard won their claim and were awarded $24 million in punitive damages and $6 million in compensatory damages by a jury.[467]

In a coordinated effort to obtain justice after failing to obtain a resolution within the Roman Catholic Church, a number of victims of abuse by priests took their complaint to the International Criminal Court, (ICC), in The Hague, Netherlands in September 2011. They asked the Court to investigate the then Pope Benedict XVI and several of his cardinals for crimes against humanity. The New York based Center for Constitutional Rights (CCR) that was representing the US-based Survivors Network of those abused by priests, "argued that the global Church, has maintained a "long standing and pervasive system of sexual violence" despite promises to swiftly oust predators."[468] However, Jeffrey Lena, the lawyer representing the Vatican called the complaint a "ludicrous publicity stunt and a misuse of international judicial process."[469] But Barbara Blaine, the president of the Survivors Network, said going to Court was a last resort"[470] arguing that:

---

[466] Ibid

[467] See "$30 Million Award for Victims of Priest" by The Associated Press, New York Times, 17/07/1998: https://www.nytimes.com/1998/07/17/us/30-million-award-for-victims-of-priest.html

[468] See "Abuse victims seek ICC case against pope." By Mike Corder, IOL, September 14, 2011: https://www.iol.co.za/news/world/abuse-victims-seek-icc-case-against-pope-1137229

[469] Ibid.

[470] Ibid.

These priests and Church officials live by some other laws. Somehow, they're not held accountable like every other citizen of the nation…what must end is shattering the innocence of even one more child."[471]

The Office of the prosecutor of the ICC in a statement following the complaint stated that:

..the evidence would be studied. We first have to analyse whether the alleged crimes fall under the Court's jurisdiction.[472]

The fact is that a case about a widespread abuse by priests who innocent children had been entrusted with on the understanding that they were men of God who are pious and could be trusted turned out to be no different to hardened criminals despised by society and the question is how best could society trust those who wear the cloaks of religious leaders even though it is a fact that the abusers might be an insignificant percentage of those who are priests in the Roman Catholic Church?

But the problem is not as much different in the protestant church which will be discussed below or even in other religions such as Islam which is not covered in this book in any reasonable detail. In Christianity, cults and protestant Christian crimes including sexual offences cannot be discussed in sufficient details except to cite a few cases to highlight the point.

13.3 Jim Jones and the Jonestown Mass Suicide in 1978[473]

The question might be asked about when it is appropriate for the State to intervene without breaching the enjoyment of individuals' rights to freedom of conscience, religious belief and practice? The answer is simple. Things usually do not just suddenly happen. They happen after a time of planning, and the planning might have been done sometimes over days,

---

[471]   Ibid.

[472]   Ibid.

[473]   An in-depth detail account can be read in the book by Jeff Guinn, The Road to Jonestown, Jim Jones and Peoples Temple © 2017 Simon & Schuster Paperbacks.

weeks, months or even years. The story of Jim Jones the American leader of the Peoples Temple show that sometimes a religious leader may start on a good note and then suddenly engage in the most despicable evil acts and these evils gradually develop to the point of a dangerous end if not duly nipped in the bud. One of the opening quotes to the chapter, taking from the book of Jeremiah chapter 17 verse 9, gives a hint to the sometimes unpredictability of the human heart and the dilemma and danger it poses. Jim Jones the founding leader of the Peoples Temple who died following a mass suicide and murder of over 900 hundred members of his Peoples Temple on 18 November 1978 aptly fits this case.

Jones was said to have been a caring religious/cult leader of the Peoples' Temple which he incorporated and started in California in the United States. He was described as a "charismatic but a paranoid leader."[474]

Although Jones was white, his initial idea that attracted people to his Peoples Temple was his active act to promote racial integration and humanitarian activities within the communities around him. Jones promotion of racial integration at a time in the mid twentieth century when racial discrimination by whites against blacks was still prevalent, made many African Americans to flock to the Peoples Temple. However, it is stated that Jim Jones engaged in humiliating, beating, blackmailing, coercing and brainwashing members of his Peoples' Temple into signing their possessions over to him.[475]

By 1977 when "members of the Press began to ask questions about Jones's operation, he moved with several hundred of his followers to Jonestown, a compound he had been building in Guyana for some three to four years."[476]

Jim Jones and members of his Peoples Temple in Guyana lived in a world of their own in a place which Jones called Jonestown. They were not even subject to the laws and authority of the government of Guyana. Noting how Jim Jones and his members were living as a law unto themselves in

---

[474]   Eldridge, Alison, Jonestown Mass Murder-Suicide in Encyclopaedia Britannica: https://www.britannica.com/event/Jonestown-massacre

[475]   Ibid.

[476]   Ibid.

Guyana, the U S Embassy in Guyana sent a cable to the U S Department of State in June 1978 stating thus:

> "During the consular visits it has been observed that the local Guyanese administration exercises little or no control over the Jonestown community, and that the settlement's autonomy seems virtually total. This is due to a variety of reasons which include the fact that the area in question is remote and thus the government's rather primitive administrative machinery is already overstrained by its obligations to the Guyanese citizens living in the region, as well as an understandable disinterest on the part of the local officials to bother with an apparently self-sufficient community of non-Guyanese who obviously are not actively seeking any extensive contact with the Guyanese environment in which their settlement is located.

What we have, therefore, is a community of American citizens existing as a self-contained and self-governing unit in a foreign land and which, for all intents and purposes, is furnishing to the residents all of the community services such as civil administration, police and fire protection, education, health care, etc., normally provided by a central government within its territory."[477]

Following the cable from the U S Embassy in Guyana to the U S Department of State in June 1978, a U S Congressman Leo Ryan in November 1978 travelled to Guyana to inspect the Peoples Temple's activities and the Jonestown compound.[478] Upon arrival in Jonestown in Guyana on 17 November 1978, whatever that came out of his inspection was never conveyed to the U S Department of State or Congress because Congressman Leo Ryan never returned back to the U S alive. The following day, 18 November when he was to leave Jonestown, some members of the Peoples Temple joined him to return back to the US with him. He was attacked by members of the Peoples Temple in Jonestown but he was able to leave Jonestown unhurt. However, he was shot and killed along with 3 members of the press and another person with 11 other persons wounded at the airstrip from which he was to board his flight back to the US.

---

[477] Ibid.

[478] Ibid.

That same day, over 900 members of Peoples Temple and Jim Jones killed themselves in a mass suicide and murder executed with "fruit drink laced cyanide, tranquilizers and sedatives". Although Jim Jones himself was found to have died of gunshot wounds.[479]

In the United States, Jim Jones was allowed to have carried out his activities under the First Amendment of the US Constitution in 1791 protecting the right to religious freedom of individual citizens. But this right does not allow for someone such as Jim Jones to hold others captive and indeed to do worst things such as causing massacre of hundreds of people so there is a failing in intervention by the State as at 1977 when evidence of abuse by Jim Jones got into public awareness and the Press were asking him questions. The State of California failed to act and even allowed Jones to move to Guyana where he had more unrestrained liberty to perfect his suicide plan of the mass deaths of over 900 people.

An interview that Jim Jones surviving sons gave to ABC NEWS on the 40th Anniversary of the Jonestown Massacre in 2018 gave some insight on the possibility that the State could have stopped the mass suicide of the over 900 people that died with Jim Jones on 18 November 2018. Stephan Jones the biological son of Jim Jones had this to say about his father and the Peoples Temple:

> I lived in a community that was filled with every walk of life, every color in the rainbow, every level of education. For the most part, we lived in harmony most of the time, especially early on. But eventually, it became "all superficial."[480]

> There was nothing spiritual about my father.[481]

Concerning what the mass suicide and murder that happened on 18 November 1978, Stephan Jones had this to say:

---

[479]   Ibid.

[480]   ABC NEWS 40 years after the Jonestown massacre: Jim Jones' surviving sons on what they think of their father, the Peoples Temple today By Alexa Valiente and Monica Delarosa. 28 September 2018: https://abcnews.go.com/US/40-years-jonestown-massacre-jim-jones-surviving-sons/story?id=57997006

[481]   Ibid

There were many times that we probably could have steered things in a different direction. We could have put a stop to what happened long before that final night, and we didn't get it done.[482]

For me it was because I was focused on myself and not enough on my community and what was best for them.

What is clear is that the state could have prevented the massacre because as Stephan Jones said it was possible to have steered things in a different direction. Lessons need to be learnt.

Sadly, another catastrophe with less number of deaths happened in the United States after the incident of Jim Jones

13.4 David Koresh and the Waco Siege Deaths of the Branch Davidians[483]

David Koresh was originally known as Vernon Howell. He assumed the name David Koresh when he became the leader of the Branch Davidians[484] in 1987 in Waco Texas.

Therefore the right application of article 9 (2) will always serve a beneficial purpose to society and the state at large. In today's world where human rights have attained universal awareness and in some cases respect and regards, we will not have popes such as Stephen and Martin V, but if we did they would face prosecutions and convictions for their crimes.

This clearly implies that the state can limit the right, but in the discussions above, the issues raised hinge on whether the state is limiting the right or emasculating the right and it seems in most cases the state

---

[482] Ibid

[483] See some useful accounts in the book by Dick J. Reavis, The Ashes of WACO, An Investigation © 1995 First Syracuse University Press; and the book by James D. Tabor and Eugene V. Gallagher, Why WACO? © 1995 The Regents of the University of California.

[484] See Waco Siege American History [1993] written by The Editors of the Encyclopaedia Britannica (last updated: 21 February 2020). "The Branch Davidians was founded by Ben Roden in 1959 as offshoot of the Davidians Seventh-Day Adventist Church, which had been established by Victor Houteff several decades earlier." https://www.britannica.com/event/Waco-siege

is not only limiting and restricting the right but as it was in the United Kingdom cases, the right to religious beliefs and practices insofar as the Christian cases discussed are concerned, it is superseded by domestic laws for State Intervention such as equality law which on the face of it seem noble but in practice, it seems to ascribe one group in society with more liberties than others. Although some may prefer to say some groups seem to be given licence to practice vices instead of human rights and equalities.

The actual instances where the right to freedom of religious belief and practice should be monitored, limited and where necessary be denied should be in the cases where any person or group of persons in the name of religion whether Christianity, Islam or any other religion indulge in criminality and threat to waste of human lives or actual destruction of human lives, and there had been several instances of such from several cases, some of which will be discussed herewith to buttress the point.

It is stated that those belonging to the Seventh-Day Adventist Church established by Houteff moved to a farm about 10 miles east of Waco, Texas, while those belonging to the Branch Davidians offshoot of Roden took possession of the settlement known as Mount Carmel. In this settlement they "lived a simple life, preparing for the imminent return of Jesus."[485]

However, following "a power struggle" in the mid-1980s, Vernon Howell became the leader of the Branch Davidians in Mount Carmel in 1987.[486]

The first sign that David Koresh was anything but a genuine religious leader or prophet came when he began "taking girls as young as 11 as his spiritual wives."[487] However, the authorities such as the police did not intervene even when one ex-member of Koresh Branch Davidians accused him of child abuse because of the "teenage spiritual wives"[488] he was taking. By the time the authorities decided to investigate David Koresh

---

[485]   Ibid.

[486]   Ibid. See also "The Real Story Behind the Waco Siege: Who were David Koresh and the Branch Davidians? By Melissa Chan, TIME, January 24, 2018: https://time.com/5115201/waco-siege-standoff-fbi-david-koresh/

[487]   Ibid .

[488]   Ibid

and the members of the Mount Carmel Branch Davidian that he led; he had already extended his criminality beyond child abuse to retail gun business.

On 28 February 1993, Federal Agents from the U.S. Bureau of Alcohol, Tobacco and Firearms (AFT) in possession of an arrest warrant and a search warrant went to arrest

David Koresh and to search the Mount Carmel compound of the Branch Davidians.

However, their attempt to arrest David Koresh met with a resistance and so a gun fire exchanged transpired between the Federal Agents and the members of the David Koresh led Branch Davidians and consequently, 4 federal agents and 6 members of the Branch Davidians lost their lives. Following that incident, the U S Attorney General granted permission to the FBI to raid the Mount Carmel Branch Davidians compound. This led to a 51-day standoff which ended on 19 April 1993 when fire engulfed the compound and destroyed it, leaving 75 people dead, although many of the dead including the cult leader – David Koresh - were found to have been killed as a result of gunshots. Out of the 75 that were dead, 25 were children.[489]

A surviving member of Mount Carmel Branch Davidians, David Thibodean, who granted Time an interview stated:

> he believes the dead Branch Davidians were shot by the FBI.[490]

> But, "The FBI claims no law enforcement officer had fired a single bullet since the initial shoot out."[491]

Clearly, the manner of intervention of the United States Security Agents in the Waco siege did not help to salvage the innocent children and even adults who were trapped in David Koresh's cult that bore the name of the

---

[489] Ibid.

[490] See "The Real Story Behind the Waco Siege: Who were David Koresh and the Branch Davidians? By Melissa Chan, January 24, 2018. https://time.com/5115201/waco-siege-standoff-fbi-david-koresh/

[491] Ibid

Branch Davidians at Mount Carmel, Waco, Texas, where David Koresh held sway as a false prophet, child abuser and a criminal disguised as a religious leader.

Jesus Christ the very Lord that the Christians put their faith and trust in for salvation warned in his teachings that such false prophets as Jim Jones and David Koresh would come:

> Beware of false prophets who come disguised as harmless sheep but are really vicious wolves.[492]

Emphasising on the matter of these wolves that will come in sheep's clothing, Jesus went on to say that not all who call on his name and claim to be prophet will do so genuinely. Some simply want to use the name of Jesus to attract attention to themselves and thereby get people they will deceive and exploit:

> Not everyone who calls out to me, 'Lord! Lord!' will enter the Kingdom of Heaven. Only those who actually do the will of my Father in heaven will enter. On judgment day many will say to me, 'Lord! Lord! We prophesied in your name and cast out demons in your name and performed many miracles in your name.' But I will reply, 'I never knew you. Get away from me, you who break God's laws.'[493]

In the case of David Koresh and the Branch Davidians, the intervention of the US federal agents did not appear to have been carried out with intention to save children and others who were trapped in David Koresh's deception and cruelty. That the federal agents threw in tear gas canisters into the compound was in itself a drastic act that was going to cause destruction of human lives. The claim of the FBI that the fire that destroyed the Branch Davidians was started from inside the compound failed to take note of the fact that the tear gas canisters thrown into the compound were capable of exploding and causing fire if it was in contact with flammable substances which a compound like the Branch Davidians in Waco could imaginably have had. The FBI and other federal agents should have deplored other better tactics and strategies for dealing with

---

[492] See Holy Bible, Matthew 7:15 [New Living Translation].

[493] Ibid. 7:21-23.

David Koresh and the Branch Davidians than keeping a siege of 51-day standoff.

To the extent that vulnerable innocent adults and children died in the standoff between the federal agents and David Koresh and the Branch Davidians, it can hardly be accepted that the type of intervention that led to the death of 75 people with some others wounded should be an interventional approach to stop any suspended criminal activities that may be perpetrated by a cult claiming to be a Christian organisation.

13.5 Criminal Conducts By Protestant Church Leaders

While the sad cases of Jim Jones and David Koresh clearly demonstrate the dangers of some of those who initially begin as Christian religious leaders sometimes impressively so then proceed to groom up dangerous cult members, there are also some who may not groom people up as cult members or for mass suicide but operate under the cloak of religious leaders only to carry out inexplicable crimes and harm to others.

While the exceptionally few cases discussed here are intended to make the point about crimes and offences going on in places where people thought they were going to worship God and practice their religious beliefs it has to be said that there are very many cases that had not been touched on either because they have not been decided in court or simply because there is no intent to chronicle all incidents here. Yet, it is also vital to say that all the incidents of abuses and injustices represent an insignificant percentage of most of the good things that are happening in Churches and Christian religious institutions.

The actual incidents of crimes and sexual offences that took place in the church as per the facts that have unfolded in the court suggest that they occur as a result of deception of ordinary people who genuinely thought they were dealing with men of God as the cases of Gilbert Deya, and Michael Olorubi that will be discussed below show.

Deya, a Kenyan citizen who was based in the United Kingdom, for a number of years as a pastor, though he called himself, "the Archbishop of

Peckham"[494] came to the United Kingdom in the early 1990s after been ordained by the United Evangelical Church of Kenya. He established the Gilbert Deya Ministries with Churches in London, Liverpool, Birmingham, Nottingham and in various other places.[495] Deya appeared to have been doing well within the context of his claim as an evangelical and pentecostal Church pastor or archbishop. However, his undoing or perhaps the dishonesty of his claim as a Christian leader more so, an

Archbishop came to light and public notice when he also claimed to possess the power to "cause infertile women to become pregnant."[496] But the veracity of his claim was said to be a hoax. Deya was said to have sent some barren women from his churches in the United Kingdom to Kenya to 'give birth' to miracle babies there. In Kenya Deya was accused of the stealing of five children from Pumwani Hospital and coordinating the trafficking to these children that were later handed to the women who followed went to Kenya for their "miracle babies."[497] The Kenya authorities sought the extradition of Deya who was based in the United Kingdom following his alleged crimes of stealing children and trafficking same. After several years of unsuccessful efforts to resist his extradition to Kenya, through the United Kingdom court processes including application for a review of his failed appeals Deya was eventually extradited to Kenya on 4 August 2017[498] where he had to stand trial for the theft and trafficking of children under 14 years of age. However, Deya was said to have been freed from the Kamiti Maximum Prison where he spent a year following his payment of a bail bond of Sh10 million.[499]

---

494 See Gilbert Deya: 'Miracle babies' pastor extradited to Kenya. 'The Archbishop of Peckham' BBC NEWS 4 August 2017: https://www.bbc.co.uk/news/world-africa-40824267

495 See "10 things you didn't know about televangelist Gilbert Deya by Lilian Kwamboka, Standard Digital, Kenya, 04 August 2017: https://www.standardmedia.co.ke/article/2001250318/10-things-you-didn-t-know-about-televangelist-gilbert-deya

496 Ibid

497 Ibid.

498 See "Fake 'Archbishop' accused of stealing babies finally deported to Kenya after ten-year delay." The Telegraph By Victoria Ward, 4 August 2017: https://www.telegraph.co.uk/news/2017/08/04/fake-archbishop-accused-stealing-babies-finally-deported-kenya/

499 See "Gilbert Deya freed on Sh10 million bond in child theft case." By Caroline Kubwa, 15 May 2018: https://www.the-star.co.ke/news/2018-05-15-gilbert-deya-freed-on-sh10-million-bond-in-child-theft-case/

After almost six years following the extradition of Gilbert Deya to Kenya to stand trial for theft and trafficking of children under age 14, Deya was acquitted under Section 210 of the Criminal Procedure Code (CPC) on Monday 17, July 2023, by a Nairobi court because the judge found that "no evidence was adduced linking the accused person to the charges of child stealing."[500]

However, Michael Oluronbi, a pharmacist, who for many years doubled as a pastor and called himself a prophet while preying on young gullible secondary school girls, as the facts of his case in the Court revealed, raped and sexually assaulted young innocent girls still in secondary school over two decades. His victims numbering seven testified of how Michael, a qualified pharmacist raped and sexually assaulted them when he asked them to have naked "spiritual bathing" in his house to cleanse them of evil spirits. By virtue of his profession as a pharmacist and with the aid of his wife Juliana, he was able to take his victims to abortion clinics for abortions when some of them became pregnant.[501] Oluronbi and his wife Juliana were tried and convicted at the Birmingham Crown Court. Oluronbi was sentenced to 34 years imprisonment following his conviction for 15 rape charges, seven counts of indecent assaults, and two counts of sexual assaults. His wife, Juliana, convicted of three counts of aiding and abetting rape after helping to arrange some of the abortions. She was sentenced to 11 years imprisonment.[502]

During his trial, the prosecutor told the court that Oluronbi's "true purpose was to serve his sexual gratification"[503] and it is difficult to think that Oluronbi might have had any other purpose than perpetrating such evil since he indulged in the raping and sexually assaulting of his victims for over twenty years while pretending to be their pastor. The

---

[500] "Court acquits televangelist Gilbert Deya in a miracle babies saga." Nation Reporter, Monday, 17 July 2023. https://nation.africa/kenya/news/court-acquits-televangelist-gilbert-deya-in-miracle-babies-saga-4306204; See also "Kenyan Court Acquits 'Miracle Baby' Televangelist of Trafficking" Aljazeera [Simon Maina/AFP], Monday, 17 July 2023: https://www.aljazeera.com/news/2023/7/17/kenyan-court-acquits-miracle-baby-televangelist-of-trafficking

[501] Michael Oluronbi: Birmingham pastor raped children after naked 'spiritual bathing' UK Sky News Tuesday 14 January 2020: https://news.sky.com/story/michael-oluronbi-birmingham-pastor-raped-children-after-naked-spiritual-bathing-11908734

[502] Ibid. See also Michael Oluronbi: 'Holy Bath' rapist jailed for 34 years. BBC NEWS 6 March 2020: https://www.bbc.co.uk/news/uk-england-birmingham-51767053

[503] Ibid. Remarks of Philip Bradley QC, who prosecuted Michael Oluronbi.

grievousness of his crimes found expression in the sentencing judge remarks that Oluronbi's crimes:

> must be one of the worst cases of sexual abuse of multiple children to come before the courts.
>
> You did this because you are an arrogant, selfish and vain man.[504]

13.6 Evaluation and Summary

The challenge that the State has in ensuring that religious leaders can carry out their duties of religious and spiritual guidance to their people without unnecessary interference is a difficult one when the cases discussed above about Jim Jones, David Koresh, Gilbert Deya, or Michael Oluronbi but it is not one that should be neglected if the responsibility to protect vulnerable people is to be ensured by the State. But every one of these cases discussed took rather too long a time before intervention or appropriate action was taken and in some cases such as those of Jim Jones or David Koresh as well as Michael Oluronbi, the belated intervention left many victims destroyed or badly damaged emotionally and psychologically, when consideration is given to the tender young girls Oluronbi raped.

---

[504]   Ibid. Judge Sarah Buckingham, sentencing Michael Oluronbi.

14

RELIGIOUS RIVALRY, POLITICAL EXPRESSIONS, AND OBJECTIONS FOR MILITARY SERVICE ON GROUNDS OF INDIVIDUAL'S RIGHT TO FREEDOM OF RELIGIOUS BELIEFS

Do not be deceived: God is not mocked, for whatever one sows, that will he also reap.

- Galatians 6:7 (English Standard Version).

Some of the decisions of the European Court of Human Rights clearly show that if the State does not intervene to protect individual citizens enjoying their rights to religious freedom when they are not a threat to others, religious rivalry in an internally divided and diverse religion such as the Christian religion where several denominations and doctrinal differences have been established, can lead members of one religious denomination to attack another. There have been instances of one denomination frustrating another from enjoying their religious right to freedom and sometimes even causing harm or injury in the bid to stop them from enjoying such right.

14.1. Unlawful Acts to Deprive Individual of the Rights to Freedom of Religion and Practice by Religious Organisations

One glaring example of this can be seen from what transpired in the case of the Members of the Gldani Congregation of Jehovah's Witnesses and others v Georgia.[505] The members of the Gldani Congregation of Jehovah's Witnesses were attacked in October 1999 by a number of assailants who were led by a defrocked Orthodox Church priest known as Father Basil. Because of the intrigues that followed the investigation and trial in the case, it is worth stating that the Orthodox Church happens to be the State recognised Church by the Constitution of the Republic of Georgia. Article 9 of the Constitution of Georgia says:

> The State recognises the special role of the Georgian Orthodox Church in Georgian history. Simultaneously, however, it declares complete freedom of religious belief and confession, as well as the independence of the Church from the State.

During the attack the assailants inflicted severe injuries to those who could not escape from the Congregation of the Jehovah's Witnesses meeting place and some of the wounded members of the congregation ended up been admitted in the hospital. The Jehovah's Witnesses stated that they alerted the police that the attack was to take place but they did not come to their rescue in time to prevent the attack and the injuries caused to them. The senior police investigator who subsequently had the responsibility of investigating the matter admitted that he held Orthodox faith and therefore would find it difficult to be impartial in investigating the case. The victims of the congregation of Jehovah's Witnesses attack complained of irregularities in the investigation and trial that followed their attack as neither Father Basil nor his supporters who attacked them were duly convicted and given any sentence that would deter such attacks by others in the future. Notwithstanding the expressed guarantee of the right of every citizen of Georgia to freedom of religious belief in Article 19 of the Constitution which says:

---

[505] To read the full details of this case see: Members of the Gldani Congregation of Jehovah's Witnesses and others's v Georgia, Application No. 71156/01 (May 3, 2007). See: https://www.servat.unibe.ch/dfr/em711560.html

"1. Everyone has the right to freedom of Speech, thought, conscience, religion and belief.

2. It is prohibited to persecute an individual for his thoughts, beliefs or religion and to oblige an individual to express his or her opinions about them.

The rights provided for in this Article may not be restricted unless:

> what happened to the members of the Gldani congregation of Jehovah's Witnesses and their experience as detailed in the Court reports suggests that in some cases people can breach the constitution and escape the penalties prescribed for breaches if they belonged to a certain group of people who have influence in the State system. That is the only explanation that can be given for the failure of the Government of Georgia to ensure that people such as Father Basil and his supporters serve custodian sentence for breaches to the constitution and for assaults and bodily harm to others who were merely exercising their right to religious freedom.

The victims of the attack on the members of the Gldani Congregation of Jehovah's Witnesses took their case to the European Court of Human Rights where they submitted in their application that their rights to freedom from degrading and inhuman treatments under Article 3, and freedom to practice their religious belief under Article 9:1, and, freedom from discrimination under Article 14 of the Convention were all violated.[506]

Although the government of Georgia denied the claims of the applicants before the European Court of Human Rights, the Court in their examinations of all the facts about the violations of these respective articles as they apply to the rights of the members of the Gldani Congregation of Jehovah's Witnesses, found that there were violations. The Court accordingly made various awards in respect of non-pecuniary damage up to the maximum sum of EUR 850 to each applicant.[507]

---

[506] Ibid.

[507] Ibid.

Besides the fact that the case shows that religious rivalry can affect the individual enjoyment of their right to freedom of religious belief and practice in a society with plurality of religions, the other danger that the case exposes is the fact that those engaged in public service such as law enforcement agents like police officers can be affected by bias when matters of religion and beliefs involving their own religious beliefs are at stake and this could be prejudicial to justice in the society.

14.2 When National Security overrides the Individual Right to Manifest Religious Expression and Practice

An individual manifestation of religious beliefs and expressions sometimes involves verbal or written expressions. Yet, there are times when verbal and written expressions of the individual who thinks he is merely manifesting his religious beliefs may pose harm and great danger to others and the State at large. In Arrowsmith v United Kingdom[508], the applicant Pat Arrowsmith was a pacifist who distributed leaflets urging soldiers not to go on posting to Northern Ireland as well as asking those serving in Northern Ireland to withdraw from their duties. The United Kingdom prosecuted and convicted Arrowsmith of committing offences under sections 1 and 2 of the Incitement to Disaffection Act 1934.[509] The applicant having lost her appeal against the conviction in the United Kingdom took the case to the European Commission where she lodged a complaint that her conviction in the United Kingdom was a violation of her right under Article 10 of the Convention which gives her the "right to receive and impart information and ideas without interference by public authority and regardless of frontiers."[510]

The Commission considered the application of Arrowsmith admissible and while examining her case referred to the US Supreme decision in the case of Cantwell v Connecticut[511] which was about the constitutional guarantee of freedom of conscience and religious belief as embodied in

---

[508]   Arrowsmith v United Kingdom, ECHR 1978 3EHRR 218, 7050/75; [1978] ECHR 7.

[509]   Regina v Arrowsmith [1975] QB 678.

[510]   See Arrowsmith v The United Kingdom, Note by E.M. Barendt in Oxford Journal of Legal Studies, Volume 1, Issue 2, Summer 1981, pp: 279-284: https://academic.oup.com/ojls/article-ab stract/1/2/279/1425882?redirectedFrom=fulltext

[511]   Cantwell v Connecticut, 310 U.S. 296 (1940)

the Fourteenth Amendment and guaranteed by the First Amendment of the US Constitution. The defendant in the case was on a public street trying to make passers-by to purchase some books that he had or make some contributions. He did this in a manner that he believed was of a true religion by playing a phonograph record describing the books he had. But the record contained some verbal attack on the religion of the listeners. Consequently, the listeners felt provoked with a desire to strike the defendant. The defendant in reaction took the books and the phonograph and left. However the defendant was convicted by the US State of Connecticut for breach of peace because under common law the offence of the breach of the peace can be committed not only by acts of violence but also by acts and words likely to produce violence in others.[512] However, it was argued that there was nothing in the defendant posture that suggested that he intended to offend listeners. The US Supreme Court quashed the defendant's conviction on grounds that:

> the defendant's conviction of the common law offence of breach of the peace was violative of constitutional guarantees of religious liberty and freedom of speech.[513]

However, upon examination of Arrowsmith case on merits it went on to uphold the United Kingdom's government contention that her prosecution and conviction of Arrowsmith was necessary for the purpose of national security and for the prevention of disorder.[514]

The Commission also considered the applicant's other complaint that her "right to freedom of belief" under Article 9 of the Convention was also violated by the United Kingdom as a result of the conviction. However, while the Commission accepted that she had right to freedom of belief under Article 9 of the Convention, it did not agree with the applicant that that right was violated by the United Kingdom. The Commission rather held that the applicant's act of distributing leaflets constituted the practice of political opposition as opposed to the manifestation of a belief under Article 9

---

[512] Ibid.

[513] Ibid.

[514] See Note by E.M Barendt in Oxford Journal of Legal Studies, Volume 1, Issue 2, Summer 1981, pp:279 – 284.

of the Convention right. It is noteworthy that Conte in discussing the European Court of Human Rights decisions concerning manifestation of religious beliefs in the Arrowsmith v United Kingdom and similar decisions such as Kalac v Turkey [1997] ECHR 37; and Stedman v United Kingdom [1997] ECHR 178, pointed out in comparison to the decision of the United Nations Human Rights Committee (UNHRC), in Boodoo v Trinidad and Tobago, Communication 721/1996, UN Doc CCPR/C/74/D/721/1996 (2002), that the decision of the UNHRC:

> appear to be more inclusive than the approach taken by the European Court of Human Rights, namely that only those manifestations which form a necessary part of the religion or belief are protected under article 9 of the European Convention on Human Rights.[515]

However, the observation of Conte above is rather too little and too narrow to make a distinguishing mark on any difference in the jurisprudence of the European Court of Human Rights and the United Nations Human Rights Committee, in their respective decisions on manifestation of religious beliefs. When the decision of the UNHRC in the complaints of Riley et al v Canada, Communication 1048/2002, UN Doc CCPR/C/74/D/1048/2002 (2002), is compared to the European Court decision in the Arrowsmith case, the observation Conte tries to make becomes unnoticeable. More significant in this regard is the decision of the UNHRC in M.A.B., W.A.T. and J-A.Y.T. v Canada[516], in which the Committee decided not to uphold the complaint of the three Canadian nationals who were leading members of the "Assembly of the Church of the Universe", whose beliefs and practices necessarily involve the care, cultivation, possession, distribution, maintenance, integrity and worship of the "Sacrament" of the Church which was what is known as cannabis or marijuana. The Canadian authorities had detained the authors for the possession and distribution of cannabis which was classified as a narcotic drug in Canada. The UNHRC decided the article

---

[515] Conte, Alex and Burchill, Richard, Defining Civil and Political Rights. The Jurisprudence of the United Nations Human Rights Committee. © 2009 Second Edition Published by Routledge 2016 at pp. 78-79.

[516] M.A.B., W.A.T. and J-A.Y.T. v Canada, Communication 570/1993, UN Doc CCPR/C/50/D/1993 (1994). Another case about a member of the Rastafari religion who claimed to manifest his religious belief by the use of cannabis was considered in Prince v South Africa, Communication 1474/2006, UN Doc CCPR/C/91/D/1474/2006 (2007).

18 right to freedom of conscience and religion did not protect the worship and distribution of narcotic drugs such as cannabis or marijuana. By this decision, the UNHRC were clearly making it obvious that it is not every claim about manifestation of religious belief that is acceptable as an integral part of worship in the spirit of Article 18 of the ICCPR right to freedom of conscience and religion. More apparent is the fact that the jurisprudence of both the UNHRC and the European Court of Human Rights is almost in tandem insofar as the decisions in freedom of religion and manifestation of religious beliefs goes.

While the individual right to freedom of religion and belief has been affirmed by the European Commission of Human Rights and the European Court of Human Rights in several complaints and cases decided by the Commission and the Court respectively, and indeed by some state parties through constitutional provision, it is also clear that the right cannot be enjoyed in a bid to avoid mandatory citizens' services. This can be seen from several cases decided by the European Commission and European Court of Human Rights respectively.

In Grandrath v Germany[517], the applicant Mr Grandrath was a minister of Jehovah's Witnesses who totally objected to military service and any substitute civilian service and sought exemption from such service. When the German authorities refused to uphold his request for exemption, Mr Grandrath lodged a complaint with the European Commission of Human Rights claiming that his right to freedom of religion and belief under Article 9 of the Convention was violated. Accordingly, the Commission examined his case. However, the Commission arrived at the conclusion that Mr Grandrath was a conscientious objector and being conscientious objector did confer upon him the right to exemption from military service. The Commission also went on to say that it was a matter for each state party to the Convention to decide whether or not to grant an individual the right to exemption. It was held that the German authorities had not violated the right of Mr Grandrath under Article 9 of the Convention.

However, in the recent case of Bayatyan v Armenia, which in many respect is similar to the case of Mr Grandrath, albeit with modest

---

[517]   Grandrath v Germany, (2299/64) Date 12/10/1966.

difference in facts, the European Court of Human Rights reached a different decision to that of Grandrath.[518]

The applicant Mr Vahan Bayatyan was an Armenian national, who refused to do military service in accordance with the Armenian Constitutional requirement. The applicant premised his refusal on grounds of his religious belief as a Jehovah's Witness. He stated that his religion does not allow him to serve in the Army. He quoted Isaiah 2:4 as a portion of the Bible that justifies his religious stance and refusal to perform military service as required in the Armenian Constitution. Following the applicant's refusal to do the military service in 2001, he was arrested and tried in 2002. He was initially sentenced to one year six months term of jail but upon appeal by the prosecutor who said that the Court of First Instance sentence was rather lenient without regard to the social danger the applicant's action could cause to the society. The Court of Appeal subsequently increased the applicant's sentence to two and half years. The applicant appealed against his conviction, reiterating that he was willing to do a civilian service and that the Armenian Constitution provides for alternative service under section 19 of the Freedom of Conscience and Religions Organisations Act. However, in their judgment in 2003, the Armenian Court of Cessation upheld the judgment of the Court of Appeal.[519]

Mr Bayatyan took his case to the European Court of Human Rights were he submitted that his right to freedom of religion and belief under Article 9 of the Convention was violated by his conviction in the Armenian court.[520]

In their response, the Government of Armenia stated that if each member of the sixty registered religious organisations including the Jehovah's Witnesses, nine branches and one agency, "a situation would arise in which both members of Jehovah's Witnesses and other religious organisations would refuse to perform their obligations towards the State including the possibility of refusing to pay taxes and duties on the grounds that it was against their religious convictions and the state would

---

[518] Bayatyan v Armenia, ECHR, (Application No. 23459/03) Judgment Strasbourg 7 July 2011.

[519] Ibid.

[520] Ibid.

be obliged not to convict them as this might be found to be in violation of the right under Article 9.[521]

The Armenian Government finally justified their conviction of Mr Bayatyan in violation of his right under Article 9 of Convention by submitting that it was in compliance with Article 9 in a democratic society because it was prescribed by law as provided in their constitution.[522]

In examining the case of Mr Bayatyan, the European Court of Human Rights decided to look at other documents and practice and was particular import to the case was the International Covenant on Civil and Political Rights (ICCPR) and the practice of the United Nations Human Rights Committee (UNHRC). This was important because the ICCPR has been in force since 23 March 1976 and Armenia ratified the Covenant since 23 June 1993.

The ICCPR Article 8 says:

"---

3 (a) No one shall be required to perform forced or compulsory labour,

----

(c) For the purpose of this paragraph the term 'forced or compulsory labour' shall not include:

(ii) Any service of a military character and, in countries where conscientious objection is recognised, any national service required by law of conscientious objectors."[523]

ICCPR Article 18

---

[521] Ibid.

[522] Ibid.

[523] Ibid.

1. Everyone shall have the right to freedom of thought, conscience and religion. This right shall include freedom to have or to adopt a religion or belief of his choice, and freedom, either individually or in community with others and in public or private, to manifest his religion or belief in worship, observance, practice and teaching ....[524]

The European Court of Human Rights proceeded to look at how the United Nations Human Rights Committee, which monitors the implementation of the International Covenant on Civil and Political Rights, handled and decided complaints about violations of Articles 8 on conscientious objections and Article 18, the right to freedom of conscience, religion and belief.

The Court looked at the UNHRC decision in L.T.K. v Finland, communication no.185/1984 UN doc. CCPR/C/25/D/185/1984, 9 July 1985) which was a complaint brought against Finland by a Finnish conscientious objector and noted that the UNHRC in their decision in that complaint surmised that Article 18 of the ICCPR did not provide for the right to conscientious objection with respect to Article 8 (3) (c) (ii) and therefore declared the complaint inadmissible on the basis that it was incompatible with the provisions of the ICCPR.[525]

However, the European Court of Human Rights further noted that there has been a fundamental shift in the decisions of the UNHRC since the case of L.T.K. v Finland. For instance, in its decision of 7 November 1991, in J.P. v. Canada (Communication no.446/1991, UN doc CCPR/C/43/D/446/1991) the UNHRC accepted that Article 18 of the ICCPR protected "the right to hold, express and disseminate opinions and convictions, including conscientious objection to military activities and expenditures".[526]

Further clarity was given to the way Article 18 of the ICCPR should be interpreted when in 1993 the UNHRC adopted its General Comment no. 22 on Article 18 of the ICCPR, providing inter alia, the following interpretation of that provision:

---

[524]   Ibid.

[525]   Ibid.

[526]   Ibid. Para. 61.

11...The Covenant does not explicitly refer to a right to a conscientious objection, but the Committee believes that such a right can be derived from Article 18, inasmuch as the obligation to use lethal force may seriously conflict with the freedom of conscience and the right to manifest one's religion or belief...[527]

The UNHRC further developed its position on Article 18 with respect to conscientious objection and with particular attention to Article 8.2 and 8.3 of the ICCPR when it considered the complaints of two nationals of Korea, Messrs Yeo-Bum Yoon and Myung-Jin Choi v Republic of Korea (Communications nos. 1321/2004 and 1322/2004, UN doc. CCPR/C/88?D/1321-1322/2004, 23 January 2007), because conscientious objection was not recognised in Korea. On 3 November 2006, the UNHRC in consideration of the two applicants' complaint, held that:

8.2 The Committee... notes that Article 8, para 3, of the Covenant excludes from the scope of "forced or compulsory labour', which is proscribed, 'any service of military character and, in countries where conscientious objection is recognised, any national service required by law of conscientious objectors – It follows that Article 8 of the Covenant itself neither recognises nor excludes a right of conscientious objection. Thus, the present claim is to be assessed solely in the light of Article 18 of the Covenant over time in view of its text and purpose.

8.3... The author's conviction and sentence, accordingly, amounts to a restriction on their ability to manifest their religion or belief. Such restriction must be justified by permissible limits described in paragraph 3 of Article 18, that is, that any restriction must be prescribed by law and be necessary to protect public safety, order, health or morals or the fundamental rights and freedoms of others...[528]

The UNHRC accordingly concluded that the Government of Korea unnecessarily interfered with the guaranteed rights of Messrs Yeo-Bun

---

[527]   Ibid. Para.62

[528]   Ibid. Para 63.

Yoon and Myung-Jin Choi in a way that violated Article 18 of the ICCPR.

The European Court of Human Rights having examined UNHRC monitoring and implementation practice of Article 18 right to freedom of conscience, religion and belief in the ICCPR, as discussed above, went on to also rely on its own authorities such as its decision in Bascarini and others v San Marino (24645/94) [1999] ECHR 7 (18 February 1999), among others, to decide that the Government of Armenia violated Bayatyan's right to manifest his religion and belief as guaranteed under Article 9 (1) of the Convention by the conviction and sentence imposed on him for failure to report for military service.[529]

The Court awarded Mr Bayatyan various sums of money in damages in respect of non-pecuniary damage and in respect of costs and expenses and ordered the respondent State Party, in this case the Government of Armenia to pay the applicant the sum awarded with interest within three months.[530]

What in essence was the major difference between the cases of Grandrath v Germany and Bayatyan v Armenia? Nothing substantial in actual fact, except that Grandrath objected to doing either a military service or a substitute civilian service in Germany, whereas Bayatyan objected to doing a military service but was willing to do a civilian service but he was not given. The real reasons as to why the Commission and the Court respectively reached different decisions in the two cases are stated in the reasoning leading to the respective decisions.

14.3 Evaluation and Summary

Interfering with the individual right to freedom of conscience, religious belief and practice where the exercise of such does not cause harm to others is a breach of the human right of the individual which in some cases in some jurisdictions is also a constitutional right of the citizen. However, in the cases such as those discussed in the latter part of this chapter about Catholic Church clergy, Jim Jones, David Koresh,

---

[529]   Ibid. Paras. 112 and 128.

[530]   Ibid. Paras 130-136.

Gilbert Deya and Michael Oluronbi, where gullible innocent people are being abused by those who are supposed to be the religious leaders of the people, there is the obligation on the part of the government to intervene, and indeed to do something swiftly, to prevent excessive abuse and damage to sometimes innocent and tender young people who have mistaken their abusers for religious mentors or religious and spiritual teachers.

PART IV

GROSS ACTS OF HUMAN RIGHTS VIOLATIONS IN RELIGIOUS NATIONALISM, ETHNIC-NATIONALISM AND SECULAR DEMOCRATIC STATES

15

IRAN: THE DAWN OF RELIGIOUS NATIONALISM

The Islamic Republic of Iran also known as Persia, is often accused by European Nations, the United States of America and the State of Israel among others as a sponsorer of terrorism and probably rightly so, but Iran also had a story that led the Islamic Republic to be anti-West and anti-Israel. The background and its human rights abusers are discussed below.

15.1 Iran and Religious Nationalism

The Islamic Republic of Iran is like any other nation-state, even like an advanced democratic state, when the institutions and structures of government are viewed from the constitutional construct. The executive, legislature and judiciary are separate arms of government except that the legislature known as the Islamic Consultative Assembly sends the laws they make to The Guardian Council which is made up of Islamic clergy for vetting to ensure that the laws are compatible with the criteria of Islam and the Constitution of the Republic.[531]

Historically, Iran is one of the world's oldest nations on earth but until 1979, it had operated a monarchical government based on their 1906 Constitution. The circumstances that led Iran to move from a

---

[531] See comments on "Jurisdiction and Access" with regards to the Constitution of the Islamic Republic of Iran in the UN Women Global Gender Equality Constitutional Database – Constitution of the Islamic Republic of Iran of 1979 as amended to 1989: https://constitutions. unwomen.org/en/countries/asia/iran-islamic-republic-of

monarchical state to a religious nationalist state is clearly stated in the preamble to the Constitution of the Islamic Republic of Iran (1979) and as revised and amended (1989).

The following excerpts from the preamble of the Constitution of the Islamic Republic of Iran lend credence to the Iranian revolution and the establishment of religious nationalism as a political system of government in Iran:

The Dawn of the Movement

> The devastating protest of Imam Khumayni against the American conspiracy known as the "White Revolution", which was a step intended to stabilize the foundations of despotic rule and to reinforce the political, cultural, and economic dependence of Iran on world imperialism, brought into being a united movement of the people and, immediately afterwards, a momentous revolution of the Muslim nation in the month of Khurdad, 1342 [June 1963].[532]

The developments that led to the final decision for a religious nationalistic state following a referendum in which 98.2% of the people of Iran voted in favour of having a religious nationalist state is detailed further in the preamble of the Constitution of the Islamic Republic of Iran as follows:

The Price the Nation Paid

> After slightly more than a year of continuous and unrelenting struggle, the sapling of the Revolution, watered by the blood of more than 60,000 martyrs and 100,000 wounded and disabled, not to mention billions of tumans' worth of property damage, came to bear fruit amidst the cries of "Independence! Freedom! Islamic government!" This great movement, which attained victory through reliance upon faith, unity, and the decisiveness of its

---

[532] See "Constitute" Constituteproject.org, Iran (Islamic Republic of)'s 1979 with Amendments through 1989. The Dawn of the Movement: https://www.constituteproject.org/constitution/Iran_1989.pdf

leadership at every critical and sensitive juncture, as well as the self-sacrificing spirit of the people, succeeded in upsetting all the calculations of imperialism and destroying all its connections and institutions, thereby opening a new chapter in the history of all embracing popular revolutions of the world.

Bahman 21 and 22, 1357 [February 12 and 13, 1979] witnessed the collapse of the monarchical regime; domestic tyranny and foreign domination, both of which were based upon it, were shattered. This great success proved to be the vanguard of Islamic government –a long – cherished desire of the Muslim people – and brought with it the glad tidings of the final victory.

Unanimously, and with the participation of the maraji' al-taqlid, the 'ulama' of Islam, and the leadership, the Iranian people declared their final and firm decision, in the referendum on the Islamic Republic, to bring about a new political system, that of the Islamic Republic. A 98.2% majority of the people voted for this system. The Constitution of the Islamic Republic of Iran, setting forth as it does the political, social, cultural, and economic institutions and their relations that are to exist in society, must now provide for the consolidation of the foundations of the Islamic system of government, and propose the plan of a new system of government to be erected on the ruins of the previous taghuti order.[533]

Putting the circumstances and the process by which Iran became a religious nationalist state in perspective, it seems plausible on the account of what is stated in the preamble of the Constitution of the Islamic Republic of Iran that a religious nationalist state premised on the criteria of Islam was a viable alternative to western democracy.

---

[533] The Price the Nation Paid. Ibid.

15.2 Political Stability and Citizenship

Every system of government is tested by the contentment of the citizens and those who live in the state. Democracy to some is a favoured form of government not because of how good it is but because of the citizens' hope and belief that they can change their elected democratic leaders at general elections.

Well over forty years, since Iran's enthronement of religious nationalism as a political system and as an alternative to a democratic government, the question is do the citizens of Iran and those who live in Iran feel that they are better-off under a religious nationalistic government than a democratic one? The evidence and what is filtering out of Iran in recent years is not affirmative.

Iran now appears to be operating religious nationalism increasingly in the same way as military regimes are known for despotism and totalitarianism because human rights of citizens are often flagrantly violated over issues that hinge on sometimes minor infractions. For example, since September 2022, various protests have taken place in Iran following the death of Mahsa Amini a 22-year-old woman who was arrested and detained by Iran's morality police on September 13, 2022, for not wearing her hijab properly to cover her hair in public.[534]

Three days following her arrest and detention for the offence of not covering her hair properly, she died in hospital as a result of injuries she sustained from police brutality during her arrest and detention, though the Iranian morality police denies causing her injuries during the arrest and detention. But the unanswered question is why did she die within three days of her arrest and detention if no harm and injury was caused to her during the arrest and detention? And the problem is that it was not the case that Mahsa Amini was not wearing hijab or covering her hair, but the claim of the morality police that her hair was not properly covered in public, and for that she was arrested and detained, leading to her death. The protests that have followed the death of Mahsa Amini and the efforts of the Iranian authorities to suppress the protesters have

---

[534] UK Parliament House of Lords Library Protests in Iran: Death of Mahsa Amini. Published Friday, 21 October 2022: https://lordslibrary.parliament.uk/protests-in-iran-death-of-mahsa-amini/

further exacerbated the violations of the human rights as some protesters have been killed and others injured by the Iranian authorities.

Paradoxically, the Constitution of the Islamic Republic of Iran guarantees the human rights of women and also minorities in Iran but the operation of the Iranian authorities suggests that everyone irrespective of religious belief is expected to dress and comport themselves as "devout Muslims" in appearance.

The following are articles to that effect in the Constitution of the Islamic Republic of Iran:

Article 13

Zoroastrian, Jewish, and Christian Iranians are the only recognised religious minorities, who, within the limits of the law, are free to perform their religious rites and ceremonies, and to act according to their canon in matters of personal affairs and religious education.

Article 14

In accordance with the sacred verse ("God does not forbid you to deal kindly and justly with those who have not fought against you because of your religion and who have not expelled you from your homes" [60:8]), the government of the Islamic Republic of Iran and all Muslims are duty-bound to treat non-Muslims in conformity with ethical norms and the principles of Islamic justice and equity, and to respect their human rights. This principle applies to all who refrain from engaging in conspiracy or activity against Islam and the Islamic Republic of Iran.

On the face of the Constitution of the Islamic Republic of Iran, there are things to admire. But in Iran's practice of religious nationalism over the last forty years, there are manifest incidents that are incongruent to what is stated in the constitution in respect of how citizens' should be treated. Citizens live in apprehension of the state in Iran, and the rest of world are in wonder about how oppressive regimes such as the Taliban in

Afghanistan continue to curry the support of Iran while carrying out the oppression of their citizens.

15.3 Evaluation and Summary

Iran's pattern of operating a religious nationalistic state stirs aw in the hearts and thoughts of people across the globe because of the sense of insecurity of the citizens of Iran, and the fact that people from other parts of the world do not feel safe when they think of travelling to Iran. However, from the portions of the preamble of the constitution and the articles quoted in this discussion, it must be said that the spirit behind Iran's revolution, and the decision for a religious nationalism state, and indeed, the Constitution of the Islamic Republic of Gross Acts of Human Rights Violations

Iran 1979 and as amended and revised 1989, bear some appeal. But the states that have sought to follow Iran in operating a form of government based on religious nationalism such as the Taliban in Afghanistan are making it worse for people to appreciate religious nationalism as a viable form of political system of government that should substitute or replace western democratic form of government or any other secular form of government.

16

AFGHANISTAN: THE TALIBAN AND THE THREAT OF RELIGIOUS NATIONALISM TO INTERNATIONAL PEACE AND SECURITY

Religious Nationalists cherish group loyalties over individual rights and personal achievements.[535]

We learned at an early age that it was men's interpretation of our religion that restricted women's opportunities, not the religion itself. Islam in fact has been quite progressive towards women from its inception: the prophet Mohammed (PBUH) had forbidden the killing of female infants common among the Arabs of the time, and called for education for women and their right to inherit long before these privileges were granted to them in the West."[536]

16.1 From Liberation from Communism to Religious Nationalism

One reason why religious nationalism seems to thrive is because people that are involved in it tend to forsake the pursuits of their own individual goals to pursuing group interests and goals. While this is noble when the

---

[535] Juergensmeyer, M., The New Cold War? Religious Nationalism Confronts the Secular State © 1993 The Regents of the University of California. P.196.

[536] Bhutto, Benazir, Daughter of the East, An Autography © Simon & Schuster1998, 2007. P.34.

goals are well defined and will profit all in the society, it is never good if a part of those that are expected to be protected by the group leaders become those who will be trampled upon or in some cases destroyed in order to achieve or sustain the existence of the leadership group goals.

The initial story of the Islamic insurgency in Afghanistan was premised on a noble cause, insofar as its goal was to liberate Afghanistan from any vestiges of communism under the then Soviet Union to a state that will exist on its own terms in line with international law. The Soviet Union invasion of Afghanistan in December 1979 to lend support to the then communist leaning government did not go well with the majority Muslim believers of Afghanistan. It was therefore attractive for Muslims to seek to liberate Afghanistan from any grip and hold of Communism. To this effect, Islamic insurgency made up of Afghans and Muslims from other Islamic countries that were determined to join in the fight to free Afghanistan from the Soviet Union and its Communism supporters within the Afghan state gained increasing support. The Afghan Islamic fighters known as mujahideen otherwise jihadists and their guerrilla approach to the war with the support of assistance from the United States that provided them with some arms resisted the Soviet Union forces in Afghanistan and the war went on for a decade. Eventually, the Soviet Union realised their losses were becoming more than reasonable to bear in terms of lives and billions of dollars, and decided to withdraw from Afghanistan. But as the Soviet Union forces left Afghanistan, various Islamic militant groups scrabbled for the control of Afghanistan until the Taliban which is a fundamentalist Islamic group finally seized power.[537]

16.2 The Taliban Control of Afghanistan and the Re-enforcement of Terrorism

Whatever joy that the withdrawal of the thousands of the Soviet Union occupation force in February 1989 from Afghanistan brought to the Afghan people, the celebration marking that joy was short-lived by the emergence of various factions of Islamic insurgents that fought for the control of the country. Between 1989 and 1997, civil unrest caused by

---

[537] See "The Soviet Invasion of Afghanistan and the U.S Response, 1978 – 1980." Office of the Historian, Department of State, United States of America. https://history.state.gov/milestones/1977-1980/soviet-invasion-afghanistan. See also Soviet invasion of Afghanistan 1979 https://www.britannica.com/place/Soviet-Union/The-Russian-Revolution

fighting for the control of Afghanistan by various Islamic group was intense. However, the northern part of Afghanistan which was under the control of Dostum who administered its provinces from Shiberghan had relative peace until 1997. But fighting for the control of the Southern part of Afghanistan between various Islamic groups of insurgencies went on until 1996 when the Taliban finally took control of Kabul under the leadership of Mullah Mohammad Omar. It is vital to point out the fact that the success of Omar taking control of Kabul was achieved with the assistant of Pakistan who had an economic interest because they:

> saw in the Taliban a way to secure trade routes to Central Asia and establish a government in Kabul friendly to its interests. Pakistani traders who had long sought a secure route to send their good to Central Asia quickly became some of the Taliban's strongest financial backers.[538]

As Mullah Omar took a firm grip of the Southern part of Afghanistan and control of Kabul with the help of Pakistan who were to reap the economic benefit, Osama bin Laden also returned back to Afghanistan in 1996, to support Omar with his fighters to have firm control of Afghanistan. However, much more than helping Omar and the Taliban in Afghanistan, bin Laden, found Afghanistan a safe haven to build camps where he would train his al- Qaeda terrorists. He did that successful without opposition from the Taliban.

By 1997, the Taliban advance into the Northern part of Afghanistan and prospect of taking full control of Afghanistan was so obvious that they renamed the country the Islamic Emirate of Afghanistan with Mullah Omar as the head of the emirate with the title of amir-ul momineen (commander of the faithful).[539]

> In areas under their control, the Taliban authorities enforced their version of Islamic law, enacting policies prohibiting women from working outside the home in activities other than heath care, and requiring corporal punishment for those convicted of certain crimes. They prohibited women from attending universities and closed

---

[538] See "Backgrounder on Afghanistan: History of the War. The Third Phase: The Taliban's Conquest of Afghanistan" https://www.hrw.org/legacy/backgrounder/asia/afghan-bck1023.pdf

[539] Ibid.

girls' schools in Kabul and some other cities, although
primary schools for girls continued to operate in many
other areas of the country under Taliban control. The
Taliban also enforced a strict dress code for women,
and required men to have beards and to refrain from
Western haircuts or dress. Arguably the most powerful
agency within the Islamic Emirate of Afghanistan, as
the Taliban renamed the country, is the Ministry of
Promotion of Virtue and Prevention of Vice (al-Amrbi
al-Ma'ruf wa al-Nahi'an al-Munkir), which is responsible
for the enforcement of all Taliban decrees regarding moral
behaviour.[540]

While the Taliban were fixated in fashioning their own idea of an Islamic
Emirate in Afghanistan even to the point of degrading women and girls
and stripping them of their human rights, Pakistan was enjoying new
opportunity of economic benefit of trade into Central Asia and bin Laden
was perfecting his own terrorists without considering the harm of how
millions of innocent and faithful Muslims all over the world would be
badly affected by the acts of terrorism that he was going to perpetrate.

About the same time that the Taliban successfully displaced all the
other Islamic groups of insurgents controlling some parts of northern
Afghanistan and took full control of the country, they were yet to have
respite from their years of fighting in Afghanistan before bin Laden's first
act of international terrorism following his al-Qaeda terrorists bombing
of US Embassy in Nairobi Kenya and Dar es Salaam Tanzania in 1998
attracted the United States reprisal launching of air strikes against bin
Laden's al-Qaeda's training camps in Afghanistan. But the problems
that the Taliban in Afghanistan had to contend with did not stop with
the US launching of air strikes against bin Laden's al-Qaeda locations
in Afghanistan. By October 1999, the matter took a new dimension as
the UN demanded that the Taliban should hand over bin Laden and
imposed various sanctions on Afghanistan and froze the Taliban assets
overseas as they failed to hand over bin Laden. The sanctions did not
make the Taliban to take any step towards handing over bin Laden.
Worst of all, bin Laden and his al-Qaeda went on to further commit the
most egregious of crimes against humanity. On September 11, 2001, bin

---

[540] Ibid.

Laden's 19 al-Qaeda militants hijacked airlines in the US and carried out several suicide attacks leading to the deaths of about 3000 people of which the majority were in the collapsed

Twin Towers of the World Trade Center in New York.[541] Among the almost 3000 dead and several other thousands of wounded persons were Christians, Muslims and people of all faiths and beliefs that were affected. It raises questions how bin Laden and those who say they believe in God would carry out such cruel acts and think that the Almighty God would allow them enter paradise after murdering their fellow Muslim believers who did not cause them any offence. The jihadists appear to forget that God is all knowing and holy and would not tolerate injustice and wickedness as their faith and religion also preaches peace. Interestingly, bin Laden who persuaded the terrorists to carry out the treacherous act in the belief that they would enter paradise after the terrorist act did not want to go to the same paradise and spent 10 years running away from being killed. Well, the United States reaction to the September 11, 2001 al-Qaeda terrorists act was to end or significantly diminish the threats and relevance of al-Qaeda as well as rid the earth of bin Laden. The United States and its allies which included the United Kingdom process of smoking out al-Qaeda and bin Laden led to the invasion of Afghanistan and the removal of the Taliban from control of Afghanistan in 2001.

16.3 A Failed Democratic Experiment

Following the al-Qaeda attacks of September 11, 2001, in New York City and Washington DC, the United States demanded that the Taliban hand over Osama bin Laden, the leader of the al-Qaeda to them but the Taliban refused. The refusal obviously was a fatal decision on the part of the Taliban because bin Laden had boastfully admitted responsibility for the September 11, al-Qaeda attacks, for which thousands of persons,

---

[541] Peter L. Bergen, September 11 attacks, United States [2001]: https://www.britannica.com/event/September-11-attacks

including those of the Muslims faith had died, and thousands more were also injured...[542]

With the Taliban's refusal to hand over bin Laden to the United States, there was only one obvious option left for the United States and her allies, whose nationals were victims of the al-Qaeda terrorists attacks to take. The United States and the United Kingdom and their allies invaded Afghanistan on November 13, 2001, to smoke out bin Laden and his al-Qaeda group. The entry of the United States forces and her allies into Afghanistan led to the immediate collapse of the Taliban government in Afghanistan because the Taliban fled from Kabul for hiding.

Afghanistan became a country without a government or any form of indigenous authority in control. However, following an agreement brokered by the United Nations with various Afghan groups in Germany in December 2001 for provisional arrangements for Afghanistan in what became known as the Bonn Agreement[543] of 5 December 2001, an interim national government headed by Hamid Karzai as interim president was established in Kabul.

The interim government of Karzai under the Bonn Agreement comprised of some warlords who were named as provincial governors, military commanders and cabinet ministers under a UN mandate that had a NATO-led international security assistance force.[544] The interim government remained in place in Afghanistan until 2004 when a democratic election was held and Hamid Karzai was democratically elected as president. The democratic elections produced elected lawmakers that took their place in the Afghanistan parliament in 2005 when it was opened. However, by 2014, Ashraf Ghani succeeded Hamid

---

[542] In his book The Rise and Fall of Al-Qaeda © Fawaz A. Gerges 2011, at page 84, Gerges states that: "In an unguarded moment, bin Laden once conceded that the September 11 attacks had exceeded his wildest expectations. His goal had been to "terrorize" Americans, to kill hundreds, and to force them to rethink their military presence in the Islamic world. He had not expected so many people to die, or the World Trade Center Towers to collapse, though he shed no tears over either."

[543] See "Agreement on Provisional Arrangements in Afghanistan Pending the Re-establishment of Permanent Government Institutions." https://peacemaker. un.org/afghanistan-bonnagreement2001

[544] See Hannah Bloch, "A Look At Afghanistan's 40 years of crisis – From The Soviet War To Taliban Recapture, Npr. August 31, 2021. https://www.npr.org/2021/08/19/1028472005/afghan istan-conflict-timeline

Karzai as president following a democratic election in which he defeated Karzai.

Meanwhile, the Taliban who fled Kabul and retreated to the country side of Afghanistan when the U.S. and her allies invaded Afghanistan, regrouped and began to manifest acts of recapturing power and taking control of Afghanistan again by seizing territories starting from South Afghanistan cities as early as 2006.

With the financial burden and military losses taking its toll on the Americans and the allies forces in Afghanistan, in the way that it did the Soviet forces who had first invaded Afghanistan, as discussed earlier, the United States and their allies who had accomplished the mission of destroying al-Qaeda network and eventually killing Osama bin Laden decided to leave Afghanistan.

During the presidency of Donald Trump, the U.S. and the Taliban signed a peace agreement in Doha, Qatar, on 29 February 2020 agreeing that the Taliban would stop attacking the Americans and the US led NATO international forces while the U.S. and international forces prepare to withdraw from Afghanistan by May 2021. In keeping with the agreement, NATO foreign and defence ministers decided to withdraw all international forces from Afghanistan by April 2021.[545].

The major withdrawal of the international forces emboldened the Taliban to swiftly move towards taking control of key cities in Afghanistan including the capital Kabul and that led to the overthrow of the elected democratic government of Afghanistan.

As the Taliban advanced towards Kabul in August 2021, the concerned and pragmatic Secretary General of the United Nations Antonio Guterres raised an alarm about the human rights violations with which the Taliban were pursuing their ambition to take over control of Afghanistan:

> United Nations Secretary-General Antonio Gutteres has called on the Taliban to immediately halt its offensive in Afghanistan...It is particularly horrifying and

---

[545]   See NATO and Afghanistan. 31 August 2022: https://www.nato.int/cps/en/natohq/topics_8189.htm

heart-breaking to see reports of the hard-won rights of Afghan girls and women being ripped away from them, he said.[546]

Against the call for the Taliban to halt its offensive, the Taliban marched into Kabul without any resistance. To ease their takeover of Afghanistan, the elected President Ghani quietly fled from Kabul, the capital of Afghanistan on August 15, and his government collapsed leaving the Taliban to simply step-in and take control of Afghanistan, once again.

16.4 The Return of the Taliban and the Worsening Dimension of Human Rights Violations

The respite that the Afghans had during the 20 years of the presence of the US-NATO led international forces that drove the Taliban leaders out of Kabul and control of Afghanistan, and the NATO/UN installed interim government that led to a democratic government in Afghanistan snapped with the return of the Taliban in August 2021.

At the end of August 2021, as the last batches of American and British military personnel and officials were leaving Kabul, Afghans who could not get into the aeroplanes to join those who were being evacuated were seen hanging onto aeroplane wings and every part of the aircraft that they could lay hold of not minding the risk to their lives that their actions would attract. It was obvious that they preferred to die while trying to escape the Taliban than to remain in Afghanistan and be violated with degrading and inhuman treatment under the Taliban.

While leaders with conscience who want to lead in ways that will improve upon the lives of the people that they are leading and the society they are in control of would moderate their actions to accommodate the legitimate concerns and feelings of the people, the Taliban did the opposite. They set out to govern Afghanistan, not according to how Muslims generally understand the Quran, and not how Islam is practiced in other Islamic states such as Iran and Pakistan but according to how they choose to interpret the Sharia law and decide to impose their ideology on the people

---

[546] ALJAZEERA, Human Rights, "Taliban imposing 'horrifying' human rights curbs, UN chief warns" 13 August 2021.

of Afghanistan. They gave no room for their own human limitations and fallibilities.

They imposed immediate restrictions on women in conspicuous violation of Article 12 (1) of the United Nations International Covenant on Civil and Political Rights, ICCPR, (1966); and on another serious note restriction of the education of girls in clear violation of Article 13 of the United Nations International Covenant on Economic, Social and Cultural Rights, ICESCR, (1966):

International Covenant on Civil and Political Rights (1966), Article 12:

1. Everyone lawfully within the territory of a State shall, within that territory, have the right to liberty of movement and freedom to choose his residence.

International Covenant on Economic, Social and Cultural Rights, ICESCR, (1966), Article 13:

1. The States Parties to the present Covenant recognize the right of everyone to education. They agree that education shall be directed to the full development of the human personality and the sense of dignity, and shall strengthen the respect for human rights and fundamental freedoms. They further agree that education shall enable all persons to participate effectively in a free society, promote understanding, tolerance and friendship among all the nations and all racial, ethnic or religious groups, and further the activities of the United Nations for the maintenance of peace.

The Taliban leaders in Afghanistan have so far demonstrated unwillingness to respect universal human rights and indeed, international human rights laws that Afghanistan as a State Party to the United Nations has acceded to.

The United Nations consider the Taliban in Afghanistan as de facto authorities and have not accorded it any recognition. However, the UN continues to communicate with the Taliban through its mission the United Nations Assistance Mission in Afghanistan, UNAMA, in a bid to minimise the excessive violations of human rights violations and allow the people of Afghanistan to live in Afghanistan with respect to their human rights.

But the presence of the United Nations Mission in Afghanistan does not appear to make any significant difference to gross human rights violations and abuses by the Taliban.

Amnesty International in their 2022 report on Afghanistan stated that:

> Afghanistan was the only country in the world where girls were banned from attending secondary school.[547]

The question is why would the Taliban ban girls from attending secondary schools when Pakistan the neighbouring country to Afghanistan is an Islamic Republic and it has not banned girls from attending secondary schools? Well, the Taliban are inventing their own ideology of Islam which is detrimental to the Muslims of Afghanistan let alone Afghans with other religious beliefs. The Taliban form of religious nationalism is not only abhorrent for its gross human rights violations but a threat to the existence of majority Muslims and all the minorities in Afghanistan.

Within 10 months of the Taliban takeover of control in Afghanistan, the atrocities and human rights violations committed were already in excess of two thousand going by the report of the United Nations Assistance Mission in Afghanistan, UNAMA, which reported the following human rights violations and extrajudicial killings for the period between 15 August 2021 and 15 June 2023 as:

> 2106 civilian casualties (700 killed, 1406 wounded) predominantly caused by improvised explosive device (IED) attacks attributed to ISIL-KP and unexplained ordnance (UXO)....

> 217 instances of cruel, inhuman and degrading punishments carried out by the de facto authorities since August 2021....

---

[547] Amnesty International, AFGHANISTAN 2022: https://www.amnesty.org/en/location/asia-and-the-pacific/south-asia/afghanistan/

Human rights violations of 173 journalists and media workers, 163 of which were attributed to the de facto authorities...[548]

When those in the leadership and governance of any nation turn against those who under their control and begin to kill these on a daily basis as the Taliban are doing in Afghanistan, it cannot be a matter for internal affairs of the country to carry on with extrajudicial killings of the citizens. It becomes a matter for the international community to rise to the defence of our common humanity.

16.5 Evaluation and Summary

The Afghan Taliban's form of religious nationalism is not only precluding Afghans who hold other forms of religious beliefs such as Hinduism and Christianity from living in Afghanistan, but it was sending Afghans who were Muslims also fleeing Afghanistan because they could not see the face of compassion and piety which they learn from the Quran, the Holy book of Islam from the practice of governance by the Taliban.

The fact is that since human rights are universally guaranteed by international treaties such as the International Covenant on Civil and Political Rights, ICCPR, (1966), and International Covenant on Economic, Social and Cultural Rights, ICESCR, (1966), the international community under the auspices of the United Nations have a duty to rise up at this time and take the necessary actions to protect the gross continuous violations of human rights of the ordinary people of Afghanistan, especially, the women who are denied their fundamental freedoms to move freely within their country and the young girls who are denied access to even secondary education among other things, which are breaches of their human rights. The lives of millions of women and children cannot be allowed to be destroyed by a group of despots with invented ideologies that do not fit the religion they are adhering to as the discussion and references show.

---

[548] United Nations Assistance Mission in Afghanistan (UNAMA),Reports on Human Rights in Afghanistan, 15 August 2021 – 15 June 2022: https://unama.unmissions.org/un-releases-report-human-rights-afghanistan-taliban-takeover

17

ARMENIA-AZERBAIJAN CONFLICT OVER NAGORNO-KARABAKH

17.1 The Fault Line in the Creation of Nagorno-Karabakh in the Republic of Azerbaijan

One of the causes of gross human rights violations and indeed on-going wars leading to the commission of crimes against humanity is the artificial boundaries created by superpower states for their own convenience but to the dispute and warring of communities and peoples affected by it. This is the case in the on-going conflict and wars between the republics of Armenia and Azerbaijan.

In 1923, the then Union of Soviet Socialist Republics (USSR) otherwise referred to as the Soviet Union established Nagorno-Karabakh as an autonomous enclave in Azerbaijan. The problem with the establishment of this autonomous enclave in Azerbaijan was that the 95% of the inhabitants of the enclave were Armenians by ethnicity[549]. The difference between the Armenians and the Azerbaijanis were multifaceted but religion was a major one. The Azerbaijanis were mainly Muslims and the Armenians were mainly Christians.

The Armenians of Nagorno-Karabakh were unable to integrate themselves into Azerbaijan republic, so by 1988, their regional legislature

---

[549] For the history of the conflict between Armenia and Azerbaijan see "Nagorno-Karabakh", Center for Preventive Action, October 26, 2023, COUNCIL ON FOREIGN RELATIONS Global Conflict Tracker: https://www.cfr.org/global-conflict-tracker/conflict/nagorno-karabakh-conflict

passed a resolution[550] to join the Republic of Armenia, in spite of it being situated in the Republic of Azerbaijan. They did not of course succeed as that would have meant Azerbaijan losing Nagorno-Karabakh, which is part of its territory, to the Republic of Armenia. While the Soviet Union lasted, the levers of control kept the disgruntled Armenians in Nagorno-Karabakh and the Azerbaijani government in a false state of relative peace.

17.2 The Effect of the Collapse of the Soviet Union on the Armenians of Nagorno-Karabakh

When the Union of Soviet Socialist Republics collapsed in 1991, both the Republic of Azerbaijan and the Republic of Armenia became independent sovereign states. Armenians in Nagorno-Karabakh being the majority also declared the autonomous enclave an independent state and war broke out as Azerbaijan had to assert its force to ensure that Nagorno-Karabakh being its territory remains under it. Even though the Republic of Armenia gave support to the Armenians in Nagorno-Karabakh, over 30,000 people were killed and several hundreds of thousands of Armenians fled from Nagorno-Karabakh as refugees.[551] In 1994, Russia brokered a ceasefire referred to as the Bishkek Protocol and Nagorno-Karabakh became a de facto independent state, but there were sporadic clashes between Armenia and Azerbaijan which by 2016 led to an intense four day fighting that claimed hundreds of casualties.

17.3 The Ethnic Cleansing of Armenians in Nagorno-Karabakh

The Armenians of Nagorno-Karabakh can be said to be on the verge of being ethnically cleansed from Nagorno-Karabakh and in essence from Azerbaijan. On 19 September 2023, Azerbaijan took over occupation of the de facto independent state of Nagorno-Karabakh. The report of the Center for Preventive Action, Council on Foreign Relations Global Conflict Tracker, quoted above, also says:

[550] Ibid.
[551] Ibid.

the separatist authorities announced that the ethnic Armenian enclave would dissolve on January 1, 2024. Faced with the prospect of rule by Azerbaijan, more than one hundred thousand people, 80 % of Nagorno-Karabakh population, fled to Armenia in one week.[552]

In a BBC Europe News report of 8 December 2023, it was stated that both Armenia and Azerbaijan have agreed to:

> move towards normalising relations, and will exchange prisoners captured during recent fighting in Nagorno-Karabakh.
>
> The two countries announced on Thursday that they would work towards signing a full peace treaty based on mutual respect for each other's territorial integrity.
>
> European Council President Charles Michel welcomed the statement as a "major breakthrough in Armenia–Azerbaijan relations."
>
> The US praised "an importance confidence – building measure."[553]

It is hard to understand whether the agreement of Armenia and Azerbaijan to sign a peace deal now following the near ethnic cleansing of Armenians in Nagorno-Karabakh by Azerbaijan is complementary or antithetical to the binding order made by the International Court of Justice against Azerbaijan on 17 November 2023, which Azerbaijan was asked to implement.

Armenia filed an application instituting proceedings against Azerbaijan on 16 September 2021, at the International Court of Justice, ICJ, alleging violations of the International Convention on the Elimination of All Forms of Racial Discrimination (1969). In its application, it also requested for the indication of provisional measures. After an unsuccessful objection from Azerbaijan and several requests by Armenia

---

[552] Ibid.

[553] See "Armenia and Azerbaijan to work towards peace deal." By Barbara Tasch, BBC News Europe, 8 December 2023. https://www.bbc.co.uk/news/world-europe-67655940

for modifications of the court orders in line with the court procedures, the ICJ by thirteen votes to two reached a binding decision on 17 November 2023, against the Republic of Azerbaijan.

In its binding order, the ICJ ordered Azerbaijan to do the following:

(1) By thirteen votes to two,

The Republic of Azerbaijan shall, in accordance with its obligations under the International Convention on the Elimination of All Forms of Racial Discrimination, (i) ensure that persons who have left Nagorno-Karabakh after 19 September 2023 and who wish to return to Nagorno-Karabakh are able to do so in a safe, unimpeded and expeditious manner; (ii) ensure that persons who remained in Nagorno-Karabakh after 19 September 2023 and who wish to depart are able to do so in a safe, unimpeded and expeditious manner; and (iii) ensure that persons who remained in Nagorno-Karabakh and who wish to stay are free from the use of force or intimidation that may cause them to flee;[554]

(2) By thirteen votes to two,

The Republic of Azerbaijan shall, in accordance with its obligations under the International Convention on the Elimination of All Forms of Racial Discrimination, protect and preserve registration, identity and private property documents and records that concern the persons identified under subparagraph (1) and have due regard to such documents and records in its administrative and legislative practices;"[555]

(3) By thirteen votes to two,

---

[554] See "Application of the International Convention on the Elimination of All Forms of Racial Discrimination (Armenia v Azerbaijan), International Court of Justice, No. 2023/69. 17 November 2023. https://www.icj-cij.org/sites/default/files/case-related/180/180-20231117-pre-01-00-en.pdf

[555] Ibid.

The Republic of Azerbaijan shall submit a report to the Court on the steps taken to give effect to the provisional measures indicated and to the undertakings made by the Agent of the Republic of Azerbaijan, on behalf of his Government, at the public hearing that took place on the afternoon of 12 October 2023, within eight weeks, as from the date of this order.[556]

Unless, the agreement that Armenia and Azerbaijan have entered is in relation to complying with the order of the International Court of Justice as stated above, the recent peace agreement between Armenia and Azerbaijan can be said to have come too late, mindful of the tens of thousands of Armenians that have been

killed over the years, and the thousands that have virtually abandoned their ancestral homes in Nagorno-Karabakh for refuge in the Republic of Armenia and elsewhere.

17.4 Evaluation and Summary

The extent of human rights violations and crimes against humanity that took place against Armenians in Nagorno-Karabakh over the last one hundred years of conflicts and wars between Armenians and Azerbaijanis may not be possibly known. However, what is undeniable is that there were gross human rights violations that could have been prevented if the international community had taken more proactive actions to prevent it.

The peace that now appears to be on the horizon between Armenia and Azerbaijan could well have been achieved several decades ago, and hundreds of thousands of lives of Armenians saved, if the part for a negotiated agreement was pursued between the Republics of Armenia and Azerbaijan instead of the path to arms conflict.

---

[556] Ibid.

18

ISRAEL-PALESTINE CONFLICT AND THE PERENNIAL VIOLATIONS OF HUMAN RIGHTS

...to understand a nation's future, one had to first understand its past.[557]

I had read enough history to know that it is consistently being rewritten.[558]

18.1 The Statehood of Israel and the Statelessness of the Palestinians

The geographical area that the British Empire put on the map and called the land of Palestine when they took over the administrative district of the Ottoman government that covers Jerusalem, Nablus and Acre[559] from 1917 – 1937 has become a theatre of war, where the most atrocious human rights violations are being committed for well over a century now. The *casus belli* is the claim of those who assert that they are the indigenous people of Palestine who own the land and the Jews who claim that it is

---

[557] Sirleaf, Ellen Johnson, This Child Will Be Great, © Harper Perennial Edition 2010 p.58

[558] Clinton, Bill, My Life © William Jefferson Clinton, Arrow Books 2005 p. 890.

[559] Bunton, Martin, The Palestinian-Israeli Conflict A Very Short Introduction © Oxford University Press 2013. Pp. 4-14.

their ancestral land and they returned to it from different parts of the world after being exiled from it during the Ottoman empire. Some accounts say the Jews began to return to Palestine from the late 19th century.[560]

Who really owns the land? Well, a meticulous pry into human development, history and civilisation over several centuries right up to the twentieth century reveals a displacement and replacement of peoples in lands and places over the course of human history, notably during the Roman Empire, Ottoman Empire and British Empire. Both Christianity and Islam which are the two most populous religions of the world today had not conducted their earlier crusades in holiness, love and peace, taking due cognizance of the fact that a place like Istanbul today was for centuries a major Christian centre and city called Constantinople. However, as discussed in Chapter 5 of this book, it became Istanbul upon Islamic conquest of the Christians and people of the city. The United States of America's European Christian settlers in the Americas in the middle of the second millennium AD were Christians who simply displaced the native-Americans and forcefully took over their lands. Against this backdrop, it is unrealistic to attempt to find a solution to the Israeli - Palestinian conflict by simply trying to establish a historic ownership of the land. The truth as Bill Clinton put it is that, history "is being constantly rewritten".[561] However the liberty of history being constantly rewritten should not be deployed as a negative freedom to deliberately attempt to distort the truth and more so, in this case of the Israeli-Palestinian conflict, to disparage the Christian faith and religion whose adherents in the twenty-first century do not see it as their duty to violently defend the God of the Bible and the sacredness of their Scriptures. Some emerging facts are indicative of the fact that the exercise of negative freedom in writing history could lead to a reckless display of barbarism of intellect which would not serve the best interest of humanity in general, and in resolving this conflict in particular. Several historians have written about the Israeli-Palestinian conflict and some make quite a lot of interesting reading. But the trajectory of Nur Masalha's own account of the existence of Palestine in the last four thousand years goes beyond a historical account to an unreasonable attack of the Holy Bible, the sacred Scriptures of the Christian religion, and it violates the religious

---

[560]   Ibid.

[561]   Bill Clinton as in footnote 550.

beliefs that not only Jews but Christian adherents hold on to as sacred religious beliefs, that are as a matter of fact internationally protected human rights. Masalha asserts:

> that the legends of the 'Israelites' conquest of Cana'an' and other master narratives of the Old Testament (or 'Hebrew Bible') – a library of books built up across several centuries – are myth-narratives designed to underpin false consciousness, not evident-based history...[562]

That assertion is not only unreasonable but evident of what was bound to come out of the wild goose chase of writing history that covers a four thousand years period in one man's life span of under 100 years with less than 60 years of a career as a historian.

However, Masalha demolishes the validity of his own historical account by citing Friedrich Nietzsche's position:

> that history is always written from and within a particular perspective and the past looks different from different perspectives, although some perspectives are empirically more truthful or less distorting than others.[563]

Clearly, Masalha chose the 'distorting' and 'less truthful' perspective of account in the way he has summed up the 'Old Testament books' of the Holy Bible as 'false narratives.' Otherwise, why would the prophets who were known for their piety by the people of their generations and were inspired of God over hundred years apart write down 'false narratives'? Was it to create a crisis four thousand years later? How could 'false narratives' give rights to any party in the present conflict of one hundred years? Any effort to examine why the Old Testament of the Bible could have been "based on myth -narratives designed to underpin false consciousness" as Masalha asserts makes his inference transparently reckless and absolutely bogus. Does the absence of a present day, evidence of events of over three thousand years ago make the accounts of the history of that time written by eye witnesses and handed down through

---

[562] Masalha, Nur, Palestine A Thousand Year History © 2018 Reprinted by I.B. Tauris in 2022, 2024 pp.2-3.

[563] Ibid. p.1.

the generations untrue? No, not necessarily so. Sacred events and their accounts do not necessarily have to be predicated on physical evidence before they would be accepted as historical truths by those who hold religious beliefs connected with it; and by those who have respect for the sanctity of religion. Even in the cases where physical evidence and facts had been available when it happened such evidence may erode or dissipate with time and not be visible after hundreds of years, let alone thousands of years later. Religion, beliefs and spirituality are matters that go beyond our finite minds' absolute comprehension and therefore beyond what the best of historians can comprehend from research and natural analysis after several thousands of years in the effort to prove the historical validity of its Scriptures. That is why they are deemed sacred and treated as religious beliefs which are protected human rights.

At the heart of the Statehood of Israel and the Statelessness of the Palestinians is the plan of the United Nations for the establishment of two states in 1947: A State for the Arab Palestinians; and a State of Israel for the Jews. While the State of Israel accepted the UN 1947 plan for the partition of Palestine into two states and proclaimed the independence of the State of Israel in May 1948 based on the UN plan, the Arab Palestinians rejected the plan with its offer of Statehood because they felt it was unjust for them to share the territory with the State of Israel. At the same time, they decided that they would not allow the State of Israel to exist and so embarked on arms conflict to annihilate the Jews and the State of Israel.

Historically, the foundation for the creation of the State of Israel in 1948 came about on the backdrop of the 1897 Basel Congress of the World Zionist Organization convened by Theodor Herzl[564] and it inspired what has become known as the Balfour Declaration of 1917. Almost as soon the British took the reins of power over the Middle East from the Ottoman government in 1917, the then British Foreign Secretary Arthur Balfour wrote a letter to Lord Rothschild, a prominent British Jew leader stating that the British would establish a national home land for the Jews in Palestine. Although the letter clearly stated that:

---

[564] Bunton, Martin, The Palestinian-Israeli Conflict. p. 1.

nothing shall be done which may prejudice the civil and religious rights of the existing non

-Jewish communities in Palestine[565]

the contrary has happened. The Palestinians, like any other people that believe that they are being deprived of what they believe is their possession decided to fight for their possession rather than just accept what fate was thrusting upon them following the UN 1947 Partitioning Plan of the territory for two states.

Understandably, the fact that the State of Israel came into existence with the help of Zionists Christians made the Arab Muslim states to also give support to the Arab Palestinians to take over the land from Israel by acts of aggression and violence. But this has brought severe detriment to the Arab Palestinians over the decades.

While the Arab states except Iran have come to the realisation that negotiation is the best way to resolve the Israeli-Palestinian conflict and the Palestinian Liberation Organization under its late leader Yasser Arafat and the current President of Palestine, Mahmoud Abbas decided to resolve the conflict by negotiation, two other organizations in Palestine have vowed to continue the violent path obviously at the expense of the lives and properties of Palestinian civilians: (1) the Harakat al-Muqawamah al-Islamiyyah, popularly known as Hamas, and (2) the Palestine Islamic Jihad.

It is a matter for the Palestinians and Arab states to convince both Hamas and Palestine Islamic Jihad that it is only negotiations that will lead to a quicker possible full statehood for the State of Palestine rather than acts of violence and aggression to destroy the State of Israel. They need to also be told that they do not have what it takes to destroy the State of Israel as their attacks on Israel have always brought greater casualties on Palestinians following Israeli reprisals.

[565] Bunton, Martin, Ibid. p.19.

18.2 The State of Israel and the Practice of Ethnic Nationalism and Religious Nationalism

As discussed above, the State of Israel came into existence on 14 May 1948, following the UN1947 partitioning plan of the then British Mandate of Palestine territory which Jews called Eretz Israel.[566] The population of Israel in 1948 was less than a million people, a mere 806,000[567] people. But today in 2023, it is close to ten million, 9,795,000.[568]

The State of Israel is unique in several ways because it manifestly practices a democratic government that so far produces only ethnic Jewish persons as presidents or prime ministers. And this has been the case from the time of its creation in 1948, and it will remain so for the foreseeable future hence, even with its democracy, it is appropriate to view it as an ethnic-nationalistic state. Israel effectively practises a democracy that is simultaneously driven by both ethnic-nationalism and religious nationalism. This is more so the case because a non-Jewish person cannot emerge as a democratically elected prime minister of Israel or President of Israel. Even though people may acquire Israeli nationality by naturalisation they cannot acquire Jewish ethnic identity as would be the case with someone that have naturalised to be a British citizen or American citizen. Jewishness is an ethnic identity and not what anyone can acquire, if he chooses to naturalise as an Israeli or even chooses Judaism as a religion. In places where religious nationalism is the form of government such as the Islamic State of Pakistan, the adherent to the Islamic religion gives you every right but in Israel the adherent to Judaism does not give a non-ethnic Jewish person the rights of a Jew. Hence, its ethnic-nationalism has a peculiarity capable of promoting second class citizenships in the State of Israel. However, it is quite within the democratic government of the State of Israel to address the incongruences that ethnic nationalism places on its citizens and ensure that all Israelis have equal rights in law and practice.

---

[566] Eretz Israel is Hebrew meaning land of Israel.

[567] See the Vital Statistics of Israel on the Jewish Virtual Library: https://www.jewishvirtuallibrary. org/population-of-israel-1948-present

[568] Ibid.

While Israel has established its sovereign state since 1948, the Arab Palestinians who were the majority that lived in the then British mandate of Palestine during the centuries of the Ottoman empire are yet to achieve the status of full statehood on the part of the territory that the United Nations defined for the State of Arab Palestine in 1947. And the consequence of the Arab Palestine's living side by side with the State of Israel without an independent State of their own is that it brews and ferments conflicts with accompanying gross violations of human rights, and escalating loss of lives, mostly on the Palestinian side over the years. Every effort to secure permanent peace has so far been elusive as the discussions that follow in the subsequent sections of this chapter will show.

18.3 The Oslo Accords, the Arab Peace Initiative and the Missed Opportunities for an Independent Palestinian State

Violence is a vicious, contagious disease, easily spread.[569]

While Palestinians blame Christian Zionists for their fate over the past 125 years, it has to be said that western nations with Christian religious affiliations led by the United States of America have also been at the forefront of the search for a peaceful solution to the Israeli-Palestinian conflict; and the need to grant the status of full statehood to the Palestinians, so as to achieve equity.

Between 1964 and 1993, the Palestine Liberation Organization, PLO, under the leadership of the late Yasser Arafat was the internationally recognised organization that led the fight for the self-determination and the sovereign state of Arab Palestine over the entire once mandatory Palestine territory that includes the State of Israel. By 1988, the PLO shifted ground from that of wanting to destroy the Jewish State of Israel to that of granting it recognition. The PLO leadership under Arafat did so in accordance with UN Security Council Resolution 242[570] of November 1967 and therefrom engaged in peaceful negotiations with Israel.

---

[569] Sirleaf, Ellen Johnson, This Child Will Be Great. P.143

[570] See UN Security Council Resolution 242: https://www.securitycouncilreport.org/un-documents/document/ip-s-res-242.php

The State of Israel that had initially refused to negotiate with the Arab Palestinians on the ground that they threaten its existence also accepted to have talks with the PLO officials, once the PLO recognised its right to exist. In what turned out as a grand opportunity for the Palestinians to have a sovereign state of their own, the Israelis and the Palestinians under the PLO leadership had talks in Oslo, Norway, in August 1993 and reached an agreement which became known as the 1993 Oslo Accords. In what was a moment of hope for a lasting peace between Israel and Palestine and for the peace loving people of the world, who wish to see an end to the almost annual gross violations of human rights and killings between Israelis and Palestinians the Palestinian and Israelis signed the Oslo Accords on 13 September 1993, in the White House Lawn in Washington DC before Bill Clinton, then President of the United States. It was followed by handshakes between the leader of the Palestinian delegation under the PLO leader Yasser Arafat and Yitzhak Rabin, then Prime Minister of Israel.[571]

However, the 1993 Oslo Accords and all that it promised to offer the Palestinians towards Statehood were antagonised by Hamas, who were in disagreement with the Palestinian Liberation Organization and from 1994, Hamas began to orchestrate acts to disrupt the peace process and the success of the Oslo Accords. To Hamas, it was not a matter of interest that the Palestinians would know peace and eventually have a State of their own, if the terms of the Oslo Accords were followed to full implementation. They took every action that would lead to the failure of the peace process including precipitating reckless acts of violence within that time to creating crises between Israelis and Palestinians. Hamas' disappointing role is well summed up in Rashid Khalidi's book, where he stated that:

> between 1994 and 2000 Hamas and Islamic Jihad had pioneered the use of suicide bombers inside Israel as part of their campaign against the Oslo Accords, killing 171 Israelis in 27 bombings.[572]

---

[571] See the signing of the Oslo Accords in the White House, Washington DC in My Life © Bill Clinton 2004, 2005.Pp. 542-544.

[572] Khalidi, Rashid, The Hundred Years' War on Palestine, A History of Settler Colonialism and Resistance, 1917 – 2017 © 2020 Picador Metropolitan Books. P. 214.

Following the failure of the full implementation of the Oslo Accords as a result of the Hamas and Palestine Islamic Jihad initiated violence and the conflict that followed, other measures to restore peace included 2002 Arab Peace Initiative otherwise referred to as the Taba accords.

With the failure of the Oslo Accords came increase in Jewish settlements, occupying parts of the Palestine's designated territory under international law based on the 1947 boundary lines defined by the United Nations as per the UN General Assembly Resolution 181 (II) of 1947. The occupation of these Palestine areas has not only led to provocations of the Palestinians in the areas but also to serious sporadic wars that claimed lives and exacerbated gross human rights violations, giving justification to Hamas and Palestine Islamic Jihad's acts of terrorism against Israelis, which have brought responses from the Israel Defence Forces that have been often disproportionate and alarming because Israel is not able to get to Hamas and Islamic Jihad agents without causing damage to civilian properties and destruction of the lives of ordinary Palestinians. This is the conundrum that is causing the deaths of Israelis and more so Palestinians against the norms and rules of international law, international humanitarian law, and international human rights law.

18.4 The Hamas terrorists attack of 7 October 2023 on the State of Israel and its Existential threat to Palestinians.

What begins with the failure to uphold the dignity of one life, all too often ends with a calamity for entire nations.

In this new century, we must start from the understanding that peace belongs not only to States or peoples, but to each and every member of those communities. The sovereignty of States must no longer be used as a shield for gross violations of human rights. Peace must be sought, above all, because it is the condition for every member of the human family to live a life of dignity and security.[573]

From the time of its formation in 1987, Harakat al-Maquwamah al-Isamiyyah, popularly known as Hamas, which the United States, the

---

[573] Annan, Kofi, Nobel Lecture delivered in Oslo on 10 December 2001: https://www.un.org/sg/en/content/sg/speeches/2001-12-10/nobel-lecture-delivered-kofi-annan

United Kingdom, the European Union, and Canada, consider as a terrorist organization because of its violent resistance to what it deems Israeli occupation of the historic Palestine"[574], stated its mission and goal clearly, which is to completely destroy the independent State of Israel. As stated earlier, this was the reason why it frustrated the PLO and Israel from the full implementation of the 1993 Oslo Accords which would have led to the full independence of the Arab State of Palestine.

Since then sporadic skirmishes have often occurred between Hamas and Israeli forces annually, but what happened on Saturday 7 October, 2023, was far more than the usual skirmishes that people around the world hear and see on television screens about Israelis and Hamas or Palestinians clashes or occasional wars. To the horror of every reasonable person in every part of the world, people woke up to see on television, Facebook or WhatsApp, videoclips of Hamas terrorists entering into the State of Israel and massacring hundreds of young people from different parts of the world who went to a music festival in Israel to enjoy themselves. Some were taken as captives. It was rather strange that the Hamas terrorists did not bother to establish the nationalities of the people they were killing in the music festival and also taking as captives. But then that is the mark of terrorists. Americans, United Kingdom citizens among others and Israelis who were at the scene were either killed or taken as captives. The attack did not stop at the music festival scene. The Hamas terrorists went into Israeli communities and killed elderly people: men, women, and even children including babies that were just a few months old. The height of the terrorists' barbaric acts was seen in their circulations of video-clips of decapitated innocent babies. While the rest of the world were shocked by these images of horror, which took place in clear breaches of international law rules in respect of the territorial sovereignty of a state, international humanitarian law and international human rights law, the only places where there were celebrations for these monstrous acts were various Palestinian cities. There were video-clips of a number of groups of Palestinians celebrating what they saw as Hamas victory over the State of Israel. This was quite strange as most people outside Palestine and Israel territories were concerned about the safety of both Palestinian civilians and Israelis as it was obvious that the Hamas terrorist attacks on the State of Israel and the acts of crimes against humanity and

---

[574] See Hamas: Background and Issues for Congress. December 2, 2010: https://crsreports.congress.gov/product/pdf/R/R41514

gross violations of human rights were bound to provoke war. It was later widely reported that Hamas killed about 1,200 people in Israel including foreign nationals and they also abducted over 200 people and took them into Gaza as hostages. These hostages again included foreign nationals and even Arab Muslims who just happened to have been in Israel for the festival or for some other reasons, and fell into the hands of Hamas and Palestine Islamic Jihad, while they were on their terrorist mission on that Saturday 7 October, 2023.

Quite predictably, the Prime Minister of Israel, Benjamin Netanyahu, announced on that same day, that Israel was at war and the Israeli "military will use all of its strength to destroy Hamas' capabilities."[575]

As Israel embarked on this war against Hamas in Gaza, Hezbollah, the military organisation armed and funded by Iran in Lebanon and labelled as a terrorist organisation by most western nations such as the United States of America and the United Kingdom of Great Britain, started firing rockets into Israel from Lebanon from 8 October, 2023. This was quite strange as it appears to be Hezbollah own invitation for the Israeli Defence Forces to also take the war to them in Lebanon.

Within days of the war, thousands of Palestinian civilians were killed and properties in Gaza were razed down by Israeli Defence Forces (IDF) bombs. People were picked from underneath the rubbles of collapsed and demolished buildings. The IDF said Hamas were using the Palestinian civilians as human shields and areas such as hospitals and schools that were meant to be safe zones under international humanitarian law were places of Hamas operations from which they launched rockets into Israel. While the rockets of Hamas were never reported to kill any Israeli because the IDF stopped the rockets from landing in places of harm, the places from where the rockets were launched enabled the IDF to direct their missiles to the areas and buildings were hit and destroyed, with sometimes hundreds of people killed.

---

[575] See "In a televised address Saturday night, Israeli Prime Minister Benjamin Netanyahu, who earlier declared Israel to be at war..." in "Hamas surprise attack out of Gaza stuns Israel and leaves hundreds dead in fighting, retaliation" by Josef Federman and Issam Adwan, AP World News, October 8, 2023. https://apnews.com/article/israel-palestinians-gaza-hamas-rockets-airstrikes-tel-aviv-11fb98655c256d54ecb5329284fc37d2

It seemed it was of no consequence to Hamas that thousands of Palestinian civilians were dying within days of the war besides the excessive destruction of residential buildings and infrastructures and the displacement of the over 2 million residents of Gaza. As if to prove the level of lack of concern for the alarming deaths of Palestinian civilians and the destruction of properties and displacement of people in Gaza, Osama Hamdan, a member of the Hamas Political Bureau that governed Gaza who was in safety in Lebanon when the Palestinians were dying as a result of the war Hamas has brought upon them, granted a television interview to Al-Jadeed TV in Lebanon. He re-instated the goal of Hamas saying: "Hamas has just one 'no' – no to the existence of Israel."[576]

The rhetoric of the Hamas Political Bureau Member Hamdan at a time that the entire 2.2 million Palestinian residents of Gaza were living in fear and more than half of the population had been displaced and thousands killed in the war, makes those outside the territories of Palestine and Israel wonder whether Hamas is a greater enemy of the Palestinian people than Israel is? And if so, should every protest against Israel for the peace and security of Palestinians be equally a protest against Hamas? There is an immediate necessity for a ceasefire but Hamas are goading Israel to continue the war by their rhetoric and the rockets that they are still firing into Israel daily even though their rockets are often intercepted by the Israeli military defence force.

As at 7 December 2023, the Reuters News Middle East correspondents stated that:

> At least 17,177 Palestinians have been killed …according to the Gaza Health Ministry figures, while 1,200 people were killed in the Hamas incursion into Israel, according to Israeli tallies.[577]

[576] See "Hamas Political Bureau Member Osama Hamdan: We Oppose Just One Thing – The Existence of Israel; We Are Willing To Help The Israelis Go Back To Where They Came From." Al-Jadeed TV (Lebanon). Oct 11, 2023: https://www.memri.org/tv/hamas-official-osama-hamdan-israel-heart-problems-region-return-countries-

[577] See "How many Palestinians have died in Gaza? Death toll explained." Reuters By Ali Sawafta and Maggie Fick, December 7, 2023: https://www.reuters.com/world/middle-east/how-many-palestinians-have-died-gaza-war-how-will-counting-continue-2023-12-06/

Most unfortunately the war continues because Hamas continues to threaten the existence of Israel even though it is apparent that such threats from Hamas are only bringing an ever-increasing death toll on the Palestinians and complete destruction of homes that they have built over many years. Israel is demanding the release of the hostages that Hamas took on 7 October during their terrorist attacks as a prelude for a ceasefire but Hamas have not, for the purpose of saving the destruction of more of Palestinians' properties and more importantly saving Palestinian lives, considered doing so. While it is incumbent upon Israel to show restraint and stop the indiscriminate killing of civilians and destruction of properties in their legitimate war against Hamas, the United Nations have also been making demands for a humanitarian ceasefire. More about this will be discussed in the section that follows.

18.5 The United Nations Enforcement Dysfunction Evidenced in the Case of the State of Palestine

Some of the world's best brains and technocrats are international civil servants with the United Nations Organization Secretariat and its specialised agencies. However, the decision-makers such as members of the General Assembly and those who are to effect, the implementation of policies are sometimes political appointees from member states of the United Nations Organization, who sometimes are not fit for the roles they are appointed to, and therefore become bureaucratic bottlenecks in the system. This can be seen in the events that have preceded the two-states plan by the United Nations General Assembly resolution 181 (II) of 1947 for the Jewish State of Israel and the Arab State of Palestine already discussed above, and the subsequent resolutions of the United Nations General Assembly and the Security Council, respectively, that have had no effect over the years as will be seen in the discussion that will follow.

A lot has been said and written about the wars that have been fought between the time of the partitioning of the then British mandate of Palestine territory in 1947 for a Jewish State of Israel and Arab State of Palestine in 1948 and 2014, when the Palestinians fought wars, initially with intent to destroy the State of Israel, but later as acts of resistance from oppression from Israel. There is no intent to rehearse the stories of those wars here but rather to discuss the extent to which the United

Nations have been unable to effect, the implementations of its resolutions to demonstrate its effectiveness in maintaining international peace and order.

Before delving into facts that show the United Nations as manifestly impaired with enforcement dysfunction, insofar as the Palestine case is concerned, it is also vital to point out one of the grand achievements of the United Nations for the Palestinian people. Following the end of the 1947 and 1948 Palestinian war, the United Nations General Assembly passed Resolution 194 of December 1948[578] to assist Palestinians. Incidentally the Arab states who were members of the United Nations in 1948 voted against the resolution which had been a lifeline for thousands, indeed, millions of Palestinians, since it came into effect in 1949. Although some aspects of the resolution which led to the establishment of the United Nations Conciliation Commission for Palestine (UNCCP)[579] did not achieve its grand purpose such as reaching a final settlement to enable Palestinians return to their homes, it served as a basis for which the United Nations General Assembly Resolution 302 was passed for the establishment of 'The United Nations Relief and Works Agency for Palestine Refugees, (UNRWA), in 1949.[580] There is no doubt about the fact that the UNRWA has done some tremendous work by assisting Palestinians over the past seventy-four years of its existence. However, the fact also that what should have been a short-term agency for assistance of Palestinian refugees to resettle had become a permanent agency is also a reflection of the gaps in policies, decisions and implementation procedures of the United Nations.

However, the real problem underlying the enforcement dysfunction of the United Nations has to do with the passing of resolutions that require the compliance of states that are parties to the United Nations Organization but which such states sometimes disregard without consequences. There appears to be a general inability or lack of will on the part of the United Nations Security Council to apply the relevant articles of the UN Charter in enforcing resolutions that state parties fail to comply

---

[578] See "United Nations The Question of Palestine and the General Assembly" https://www.un.org/unispal/data-collection/general-assembly/#:~:text=The%20question%20of%20Palestine%20was,under%20a%20special%20international%20regime

[579] Ibid.

[580] Ibid.

with. For instance, following the end of the six days 1967 war between Israel and the Arab States of Syria, Jordan and Egypt that joined forces with the Palestinians against Israel and were defeated by Israel within six days, Israel took over Gaza from Egypt, and the West Bank from Jordan, and the Golan Height from Syria. The United Nations Security Council passed Resolution 242[581] (1967) calling on Israel to withdraw from the territories it occupied in the aftermath of the 1967 war. Israel did not comply with that resolution and the United Nations is still suffering from enforcement dysfunction in taking any action to enforce that resolution against Israel. The United Nations General Assembly further addressed the question of Palestine in 1974 and passed Resolution 3236 on 29 November 1974 recognizing the right of the Palestinian people to self-determination that has not led to the full statehood of Palestine.

In December 2003 the Secretary-General of the United Nations officially communicated the decision of the General Assembly for an advisory opinion to the International Court of Justice, ICJ, asking that they advise on:

"What the legal consequences arising from the construction of the wall being built by Israel, the occupying power, in the Occupied Palestinian Territory, including in and around East Jerusalem, as described in the report of the Secretary-General, considering the rules and principles of international law, including the Fourth Geneva Convention of 1949, and relevant Security Council and General Assembly resolutions.[582]

The ICJ took time to establish its jurisdiction to give the requested advisory opinion not least because the State of Israel objected to the ICJ giving the advisory opinion on the grounds that the ICJ could not effectively do so:

[581] See UN Security Council Resolution 242: https://www.securitycouncilreport.org/un-documents/document/ip-s-res-242.php

[582] See International Court of Justice Advisory on the Legal Consequences of the Construction of a Wall in the Occupied Palestinian Territory. https://www.icj-cij.org/sites/default/files/case-related/131/1677.pdf

without enquiries first into the nature and scope of security threat to which the wall is intended to respond.[583]

After the ICJ established that it had jurisdiction to give the required advisory opinion to the General Assembly it went on to examine the facts available to it and concluded that Israel was in breach of international law by constructing the wall. By fourteen votes to one, the ICJ decided on 9 July 2004, that:

> Israel is under obligation to terminate its breaches of international law; it is under obligation to cease forthwith the works of the construction of the wall being built in the occupied Palestinian Territory, including in and around East Jerusalem, to dismantle forthwith the structure therein situated, and to repeal or render ineffective forthwith all legislative and regulatory acts relating thereto, in accordance with paragraph 151 of this opinion. [584]

Judge Buergenthal who was the only Judge that voted against the decision stated in his dissenting opinion that in his view:

> the court should have exercised its discretion and declined to render the requested opinion because it lacked sufficient information and evidence to render the opinion. The absence in this case of the requisite factual basis vitiates the court's sweeping findings on the merits, which is the reason for his dissenting votes.[585]

Although Judge Higgins voted in favour of the decision that Israel has breached international law by the construction of the wall she also expressed reservation in the Court's decision to give the advisory opinion in a separate opinion where she stated inter alia that:

> in her view, a condition elaborated by the court in the Western Sahara Advisory Opinion is not met – namely,

---

[583]   Ibid at para. 55

[584]   Ibid. See para. 163.

[585]   Ibid. See "Declaration of Judge Buergenthal"

that where two states are in dispute, an opinion should not be requested by the General Assembly.[586]

The ICJ sent its advisory opinion to the General Assembly and the evidence of what follows is a proof of the enforcement dysfunction of the Organization.

Following a series of other resolutions, the United Nations General Assembly passed Resolution 67/19 on 29 November 2012 granting observer status to the State of Palestine.[587] But being an observer state does not give the State of Palestine the rights of a state party/member of the United Nations Organization.

With Israel still acting as an occupied power following victories over the wars they have fought to defeat those who say they are going to destroy them, such as Hamas, the conflict between Israel and Palestine seem so intractable that even the United Nations best endeavours appears to achieve little or nothing in turn to make a difference.

As a result of the increasing number of Palestinian casualties in the on-going Israel-Hamas war in Gaza and in order to stem further killings of Palestinian civilians and the destruction of properties in Gaza, the United Nations Secretary-General Antonio Guterres, exercised the powers vested on him under article 99 of the United Nations Charter and sent an urgent letter on 6 December 2023[588] to the President of the United Nations Security Council, requesting that they pass a resolution for an immediate humanitarian ceasefire of the Israel-Hamas war and for immediate and unconditional release of hostages as well as humanitarian access into Gaza.

Although the President of the Security Council convened a meeting of the Security Council on 8 December 2023 with intent to pass a resolution

---

[586] Ibid. See "Separate opinion of Judge Higgins"

[587] See "The United Nations Question of Palestine: https://www.un.org/unispal/data-collection/general-assembly/#:-:text=The%20question%20of%20Palestine%20was,under%20a%20special%20international%20regime

[588] See "The 6 December 2023, Letter of the UN Secretary-General to the President of the UN Security Council: https://www.un.org/sites/un2.un.org/files/sg_letter_of_6_december_gaza.pdf?_gl=1*y02737*_ga*OTI3NDg5NzM0LjE2Njk4MzUxNTg.*_ga_S5EKZKSB78*MTcwMTg5OTY5Mi44LjEuMTcwMTg5OTY5Ny41NS4wLjA.*_ga_TK9BQL5X7Z*MTcwMTg5OTY5My41MTMuMS4xNzAxODk5Njk2LjYwLjAuMC4w

drafted by the United Arab Emirate and backed by over 90 member states, "demanding an immediate humanitarian ceasefire, and the immediate and unconditional release of hostages as well as humanitarian access"[589], the resolution was not passed. While thirteen members of the Security Council voted in favour and the United Kingdom abstained on grounds that the resolution did not condemn the terror attack perpetrated by Hamas on 7 October against Israel[590]. The United States vetoed the resolution on grounds that "all recommendations of the US were ignored leading to an "imbalanced resolution that was divorced from reality."[591] The US stated that it could not understand "why the resolution authors declined to include language condemning "Hamas's horrific terrorist attack" on Israel on 7 October. It killed people from a range of nationalities, subjecting many to "obscene sexual violence."[592]

However, on 12 December 2023, the United Nations General Assembly met in an Emergency Special Session to deliberate on the decades of Israel-Palestine conflict and on the on-going Israel-Hamas war in Gaza[593].

At the Special Session the General Assembly adopted a resolution which was supported by 153 members with only 10 voting against and another 23 states abstaining.[594] The resolution demands "an immediate ceasefire", "the immediate and unconditional release of all hostages and as well as "ensuring humanitarian access."[595] The General Assembly also reiterated its demand that all parties should comply with their obligations under international law, including international humanitarian law, "notably with regard to the protection of civilians."[596]

---

[589] See "United Nations The Question of Palestine, US vetoes resolution on Gaza which calls for 'immediate humanitarian ceasefire." 8 December 2023: https://www.un.org/unispal/document/us-vetoes-resolution-on-gaza-which-called-for-immediate-humanitarian-ceasefire-dec8-2023/

[590] Ibid. See comments of Ambassador Barbara Woodward, Permanent Representative of the United Kingdom to the United Nations.

[591] Ibid. See comments of US Deputy Permanent Representative Robert A Wood.

[592] Ibid.

[593] See "UN General Assembly votes by large majority for immediate humanitarian ceasefire during emergency session 12 December 2023: https://news.un.org/en/story/2023/12/1144717

[594] Ibid.

[595] Ibid.

[596] Ibid.

Though the UN General Assembly resolutions have some moral weight on any given matter, it is not binding, so it was not too surprising that a day following the resolution demanding an immediate ceasefire and release of all hostages, neither a ceasefire nor the release of hostages have taken place. This is indicative that neither Hamas nor Israel, took the UN resolution seriously. In fact, Israel's foreign minister told BBC News correspondent that Israel will continue the war "with or without international support."[597] He stated that: "A ceasefire at this stage of the conflict would be "a gift" to Hamas and allow it to return, Eli Cohen warned."[598]

It has to be said that the inability of the member states of the United Nations to approach things objectively and to reconcile politics with realities when it is necessary to do so have often led to delays in taking actions that would have saved lives, and protected people, in times of conflict from suffering gross violations of human rights. There is no reason why the cause of the Israel-Hamas war such as condemning the Hamas terrorist attack on the State of Israel on 7 October should be omitted from a resolution that seeks to oblige Israel to end the war. The causalities on the Palestinian side are astronomical and so every reasonable compromise should have been reached so that the member states that can influence Israel to end the war, such as the United States should have been able to have some negotiating lever to get Israel to end the war.

Ten days following the UN General Assembly resolution of 12 December 2023, discussed above, the United Nations Security Council eventually passed a resolution to speed up humanitarian aid into Gaza, to free hostages and 'create conditions for 'sustainable cessation of hostilities.' But in absence of emphasis on immediate ceasefire, the UN Security Council resolution 2720 (2023) of 22 December 2023, which recorded a vote of 13 in favour to none against, with 2 abstentions (United States,

---

[597] See "Israel to continue Gaza war with or without international support, FM says" BBC News report by David Gritten and Hugo Bachega, BBC News, London and Jerusalem. https://news.un.org/en/story/2023/12/1144717

[598] Ibid.

Russian Federation)[599], leaves a lot to be desired, because it simply aims at making aid available for the people in Gaza to sustain themselves pending when bombs from Israel or misguided rockets from Hamas will land on them and destroy them, as has been the case, since the war began on 7 October. Rather than dwelling on achieving the passing of resolution 2720 (2023) which did not call for an immediate ceasefire, the energy expended in achieving this resolution should have been expended in persuading Hamas to release the hostages which Israel says is a pre-condition for them to have a ceasefire. With the Israeli Defence Force and Hamas daily exchanging fires, even though the rockets from Hamas never land to kill any Israeli, as they are intercepted by Israeli forces mid-air, more should have been done to get Hamas to realise that their daily rocket fires into Israel are acts provoking Israel to destroy whatever is left of Gaza and the Palestinians in it.

The most serious act in the effort to save Palestinians from continuous destruction in the hands of Israeli Defence Forces in the on-going Israel-Hamas war is the action South Africa has taken against Israel at the International Court of Justice, ICJ.

On 29 December 2023, The Republic of South Africa filed an application instituting proceedings against the State of Israel at the International Court of Justice alleging violations by Israel of its obligations under the Convention on the Prevention and Punishment of Genocide in relation to Palestinians in the Gaza Strip.[600]

In the application, South Africa states that since 7 October, Israel "has failed to prevent genocide and has failed to prosecute the direct and public incitement to genocide". South Africa also made requests for the indication of provisional measures in order to "protect against further, severe and irreparable harm to the rights of the Palestinian people under the Genocide Convention"[601] and to ensure Israel's compliance with its

---

[599] See "Security Council Requests UN Coordinator for Humanitarian Aid to Gaza, Adopting Resolution 2720 (2023) by recorded vote." https://press.un.org/en/2023/sc15546.doc.htm. See also "Full text of UN Security Council resolution calling for Gaza pauses, boost in aid." The Times of Israel, 23 December 2023. https://www.timesofisrael.com/full-text-of-un-security-council-resolution-calling-for-gaza-pause-boost-in-aid/

[600] See 192 – Application of the Convention on the Prevention and Punishment of the Crime of Genocide in the Gaza Strip (South Africa v. Israel) Document Number 192-20231229-PRE-01-00-EN: https://www.icj-cij.org/index.php/node/203395

[601] Ibid.

obligations under the Genocide Convention not to engage in genocide, and to prevent and to punish genocide."[602]

The State of Israel, however, in its response at the International Court of Justice, stated that "South Africa, has regrettably put before the court a profoundly distorted factual and legal picture"[603]. Interestingly, voices from some other member states of the United Nations such as the German government and UK Prime Minister had these to say in support of Israel.

> The German government issued a statement on Friday, saying it expressly rejects the accusation of genocide" against Israel, and that the accusation had "no basis whatsoever.[604]

Similarly,

> A spokesperson for UK Prime Minister Rishi Sunak said Mr Sunak believed South Africa's case was "completely unjustified and wrong.[605]

18.6 Evaluation and Summary

> The just war is the war that must be fought to defend the common good and avert evil; and it must be fought when there is a reasonable prospect of success.[606]

The Israeli – Palestinian conflict is not one that can be resolved by victory in battle or in the war front. If it could be resolved by victory in battle or in the war front, then by now the wars that have been

---

[602] Ibid.

[603] See "Israel says South Africa distorting the truth in ICJ genocide case" BBC Middle East by Raffi Berg in London & Anna Holligan at The Hague. BBC NEWS 12 January 2024: https://www.bbc.co.uk/news/world-middle-east-67944903

[604] Ibid.

[605] Ibid.

[606] Thomas Aquinas is best known for his theory of the Just War in his Five Volumes of The Summa Theologica. What I have stated above is a paraphrase of my summation of Aquinas position in his The Summa Theoligica, hence no page reference quoted.

fought between Israeli and the Palestinians and Arabs in defence of the Palestinians, would have brought an end to the matter. However, the

State of Israel should realise by now that even though they have been victorious in battles and wars over the Palestinians and Arab nations such as Egypt, Jordan, Lebanon and Syria who had either given support to the Palestinians or actually joined them in battle in the past against Israel, they cannot live in peace except they seek to let the Palestinians live in dignity and peace instead of as a defeated and subjugated people. And the Palestinians should realise that whether it is Hamas or any other terrorist organisation that seeks to destroy the State of Israel in the guise of freeing them, they will be plunging them on a mass suicide voyage, as the response of the Israeli Defence Forces to the Hamas gross acts of crimes against humanity on 7 October 2023 in Israel now shows.

Both Israel and Hamas have thrown the international communities under the United Nations Organization the challenge of taking a fresh look at the definition of the use of force in armed conflict when a sovereign nation such as Israel engages a terrorist organization that deliberately uses places such as mosques, churches, and schools that are designated safe zones under international humanitarian law as places from which they could launch attacks towards their enemy, in the hope that they would not receive retaliatory attacks at such places. But the question is, is it safe to conclude that whenever such places are used to launch attacks that they become automatic military targets? Should the international community sanction any organization such as Hamas that uses civilians as shields and launches attack from such places in breach of international humanitarian law in order to ensure that the sanctity of international humanitarian law is maintained in war times?

While the answers to these questions will unfold in the near future by what the United Nations will do at the end of the war, for now, it should be clear to the State of Israel that there should be a need for a change of strategy in the bid to defeat Hamas in order to minimise innocent civilian casualties in Gaza. A government with conscience should show responsibility for respect for international humanitarian law and civilian lives. As for Hamas, it should be clear to them that freedom fighters do not expose their people to the level of destruction that Hamas have exposed Palestinians to. The only people that expose their people to destruction are terrorists. Hamas members should search their consciences as to whether it is worth denying themselves and Palestinians peace and freedom in the quest to destroy the State of Israel, when it is obvious that such pursuit will turn out to be a course on self-destruction.

For the benefit of the Palestinian people, and in order to end the mutually damaging competitive cycle of violence that has so far delayed Palestine from having its own independent sovereign state, the leaders of the various militant factions whether they be Fatah, Hamas or Islamic Jihad and any other group involved in violence should forsake violence and unite to pursue full independence for the State of Palestine.

Unless they choose to do so, it is more difficult for the United Nations, the Arab League or any other external agents to help Palestine attain the status of a sovereign independent state. A lot of things are going wrong in the world in the twenty-first century because there is a drift from applying the benefits of the experience of others in the past to what should be done now. Yasser Arafat decided to give up arms struggle and pursue political negotiations in order to secure the independence of Palestine. The following words of Arafat at the signing of the Oslo Accords in 1993 ought to guide Palestinian leaders today:

> Our people do not consider that exercising the right to self-determination could violate the rights of their neighbours or infringe on their security. Rather, putting an end to feeling of being wronged and of having suffered an historic injustice is the strongest guarantee to achieve coexistence and openness between our two peoples and future generations.[607]

The rhetoric of Hamas as per the interview of Osama Hamdan that was referred to earlier shows that Hamas is not seeking the path of peace but that of violence which is against the wise counsel of Arafat, as per the above quoted statements, which he made during the signing of the Oslo Accords. In the same vein, the leaders of Israel should remember the wise words of Rabin on the same occasion when he stated that:

---

[607]   See Remarks of Yasser Arafat in Bill Clinton, My Life © 2004, 2005 at page 544.

We are destined to live together, on the same soil in the same land. We, the soldiers who have returned from battles stained with blood …., say to you today, … in a loud and clear voice:

Enough of blood and tears. Enough!…We, like you want to build a home, to plant a tree, to love, to live side by side with you in dignity, in affinity as human beings, as free men.[608]

It might be expected that the experience of Rabin that led him to make the above statement during the signing of the Oslo Accords should guide other leaders of Israel in the path of finding lasting peace with the Palestinians. However, the prevailing empirical evidence of daily settlements of Israelis in Palestinian defined territory suggest that due regards is not given to what their past leader Rabin has said as quoted above.

Insofar as the application of South Africa against Israel at the ICJ is concerned, it is plausible that a member state of the United Nations such as South Africa can initiate an action against another state such as Israel with intent to prevent what seems manifestly apparent as acts of genocide in the Israel-Hamas war. However, it is difficult to see how the ICJ can grant the request of South Africa's application by ruling that Israel has committed genocide, mindful of the genocidal attacks by Hamas against Israel on 7 October 2023, and the interview referred to in this chapter about a member of the Hamas Political Bureau still threatening genocide against Israel in the TV interview on 11 October in Lebanon. The intent to commit genocide seems to be more demonstrably evidence by Hamas actions and declarations than that of Israel who have only declared intent to eradicate Hamas. Nevertheless, as per Article 7 (1) (d) and (k), of the International Criminal Court, there are undeniable cases of crimes against humanity committed by Israel in the way they are conducting the war against Hamas in Gaza.

Thousands of Palestinian civilians including children have been killed and others displaced and transferred from their homes.

---

[608] Ibid. The remarks of Yitzhak Rabin.

19

ACTS OF STATES THREATENING INTERNATIONAL PEACE AND SECURITY

Look beneath the surface so you can judge correctly.[609]

19.1 A Stable Society as a Foundation for Human Rights Protection and Enforcement

A lot can be said about the odds against human rights protection and enforcement but one common denominator that affects human rights protection and enforcement is a stable or unstable political and economic condition of a nation-state. A society has to be stable and orderly in order for people to enjoy rights and freedoms. No one can assert their rights in a lawless society that is in anarchy and chaos. In a lawful society where there is public order and security, people enjoy lawful rights in a corresponding order to their respective legal obligations and conducts. For a society to be stable argues the economist Paul Collier:

> Accountability and security are vital: without them a country cannot develop. The societies of the bottom

---

609   John 7:24, Holy Bible, New Living Translation [NLT].

billion have not, individually, been able to supply either accountability or security.[610]

Since human rights are exceptional rights and freedoms that people are universally accorded in a number of cases without any corresponding duty or obligation, in some ways, human rights are like a luxury to people in certain societies where there are conflicts and disorder. The typical example here is the case of Afghanistan discussed in the chapter 16.

However, every nation-state, irrespective of how rich it might be, would face social and economic upheavals from time to time, sometime as a result of its citizens reaction to government policies. So human rights and fundamental freedoms can at such times be suppressed or relegated to the background in a bid to avert anarchy and secure peace and public order. But if it were the case that incidents of human rights violations were occasional minimal occurrences to prevent a state from descending into anarchy, the world would have been more peaceful and secure. The reality is that there are cases where the abuse of office by public officers and those who are heads of government have led to widespread violations of human rights and in some cases crimes against humanity and genocide. Two examples of what occurred during the last decade of the twentieth century might suffice to prove this point. One was what happened following the killing of President Habyarimana of Rwanda whose plane was shot down on April 6, 1994, and closely followed by the killing of Prime Minister Uwilingiyimana of Rwanda on April 6, 1994, and the instance genocide that was unleashed against the Tutsi people of Rwanda.[611] While the Rwandan genocide took place in Africa, the second case was that of gross violations of human rights, crimes against human rights and genocide committed on a large scale in the former Federal Republic of Yugoslavia under President Slobodan Milosevic who was intentionally complicit or deliberately feigned oblivion of the violations of

---

[610] Collier, Paul, WARS, GUNS & VOTES DEMOCRACY IN DANGEROUS PLACES © 2009 p.189. On pages 239 and 240 of the book Professor Collier lists over 30 countries in Sub-Saharan Africa among the bottom billion people in world in the world. Incidentally, human rights protection and enforcement is not given prominence in these countries. Thus, proving the fact that people cannot enjoy human rights in politically and economically unstable countries.

[611] See "The Rwandan Genocide: How It was Prepared", April 7, 1994: Massive Killing Begins A Human Rights Watch Briefing Paper, April 2006, Number 1. https://archive.hrw.org/legacy/backgrounder/africa/rwanda0406/index.htm

human rights, crimes against humanity and genocide which were taking place against the Kosovo Albanians and Bosnian Muslims.[612]

In the case of the former Federal Republic of Yugoslavia, the United Nations reacted by setting up a United Nations International Criminal Tribunal for the former Yugoslavia, ICTY, in 1993 and 161 persons across all the ethnic groups were indicted. The Tribunal functioned from 1993 and closed officially on 27 December 2017. The trial of those who were indicted led to the convictions and sentencing of 91 persons, while 37 indictments were withdrawn, 18 acquitted, and others referred to national jurisdictions. Quite disappointingly, Slobodan Milosevic who was the president of the former Federal Republic of Yugoslavia and 6 others who were indicted for gross human rights violations and genocide died at the International Criminal Tribunal for Yugoslavia in The Hague, before their prosecution and trial could be concluded.[613]

Following the United Nations Security Council Resolution 955, an International Criminal Tribunal for Rwanda, ICTR, was equally established in November 1994 for the prosecution and trial of the people responsible for the genocide in Rwanda.[614]

The ICTR indicted 93 persons. Out of that number, 62 individuals were convicted and sentenced, 14 were acquitted, 10 were referred to national jurisdiction for trial, 3 fugitives were referred to the MICT, 2 died before the judgement while 2 indictments were withdrawn.[615]

While the work of United Nations International Criminal Tribunals for the former Federal Republic of Yugoslavia and Rwanda, respectively, did some commendable work by the prosecution of human rights violators, and those who committed crimes against humanity and genocide, the United Nations has not been able to devise measures to prevent such occurrences in the future. Much as it is important to prosecute and convict those who breach international law norms and commit gross

---

[612] See "Kosovo, Croatia & Bosnia (IT-02-54) SLOBODAN MILOSEVIC", International Criminal Tribunal for the Former Yugoslavia (Case Information Sheet)

[613] The ICTY Indicted 161 Individuals https://www.icty.org/en/cases/key-figures-cases

[614] International Criminal Tribunal for Rwanda, UNICTR. https://www.loc.gov/item/lcwaN0010101/

[615] United Nations International Residual Mechanism for Criminal Tribunals. Legacy Website of the International Criminal for Rwanda. The ICTR in Brief: https://unictr.irmct.org/en/tribunal

violations of human rights, it is far better to prevent the occurrence of such atrocities.

19.2 Russia's invasion of Ukraine and the Threat to International Peace and Order

To ensure that human rights are taken seriously, after the Second World War, the United Nations came up with two treaties on human rights following the Universal Declaration of Human Rights, UDHR, (1948). They are: One, the International Covenant on Economic, Social and Cultural Rights, ICESCR, (1966)[616]; and two, the International Covenant on Civil and Political Rights, ICCPR, (1966).[617]

Much is not often heard about economic, social and cultural rights, as we do about violations of people's civil and political rights. Often, it is only - "Article 1. All peoples have the right to self-determination" - of the International Covenant on Economic, Social and Cultural Rights, that we hear about. On the other hand, we daily hear about mass violations of people's civil and political rights, especially, in places of conflicts. An on-going example is President Vladimir Putin of the Russian Federation decision to invade Ukraine. Not minding the fact that Ukraine is a sovereign state, and not considering the mass and gross violations of human rights that will accompany the invasion, Putin sent in thousands of Russian troops to invade Ukraine on 24 February, 2022. His grounds for the invasion were to "demilitarise and denazify" Ukraine.[618]

Putin further stated that his basis for the invasion of Ukraine was to prevent "Nato from gaining a foothold in Ukraine" and "ensuring Ukraine's neutral status."[619] In essence, based on distrust of what Ukraine

---

[616] International Covenant on Economic, Social and Cultural Rights, ICESCR https://treaties. un.org/Pages/ViewDetails.aspx?src=IND&mtdsg_no=IV-3&chapter=4

[617] International Covenant on Civil and Political Rights, ICCPR https://treaties.un.org/doc/ publication/unts/volume%20999/volume-999-i-14668-english.pdf

[618] Kirby, Paul, "Has Putin's war failed and what does Russia want from Ukraine? Russia – Ukraine war. BBC News Europe 24 February: https://www.bbc.co.uk/news/world-europe-56720589

[619] Ibid.

as a sovereign state may choose to do with NATO, Putin decided to unleash a force of terror that has caused the displacement of 13 million[620] Ukrainians who are either displaced in their country or are refugees abroad following the invasion. More serious is the fact that thousands of people on both sides have died as a consequence of Putin's invasion of Ukraine. "The UN human rights commissioner says at least 8,006 civilians have died and 13,287 have been wounded in 12 months of the war, but the true number is likely to be substantially higher."[621]

At the global level, the impact of Russia's invasion of Ukraine has taken several nations of the world by surprise and the economic consequences and deaths that must have followed will remain incalculable. The World Bank confirmed this in a Press Release saying:

> Russia's invasion of Ukraine has triggered one of the biggest human displacement crises and exacted a heavy toll on human and economic life," said Anna Bjerde, World Bank Vice President for the Europe and Central Asia region." Ukraine continues to need enormous financial support as the war needlessly rages on as well as for recovery and reconstruction projects that could be quickly initiated.
>
> The global economy continues to be weakened by the war through significant disruptions in trade and food and fuel price shocks, all of which are contributing to high inflation and subsequent tightening in global financing conditions.[622]

The United Nations response to Russia's invasion of Ukraine and the gross violation of human rights and associated crimes against humanity that has taken place has not been effective so far, though the UN has strongly condemned the invasion. On the eve of the second year of the invasion it held

---

[620]   Ibid.

[621]   Ibid.

[622]   "Russian Invasion of Ukraine Impedes Post-Pandemic Economic Recovery in Emerging Europe and Central Asia." https://www.worldbank.org/en/news/press-release/2022/10/04/russian-invasion-of-ukraine-impedes-post-pandemic-economic-recovery-in-emerging-europe-and-central-asia

an emergency session and its General Assembly adopted a resolution demanding that the "Russian Federation Withdraw Military Forces"[623] from Ukraine.

19.3 Sudan: The War of the Generals at the Expense of National Security and Peace

But the forces that are compounding the violations of human rights, orchestrating incidents of crimes against humanity and threatening the peace of the world are not just dictators like Putin. They are also people that want to achieve political power and authority at all costs, as we are seeing in Sudan where two self-seeking rival army generals have decided to visit the citizens and people of Sudan with an arms conflict that has resulted in gross violations of human rights and crimes against humanity, since 15 April, 2023. Rather than facilitate a smooth transition to a democratic government, the two factions of armed forces in Sudan led by General Abdel Fattah al-Burhan, the country's de facto ruler and the Rapid Support Forces (RSF), led by General Mohammed Hamdan Dagalo, known as Hemedti, have engaged in a war of attrition to the detriment of all who are resident in Sudan.[624]

While the two Sudanese army generals should be principally held responsible for this unnecessary armed conflict and the gross violations of human rights that was occasioned by it, the fact remains that Sudan is not known to be a major arms manufacturer. It is therefore the case that nations with arms industries that are supplying the arms with which the war is being fought should be held to be complicit in the violations of human rights and crimes

---

[623] See "Eleventh Emergency Special Session 18th & 19th Meetings (AM + PM) GA/12492 23 February 2023 "Hours Before Ukraine Conflict Enters Second Year, General Assembly Adopts Resolution Demanding Russian Federation Withdraw Military Forces." https://press.un.org/en/2023/ga12492.doc.htm

[624] For a background understanding to the conflict see: - Adam Fulton and Oliver Holmes "Sudan Conflict: Why is there fighting and what is at stake in the region? Power struggle between military factions erupted after faltering transition to civilian led-government" The Guardian, Explainer, Thursday, 27 Apr 2023: https://www.theguardian.com/world/2023/apr/27/sudan-conflict-why-is-there-fighting-what-is-at-stake#:~:text=A%20central%20cause%20of%20tension,into%20the%20regular%20armed%20forces

against humanity that is taking place now in Sudan, even if these arms industries and their dealers are situated in superpower nations such as the United States and Russia. Unless those who supply arms to people involved in morally unjustified conflicts such as what is now seen in Sudan are also held responsible for crimes against humanity and human rights violations, protection and respect for human rights will remain an elusive and theoretical concept in most places of the world.

19.4 The United States and Acts of Gross Violations of Human Rights

With the Two World Wars fought in the first half of the twentieth century, many might have thought that world leaders have learnt their lessons from history and so the twenty-first century will be a century of peace. Well, such thoughts became illusions from the very start of the twenty-first century. An international conflict and war in the very first year of the first decade started as a result of Osama bin Laden's al-Qaeda attacks on the World Trade Center in New York and the Pentagon, on September 11, 2001, as discussed in chapter 16 on Afghanistan.

While the US led forces to invade Afghanistan for harbouring Osama bin Laden and that war against al-Qaeda was on-going, it also ordered the invasion of Iraq on the allegation that the then President of Iraq, Saddam Hussein, was developing Weapons of Mass Destruction (WMD). In agreement with the assertion of US President George W Bush, the then British Prime Minister, Tony Blair, stated that it was "beyond doubt" that Saddam Hussein was continuing to produce WMD."[625] However, not all the European nations bought into the story of invading Iraq on the grounds that Saddam Hussein was developing weapons of mass destruction. The then French Foreign Minister Dominique de Villepin for instance stated that "military intervention would be "the worst possible solution."[626] Mr Dominique de Villepin turned out to be prophetic but as it is often the case with prophets, their expressions and advice is never taken seriously.

---

[625]   "Why did the U.S. and allies invade Iraq, 20 years? BBC World News 20 March 2023: https://www.bbc.co.uk/news/world-64980565

[626]   Supra.

After their overthrow of the Saddam Hussein's government and the destabilisation of Iraq as a sovereign state in international law, the United States and United Kingdom then stated that they did not find any weapons of mass destruction and they had acted on a false intelligence report. However, between the time of the invasion of Iraq in 2003 and 2011, when the US troops and their allied forces withdrew from Iraq, "it is estimated that 461,000 people died in Iraq from war-related causes between 2003 and 2011 and that the war cost the US $3 trillion."[627]

The displacement of millions of Iraqis as a result of the invasion and the gross human rights violations and crimes against humanity that were committed in Iraq during the period of invasion and after because of the instability caused by the invasion is yet to be accounted for.

As the American forces withdrew from Iraq in 2011, after destabilising the country completely following their invasion, the United States had another president because George W Bush had completed his constitutional tenure as president. The president in power after Bush was Barack Obama, a son of a Kenyan man who many thought, might make a difference in promoting better relationships between the United States and African nations, mindful of his African roots in Kenya, did exactly the opposite. However, as the US sought to assert and exert its power globally as the major super power, consideration and respect for human rights protection seemed like an inconsequential matter. President Obama set out to have his presidential turn of invasion but this time he picked on Libya.[628] Under Muammar Gaddafi, Libya was the only African nation that had a stable economy and its citizens lived in conditions that were better than some citizens of the United States in the US.

To get what would be accepted as a legitimate ground for invasion of Libya whose president Muammar Gaddafi had ruled for over forty years as at 2011, President Obama sponsored and secured a UN Security Council Resolution 1973 to go into Libya and protect the Libyan people from Gaddafi's "crackdown".[629] Protesters in Libya were taking their cue

---

[627] Supra.

[628] See Kuperman, Alan J., "Obama's Libya Debacle How a Well-Meaning Intervention Ended in Failure" Foreign Affairs March/April 2015. https://www.foreignaffairs.com/articles/libya/2019-02-18/obamas-libya-debacle

[629] Supra

from the Arab Spring that had brought about changes of governments in some of the North African states and Gaddafi were resisting being a victim to it.

On the order of President Obama, in March 2011, the United States and NATO allied forces entered Libya under the code name of "Operation Unified Protector (OUP)[630] and by 20 October 2011, Muammar Gaddafi was killed and Operation United Protector "was successfully concluded on 31 October 2011."[631] Libya has not been able to return to political stability and order since 31 October 2011, and no one in the international community has raised the issue of crimes against humanity and gross human rights violations against those who ordered the invasion that had caused gross violations of human rights and crimes against humanity. What was tagged "Operation Unified Protector" by the then US President Obama and the NATO led forces can be correctly described in every respect as "Operation Unified Destruction" of Libya.

The forces that are impinging on the protection and enforcement of human rights and posing threats to international peace and order are not just dictators like the executed Saddam Hussein or assassinated Muammar Gaddafi. The actions of some the presidents of United States such as George W Bush and Barack Obama, as discussed above, show that their orders for invasions of Iraq and Libya, respectively, were void of plans for the peace and security of these states to ensure the protection and enforcement of human rights. By their actions it would be correct to say secular democracy is just as harmful as military dictatorships, if elected leaders cannot be held accountable for such evil as crimes against humanity and gross violations of human rights.

19.5 China's Passive Threats to International Peace and Order

The People's Republic of China for almost the entire second half of the twentieth century was known for gross violations of human rights of its citizens, especially, unlawful detentions and killings. However, China

---

[630] See "NATO and Libya" (Archived) 09 Nov 2015: https://www.nato.int/cps/en/natohq/topics_71652.htm

[631] Supra

appears to have made some improvement on its human rights record just before the entrance of the twenty-first century.

A visit by the United Nations High Commissioner for Human Rights Michelle Bachelet is indicative of a measure of improvement of China's human rights records as the following excerpts from the High Commissioner Statement on the 28 May 2022, suggests:

> For the first time in 17 years, a UN High Commissioner for Human Rights has been able to travel to China and speak directly with the most senior Government officials in the country, and other interlocutors on key human rights issues, in China and globally.
>
> We also agreed to establish a working group to facilitate substantive exchanges and cooperation between my office and Government through meeting in Beijing and in Geneva, as well as virtual meetings. This working group will organize a series of follow-up discussions about specific thematic areas, including but not limited to development, poverty alleviation and human rights, rights of minorities, business and human rights, digital space and human rights, judicial and legal protection and human rights, as well as other issues raised by either side.[632]

But if China's human rights record concerning how it deals with her citizens is improving, the threat it poses to the international community is rising with its claim over Taiwan.[633] China is asserting the intention to take over Taiwan without the consent of the Taiwanese people, which is clearly in violation of international law and the United Nations Charter. Although, the United Nations General Assembly Resolution 2758 passed on 25 October 1971, subjects Taiwan to the sovereignty of the People's Republic of China, Taiwan still has the right to self-determination under international law and under the UN Charter. Rather than seize Taiwan as its territory by military fiat as China threatens to do, it should conduct

---

[632] "Statement by UN High Commissioner for Human Rights Michelle Bachelet after official visit to China 28 May 2022: https://www.ohchr.org/en/statements/2022/05/statement-un-high-commissioner-human-rights-michelle-bachelet-after-official

[633] Brown, David, "China and Taiwan: A really simple guide. BBC News China 6 April 2023: https://www.bbc.co.uk/news/world-asia-china-59900139

a referendum in Taiwan to see if the majority of the Taiwanese people are inclined to becoming a province of China as opposed to being a sovereign state as they have been seeking to do and are legally entitled to do. In the absence of a referendum that will show the decision of the Taiwanese people as to whether or not they want to be a part of the People's Republic of China, any act by China to take over Taiwan will amount to an act of aggression that may result to international conflict in breach of international peace and security.

19.6 North Korea: Perpetrator of Crimes against Humanity and Threat to International Peace and Security

It is impossible to write about human rights violations and crimes against humanity by a State and not cite North Korea as the foremost case. No other nation-state in modern history has the catalogue of human rights abuses and crimes against humanity that are ascribed to the Democratic People's Republic of Korea popularly known as North Korea.

The following excerpts from a 2013 UN Commission of Inquiry[634] on human rights violations in the Democratic People's Republic of Korea (DPRK) tell the story of the sad state of affair there.

> GENEVA (17 February 2014) – A wide array of crimes against humanity, arising from "policies established at the highest level of State," have been committed and continue to take place in the Democratic People's Republic of Korea, according to a UN report released Monday, which also calls for urgent action by the international community to address the human rights situation in the country, including referral to the International Criminal Court.[635]
>
> The gravity, scale and nature of these violations reveal a State that does not have any parallel in the contemporary world," the Commission – established by the Human

---

[634] For a more detailed read of the report of the 2013 UN Commission of Inquiry on human rights in DPRK, see: https://www.ohchr.org/en/press-releases/2014/02/north-korea-un-commission-documents-wide-ranging-and-ongoing-crimes-against?LangID=E&NewsID=14255

[635] Supra

Rights Council in March 2013 – says in a report that is unprecedented in scope.

These crimes against humanity entail extermination, murder, enslavement, torture, imprisonment, rape, forced abortions and other sexual violence, persecution on political, religious, racial and gender grounds, the forcible transfer of populations, the enforced disappearance of persons and the inhumane act of knowingly causing starvation," the report says, adding that "Crimes against humanity are ongoing in the Democratic People's Republic of Korea because the policies, institutions and patterns of impunity that lie at their heart remain in place.[636]

It is estimated that between 80,000 and 120,000 political prisoners are currently detained in four large political prison camps, where deliberate starvation has been used as a means of control and punishment. Gross violations are also being committed in the ordinary prison system, according to the Commission's findings...

The Commission also found that, since 1950, the "State's violence has been externalized through State-sponsored abductions and enforced disappearances of people from other nations. These international enforced disappearances are unique in their intensity, scale and nature.[637]

In a letter to Kim Jong-un, the Commissioner stated that it would recommend referral of the situation in DPRK to the International Court "to render accountable all those, including possibly yourself, who may be responsible for the crimes against humanity referred to in this letter and in the Commission's report.[638]

While the issues stated in the UN Commission of Inquiry report about gross violations of human rights and crimes against humanity have remained unaddressed by the North Korean supreme leader Kim

---

[636]   Supra

[637]   Supra

[638]   Supra

Jong-un's government, the DPRK has taken to another height disregard for international peace and order by posing threats to international peace and security through ballistic missiles testing. The DPRK has been launching nuclear missile tests to the discomfort of its neighbouring countries such as South Korea officially known as the Republic of Korea.

In 2022 DPRK launched a series of missiles following its nuclear testing to the disturbance of the international community. The United Kingdom Ambassador to the United Nations, Ambassador Dame Barbara Woodward DCMG OBE in a speech on 4 November 2022, to the United Nations Security Council, asked the Council to take steps to "urge DPRK to end these provocations"[639] and threats to international peace and security.

North Korea's simultaneous acts of internal gross violations of the human rights of its own citizens and the external threats to the international community have reached such an inexplicable despicable level that if the United Nations Security Council and the United Nations General Assembly together with States parties that make up the United Nations Organization fail to act decisively, the international community will have no one to blame at what might befall it from the DPRK. As recent as May 2023, Isabel Keane of the New York Post reported that:

> A two-year-old North Korean was sentenced to life in prison after officials found a Bible in the toddler's parents' possession, as the totalitarian regime continued to "execute" and "torture" religious worshippers.[640]

A world in which a two years old boy would spend his entire life in prison because his parents were found with a religious book – the Christian Holy Bible - is a lawless country that flagrantly disregards international

---

[639] "These actions are an unacceptable threat to international peace and security." Statement by Ambassador Barbara Woodward at the Security Council open briefing on the Democratic People's Republic of Korea's Ballistic Missile Test. From: Foreign, Commonwealth & Development Office and Dame Barbara Woodward DCMG OBE. Published 4 November 2022: https://www.gov.uk/government/speeches/these-actions-are-an-unacceptable-threat-to-international-peace-and-security

[640] Keane, Isabel, "North Korea toddler, parents jailed for life after being caught with Bible." New York Post. May 28, 2023: https://nypost.com/2023/05/28/north-korea-toddler-parents-jailed-for-life-after-being-caught-with-bible/ Isabel Keane's report refers to a new International Religious Freedom Report by US State Department that can be read at: https://www.state.gov/reports/2022-report-on-international-religious-freedom/north-korea/

law and norms and cannot be safe for anyone. It brings to bear the remark by Johan Galtung that 'to the man with a hammer the world looks like a nail.'[641] Invariably, the same lawless country that degrades and tortures its citizens will in a matter of time turn on the rest of the world, if not checked, because lawlessness has no limits to barbaric and destructive acts.

19.7 Australia and the Constitutional Degradation of the Indigenous (Aboriginal) and Torres Strait Islander Peoples

The international community under the auspices of the United Nations appears to turn its attention to human rights violations mostly to places where oppressed people have resorted to arms conflicts or outright war against their oppressors. This method of pursuing human rights protection and enforcement obliquely makes acts of arms conflict attractive to those who are oppressed and want the human rights addressed. While the principle of respect for the sovereignty of the state and non-interference in the internal affairs of a state is sacrosanct in international law, a situation such as in Australia where the Constitution was deliberately written to the effect that the indigenous peoples "were considered a "dying race" not worthy of citizenship or humanity"[642] and are degraded without being mentioned in the constitution should not be acceptable in the twenty-first century to the rest of humanity and the comity of nations.

About one million[643] people today are descendants of people who have been disregarded as human beings since 1901 when the constitution of Australia was created. But this should now be a matter for the concern of the international committee as it breaches Australia's international human rights law enforcement obligations.

---

[641] Galtung, Johan, Peace by Peaceful Means © SAGE Publications Ltd 1996 p.268.

[642] See "The Indigenous World 2023: Australia" especially, the section on "Referendum on constitutional recognition." Written on 30 March 2023. https://www.iwgia.org/en/australia/5143-iw-2023-australia.html#:-:text=The%20Aboriginal%20population%20in%20Australia,the%20total%20population%20of%2024%2C220%2C200

[643] Ibid. The figure given as the population of the Aboriginal and Torres Strait peoples (otherwise indigenous peoples) is 984,000 as at 30 June 2021.

The extents to which the degrading and inhuman treatments of the indigenous (Aboriginal) and Torres Strait Islander peoples have reached has not been a matter of secrecy. According to a BBC Australia News report:

> In the past three decades, more than 400 Aboriginal people have died in custody, either being held in prisons or under the arrest of the police – despite findings and recommendations from a national inquiry in 1991. Many have died under suspicious circumstances, some due to negligence or lack of medical assistance. No-one was convicted for any of these deaths.[644]

In the same report it is stated that:

> In February 2008, then-Prime Minister Kevin Rudd formally apologised to Australia's indigenous people for the policies that have caused centuries of continued suffering and in which the police have played a big part.
>
> It was a key moment. But for many, the moment passed with no real change.[645]

The apology by the then Prime Minister Kevin Rudd was made in 2008 but 12 years later in 2020, as the BBC News report shows:

> the justice system has unfairly targeted young Aboriginal people..[646]

> While indigenous Australians make up less than 3% of the population, they represent more than a quarter of adult prisoners.[647]

---

[644] See "Aboriginal Australians 'still suffering effects of colonial past' BBC Australia News Report by Shaimaa Khalil, BBC News, Sydney. 16 July 2020. https://www.bbc.co.uk/news/world-australia-53436225

[645] Ibid. See the section entitled: "The Stolen Generations."

[646] Ibid.

[647] Ibid. See the section entitled: "Colonial roots."

Massacres and jailing of indigenous Australians enabled British settlement here from the late 18th century.[648]

The Australian government in its interactive dialogue on 24 September 2020 with Mr Francisco Cali Tzay, the United Nations Special Rapporteur on Rights of Indigenous People simply reaffirmed "its support for the UN Declaration on the Rights of Indigenous Peoples."[649] However, as at date, 26 December 2023, nothing manifestly evident has been done to accord the indigenous peoples the rights of citizens of Australia, in the constitution of Australia. Effectively, the indigenous people of Australia are stateless in their own ancestral lands.

19.8 Evaluation and Summary

Besides the case of Australia which as at now in the twenty-first century is still depriving the indigenous people in their ancestral homes in its territory, the rights of citizens as enshrined in the constitution, the discussions in this chapter evidently show that the main perpetrators of human rights violations are the states that are Super powers. Though the worst violator, North Korea cannot be categorised as a superpower but the states presently known as superpowers such as the United States, China, and the Russian Federation are as well violators of human rights and perpetrators of crimes against humanity in quite despicable ways.

A world where the most powerful states can decide to invade the less powerful and destabilise the less powerful states with millions of citizens displaced from their home countries, and hundreds of thousands, sometimes even millions died, because of a war predicated on mistrust is not safe. It cannot be said that a world in which such happens upholds human dignity and respect for human rights based on the laws and treaties of human rights that have been signed into force.

---

[648] Ibid.

[649] See "Australian Statement for the Interactive Dialogue with the Special Rapporteur on the Rights of Indigenous Peoples, 24 September 2020": https://www.dfat.gov.au/international-relations/themes/human-rights/hrc-statements/45th-session-human-rights-council/australian-statement-interactive-dialogue-special-rapporteur-rights-indigenous-peoples#:~:text=Australia%20welcomes%20Mr%20Francisco%20Cali,the%20Rights%20of%20Indigenous%20Peoples

While warrant of arrest has been issued by the International Criminal Court for the arrest of Vladimir Putin and it is expected that he will be arrested to account for human rights violations and crimes against humanity in Ukraine, the unlawful invasion of Iraq by the United States of America during the presidency of George W Bush in 2003, and the incalculable human rights violations and crimes against humanity that followed that invasion is yet to receive a formal international condemnation by the international community. As if the United States Presidents are entitled to act with impunity, no condemnation has been redirected to President Barack Obama directing US forces and NATO to invade and violate the human rights and peace of the people of the Libya. The countless deaths that followed the invasion in Libya and the destruction of that country which was for many years the only economically stable African nation is now almost beyond remediation. Again, no formal international condemnation let alone the idea of the issue of a warrant of arrest by the International Criminal Court for Crimes against humanity.

PART V
CONCLUSION AND RECOMMENDATION

20

TOWARDS GUARANTEEING HUMAN RIGHTS ENFORCEMENT AND ELIMINATING THREATS TO INTERNATIONAL PEACE AND SECURITY

...let justice roll down like waters, and righteousness like an ever-flowing stream.[650]

20.1 The Decline of Christian Religious Nationalism and Rights

As the account in the early chapters of this book show religious nationalism was started with Christianity when it became the religion of the Roman Empire and through the European nation-states during European colonisation of Africa, Asia, and the Americas. However, the secular state emerged out of Christian religious nationalism following several revolutions. Christians are now among those restricted from exercising their rights to freedom of thought, conscience, and religious beliefs as the cases discussed in various chapters of this book reveal. Utilitarian Christian rights are now increasingly being dwarfed by deontological rights in most western nations across Europe and the Americas.

---

[650] Amos 5:24, Holy Bible, English Standard Version [ESV].

The case for the protection of religious freedom and prevention of human rights violations have been made in the preceding discussions. However, the forces that precipitate human rights violations and crimes against humanities by their actions are powerful forces such as the heads of governments of super-power states such as president Vladimir Putin and more seriously some of the presidents of the United States such as George W Bush and Barack Obama whose respective actions in Iraq and Libya have caused gross human rights violations and crimes against humanity that are on-going and appear to be overlooked because of the super power status of the United States.

The economic and military might of a nation-state like the United States simply gives it an uneven advantage that makes it to decide when and how to respect or violate human rights while policing others who may be less harmful offenders. As the discussions in chapter one reveal, the law and justice system that was spread by the Roman Empire had political colouring that sometimes allows the rich and strong to get away with some offences in the way that the United States has sometimes gotten away

with human rights violations, while trumpeting the needs for other states to respect human rights.

20.2 Human Rights and Justice

From the discussions in chapter one and subsequent chapters of this book, the extent to which European nations laws and justice systems became universal laws and justice systems in most nations of the world and became the source of international law cannot be denied following the Roman Empire's rule over the world in the middle ages; and the British Empire's domination of the world after that right through into the twentieth century.[651]

---

[651] In her book, A Short History of European Law © 2018 Harvard University Press, p.3, Tamar Herzog, made a remark which buttresses this position by saying: "some scholars' criticisms of contemporary international law, which they trace back to Europe and which they consider a European rather a truly global human heritage." She further discussed Making European Law Universal I & II in chapters 9 and 12 of the same book.

It is also what has defined the freedoms and rights enshrined in the universal declaration of human rights premised on Christian precepts of equality of all men before God.[652] The universal declaration of human rights as discussed in earlier chapters mutated into various international human rights law treaties.[653] However, the question is whether the European legal processes and justice system suffices in every situation in its procedures of administration of justice? This remains a matter for comparative evaluation.

20.3 Christianity as Europeans' Religion[654] and Human Rights

As the discussions in chapter 2 and the subsequent chapters that followed leading up to the discussion about the thirty years Christian religious war between European nations which ended with the Treaty/Peace of Westphalia (1948) shows white people[655] of western European nations under the Roman Empire rejected Christianity at the onset and for over 300 years they were killing Jewish and African Christians who refused to renounce their faith at the behest of the Roman Empire authorities. When western Europeans under the Roman Empire eventually accepted Christianity, following the conversion of Emperor Constantine the Great, unholy men such as Pope Martin V discussed earlier were made popes and these went to alter the soul and heart of the Christian faith

---

[652]   The Holy Bible's account of creation says: "So God created human beings in his image." – Genesis 1:27. (New Living Translation).

[653]   In his book, Christian Human Rights © 2015 University of Pennsylvania Press, Samuel Moyn, stated: "The truth is that Europe and the modern world drew nearly everything from Christianity in the long term." Moyn went on to say: "Without Christianity, our commitment to the moral equality of human beings is unlikely to have come about, but by itself this had no bearing most forms of political equality – whether between Christians and Jews, whites and blacks, civilized and salvage, or men and women." P.6.

[654]   Christianity is often said to be western Europeans or white people's religion with reference to colonisation and how the colonial masters such as Britain, France etc. pretended to have brought Christianity to people outside Europe while actually exploiting their resources contrary to the Christian teachings of love and compassion. In actual fact the Bible makes it clear for instance in Matthew 2:1-23 - that Jesus Christ was born in Bethlehem in Judea in present day Israel and was raised partly in Egypt which is in Africa which means he was a Middle Easterner with African upbringing and therefore far from being a European. Christianity also was mostly flourishing in the Middle East and Africa until the fourth century. How Christianity became European religion has been discussed in Chapter two of this book following the conversion of Emperor Constantine.

[655]   The use of the term white people here only have relevance with regards to the claims made by those who want to falsity history that Christianity was the religion of white people or Western Europeans.

and religion by their failure to be guided by the fear and love of God, over and above, their aspirations for power, control and subjugation of people. Until the conversion of Constantine the Great, the denial of religious freedom, and the persecution and execution of Christians was an expected experience for Christian believers.[656] As the discussions in the earlier chapters also show, persecutions and killings of Christians paused during the Roman Empire at the behest of Emperor Constantine the Great, well before Christianity eventually became a world religion that was mandatory for everyone in the entire Roman Empire. But what the world was to witness for well over a millennium and a half of the Roman Empire and the subsequent empires that were claiming Christianity as their traditional belief and religion was a torrent of human degradation and destruction of a large population of human lives in ways abhorrent to Christianity and the teachings of Jesus Christ who taught the love of God and the love of humanity as the two categorical imperatives for the Christian believer.[657] But out of the centuries of human inhumanity to human came revolutions, wars and protests that set the course for the development of civil liberties and human rights that are enforceable in some parts of the world today, especially, in western Europe and North America, where there are stable political and economic conditions. However, the cases discussed in some of the chapters above about Christians whose human rights to freedom of belief and religion were breached or denied such as Eweida and Others v. United Kingdom [2013] is indicative of the fact that even in European nations Christians are not quite free to practice their human rights without undue constraints.

20.4 Slave Trade, Colonialism and the Vestiges of Crimes against Humanity

As discussed in Chapter 2, with the conversion of Emperor Constantine to Christianity and the later proclamation of the entire Roman Empire as

---

656   Theologians and commentators to the book of Hebrews hold the view that the book of Hebrews was written to encourage Jewish Christians who were forced to renounce their faith following persecutions by the Roman Empire Authorities. See "Jewish believers" in David Pawson, Unlocking the Bible Omnibus © 2003 Harper Collins Publishers pp.1117-1118; See also David Petersen's commentary on the book of Hebrews especially "What was the situation of the first recipients and why was Hebrews written?" at pages 1322 – 1323 in the New Bible Commentary © Universities and Colleges Christian Fellowship, Leicester, England, 1953, 1954, 1970, 1994..

657   See Matthew 22:37-39 Where Jesus said: "You must love the LORD your God with all your heart, all your soul, and all your mind.'Love your neighbour as yourself.'

a Christian world, European nations' kings and rulers found Christianity as a means of controlling and suppressing their people prior to human rights development.

Between AD383 when Christianity became the official religion of the Roman Empire and AD1648, when the European religious war ended with the loss of millions of lives across European nations, of which Germany was worst hit, the European nations turned much of their political and economic interests outside the European continent to other continents for trade and exploitation of valuable resources. Consequently, they went on to perpetrate the worst form of evil on humanity globally in acts of conquests that saw the territories of China, India, America and Africa as fields for plunder while the peoples were used as tools for agricultural farming and economic advancement. The worst act of human degradation that followed was the transatlantic slave trade that took place between the fifteen century and nineteenth century; and the colonisation which followed between the seventeenth century and twentieth century. Both largely and badly affected the African continent - the people and their resources. The colonisation which was rather organised because it was the aftermath of the Berlin Conference of 1884/85, left African kingdoms and ethnic-nationalities fragmented and mostly on faulty boundary lines and countries. While the end of the Second World War and the emergence of the United Nations brought an end to colonisation and initiated the promotion of self-determination, the Christian religion by this time happened to be suspected as European nations religious propaganda employed as a tool of colonisation. There was a dimension of pseudo-Christianity that Europeans presented in several places. Firstly, it was promoted by European slave traders and subsequently by European Towards Guaranteeing Human Rights Enforcement colonialists in their dealings with the people they were colonising. It was largely pseudo-Christianity because neither the fear of God nor the love of one's neighbour which are the essential pillars of the Christian faith were manifestly evident in the way the agents of the colonial powers presented the gospel and how they dealt with the natives. However, there were a few exceptionally humane missionaries who manifested their Christian faith by their commitments and support to the peoples of the communities they served.

But the bitterness of the slave trade and colonialism have left some Africans in the twentieth century and even into the twenty-first century disenchanted and suspicious about the authenticity of the Christian faith. Most display pluralistic ignorance of the history of Christianity and the Church in their speeches by erroneously asserting that Christianity is a religion imported to Africa from Europe. Such remarks are made in dishonour to the great African Christian Church martyrs such as the second century martyr Perpetua who was martyred for refusing to renounce her Christian faith by the Roman Empire authorities even as a mother with a baby that had not weaned from breast milk. More prominent were the renowned Christian Church fathers of African nationalities in the fourth century such as Pope Miltiades, who was pope at the time of the earlier reign of Constantine the Great, to Athanasius of Alexandria, and the ever-memorable St. Augustine of Hippo who remains one of the foremost Church fathers to this day. All of these Africans were in the centre stages of the Christian faith and advancement at a time when the entire nation of Britain and other European nations such as France who were to become the colonial powers were wallowing in paganism and idolatry until AD383 and in the case of Britain around the end of the sixth century when Pope Gregory I, also known as Gregory the Great sent missionaries to evangelise England.[658]

However, there were European nationals who were genuine Christian believers and who stood for truth in the practice of their Christian beliefs and exercise of their faith than to toe the dictates of their Kings or rulers in carrying out acts of political deception and affliction of the Africans and Asians during colonisation. As discussed in chapter 8, Christians such as Thomas Beckett were cruelly murdered by the King's agents because he stood up to honour Jesus Christ rather than do the bidding of the King in disobedience to the word of God.

However, the British did not succeed in selling their version of the protestant Christian religion to the Chinese who were already firmly rooted in their belief in Buddhism by the time Britain got to China. The British decided to pursue only their economic interest in China by subjugating the Chinese in the nineteenth century to opium trade.

---

[658] See Gregory I in the Oxford Dictionary of the Christian Church Edited by F.L. Cross and E.A. Livingstone © 1957, 1974. Pp. 594-595; also see Gregory the Great in 131 Christians Everyone Should Know Edited By Mark Galli and Ted Olsen © 2000 Christianity Today Inc. pp.317-319.

They forced the Chinese to buy opium which the Chinese soon got addicted to and ended up destroying themselves with it. When the Chinese government realised that opium was addictive and destructive to the lives of their citizens and attempted to block Britain from carrying on the trade in China, the British went to war with the Chinese and after defeating them humiliated them to continue to do their bidding by facilitating the opium trade at the expense of the well-being of their citizens.[659]

However, as the discussions on the historical and doctrinal divisions within the Christian religion show, by the end of the European thirty years religious war in 1648, the values and traditions of the Christian religion had not only become internally diverse, but it had also become a contest between the traditionalists who wanted to maintain what they believed were the original values; and those who were of liberal tendencies that radically wanted to change the values and precepts of the religion to reflect what the liberal changing world would accept. For instance, from the time of its foundation through to almost one thousand and five hundred years of its existence, the Church of England opposed the Ordination of Women Bishops. But at its General Synod in 2014, it voted in favour of the ordination of Women Bishops.[660]

Fundamentally, what is strange about Christianity in the twenty-first century is the fact that it is doubtlessly the most populous religion in the world yet the adherents of the Christian religion are the most persecuted in the world. Whether it is in England, the United States of America, or Nigeria, it is not strange to hear of Christians being persecuted for exercising their Christian belief as some of the cases cited in various chapters above show about Lilian Ladele or Nadia Eweida.

The trend simply has continued from the crucifixion of Jesus Christ to the persecution of the first century Christian martyrs such as the apostles James, Peter, and others who were Jesus' own disciples or other martyrs

---

[659] James, Lawrence, The Rise & Fall Of The British Empire © 1994, 1998 Abacus. Pp. 236-238.

[660] Church of England General Synod backs Women Bishops BBC News, 14 July 2014: https://www.bbc.co.uk/news/uk-28300618

such as Bishop Polycarp[661] of the first century to twenty-first century Christian martyrs such as Eunice Olawale,[662] the Christian woman who was hacked to death at the rising of the sun on the morning of 16 July 2016 in Abuja, Nigeria, while evangelising on the street.

In a world where individual right to religious freedom is universally accepted as a human right with various international treaties guaranteeing it, it is despicable and inexplicable that the same nations that ratified these treaties making them rights in law in their states are abdicating responsibilities to protect their citizens from the enjoyment of these rights in compliance with their international obligations. If in Abuja, the capital of Nigeria, a citizen such as Eunice Olawale can be killed in broad day light without the security agents apprehending and prosecuting the killers then what could possibly be happening in remote suburban areas of Nigeria? Can the Federal Government of Nigeria be said to be taking their obligations to protect and guarantee their citizens human rights seriously? Absolutely doubtful!

---

[661] Polycarp, [69AD- 156AD] referred to as the aged Bishop of Smyrna, is said to have lived at the end of the age of the original apostles of Jesus Christ. He died as the martyr that was burned alive. See Galli, Mark and Olsen, Ted, 131 Christians Everyone Should Know © 2000 Christianity Today, Inc., Polycarp, pp.360/361

[662] Mrs Eunice Olawale, was a Christian preacher who was murdered just as she was preaching in one of the resident areas of Abuja Nigeria in the morning of Saturday, 16th July 2016. Sadly, the government of President Muhammadu Buhari under which a number of Christians across the breadth of Nigeria had been killed in the guise of Herdsmen and Farmers clashes had not apprehended the killers of Mrs Olawale in the country's capital. See the worrying reports of two of the nationally media outlets in Nigeria on the matter: The Sun Nigeria https://www.sunnewsonline.com/the-murder-of-eunice-olawale/; The Premium Times of Nigeria https://www.premiumtimesng.com/news/headlines/233533-no-suspects-arrests-in-abuja-preachers-murder-nearly-a-year-after.html;

21

CONCLUSION AND RECOMMENDATION

"What begins with the failure to uphold the dignity of one life, all too often ends with a calamity for entire nations.

In this new century, we must start from the understanding that peace belongs not only to States or peoples, but to each and every member of those communities. The sovereignty of States must no longer be used as a shield for gross violations of human rights. Peace must be sought, above all, because it is the condition for every member of the human family to live a life of dignity and security."[663]

21.1 The Development of Human Rights in the Twentieth Century

Taking cognisance of the overall discussions thus far, it is not incongruous to assert that Samuel Moyn was right when he stated in his book, Christian Human Rights, that: The truth is that Europe and therefore the modern world drew nearly everything from Christianity in the long term.[664]

---

[663] Annan, Kofi, United Nations Secretary-General, Nobel Lecture delivered in Oslo, on 10 December 2001: https://www.un.org/sg/en/content/sg/speeches/2001-12-10/nobel-lecture-delivered-kofi-annan

[664] Moyn, Samuel, Christian Human Rights © 2015 University of Pennsylvannia Press. P.6

Without Christianity, our commitment to the moral equality of human beings is unlikely to have come about, but by itself this had no bearing on most forms of political equality – whether between Christians and Jews, whites and blacks, civilised and savage, or men and women.[665]

However, the contemporary state of the world with the prevailing threats of terrorism, global poverty, especially in the developing nations, economic recessions and global pandemics threatening human existence, the question is whether the world is still being sustained by the Christian foundation bequeathed to it by the Roman Empire or whether it has fallen off its Christian hinges and needs a new compass?

Opinions will of course vary in any attempt to address this question but based on the discussions and the cases examined in this book, the constitutional foundation and constitutional structure of most nation-states whether it is the Islamic Republic of Pakistan or the United Kingdom of Great Britain and Northern Ireland, are not as much the problem as the operation of the justice system. The pain and indignity that Asia Bibi discussed above suffered in Pakistan prison in the early years of this twenty-first century with the fear of death by execution hanging over her head for an offence that was trumped up against her is beyond imagination. Yet that pain could have been cut short, if the wheels of justice ran faster and smoother than the ten years it took for the case to get to the Supreme Court of Pakistan and for her to be acquitted. But this has been the down side of the Roman Justice system over millennia, as the case of Paul who spent four years waiting for a decision to acquit him of false charges levied against him by the Jewish authority as discussed in Chapter one showed. In the same vein, the psychological pain, indignity and emotional turmoil that Nadia Eweida suffered before winning her case at the European Court of Human Rights after exhaustion of domestic remedies through the English Courts right up to the United Kingdom Supreme Court might just as well be better imagined than experienced. But in all these, the worst of it, perhaps, was the outcome of the case of Mrs Lillian Ladele who failed to get justice in the United Kingdom and at the European Court of Human Rights, where the dissenting opinion of the two judges who agreed with her claim bear more convincing arguments than the majority who ruled against her and in favour of the United Kingdom. The decision in the Ladele case in

---

[665]   Ibid

the United Kingdom courts unfairly places emphasis on discrimination and equality in a manner that quite obviously traded off Mrs Ladele's own right not to be discriminated against and unfairly treated while denying her the right to her freedom of conscience, religion and belief. The decision of the Court in Ladele becomes disconcerting when due consideration is given to the decision of the United States Supreme Court in Sherbert v Verner, 374 U.S. 398 (1963), where the Court stated that if a law such as the law the London Borough of Islington Council relied upon in the Ladele case burdens an individual's exercise of religion then the person should be exempted from complying especially where there are alternative means of achieving the purpose, it should serve. While the US Supreme Court ruling was based on the free exercise of religion clause of the First Amendment of the U S Constitution, it should well apply to Mrs Ladele's entitlement to enjoyment of the right to freedom of conscience and religion under Article 9 of the European Convention on Human Rights.

In general, while the enjoyment of some human rights may be subject to certain qualifications and can be restricted by the state for the purpose of public order and national security, the restrictions and denial of such rights should not be arbitrarily done.

And the courts should not encourage it by its decisions, so as not to undo that which necessitated the making of such human rights laws and fundamental freedoms for the individual in the society.

What these cases reveal are the facts that unlike Islamic cases that are decided by judges specialising in Islamic laws, cases having to do with Christians' religious beliefs and practises are decided by judges who have no profound knowledge of the Holy Bible, let alone the prescribed behaviour or conduct for Christians. Therefore the interpretation of the judges done without due cognisance of what the Sacred Scriptures of the beliefs of the person concerned say about how he or she can exercise their religious beliefs, bearing in mind the right to freedom of conscience, religious belief and practice.

Fundamentally, the years it took to decide these cases should be cut short. The relevance of the legal dictum "*Iustitia negavit moratus est iustitia*

– *justice delayed is justice denied"* must be brought to bear on the time within which each and every case should be decided.

The cases discussed in this book are quite demonstrative and proof of the inherent delays in the courts deciding cases whether at the national level or international level. Whatever it will take to address the issue of delay in deciding cases whether it will mean employing more judges, training more judicial personnel or building more courts, needs to be addressed as a way of improving the justice system both at the national and international levels. On average each of the applicants spent five years to go through the national courts and exhaust domestic remedies before taking their case to the European Court of Human Rights. To spend five years pursuing a case is too long a period of time. In respect of duration, it was even worse for Asia Bibi who was in prison in Pakistan for about 10 years over a false accusation. But in some instances, there are cases that take much longer to resolve and that leaves the claimant unable to really recover even if they end up winning the case. Justice cannot be said to be done in the Courts of Law and Justice, if people continue to suffer in this way in the cause of seeking justice to actualise their human rights.

Since there has to be stability and public order in any society or nation for people to enjoy rights and freedoms, it has to be said that nothing threatens the peace and stability of the nations of the world more than religious illiteracy, religious rivalry, ethnic-nationalism and religious nationalism. It should be understood that people stick to individual religious beliefs and practise based on certain innate factors that sometimes define their existence. Whether it is the case of Cassius Marcellus Clay Jr. changing religion in adulthood to become a Muslim and taking on the name Muhammad Ali or it is the case of a Muslim woman such as Bilquis Sheikh converting to Christianity the reasons for the religious convictions that they individually hold as the basis of their belief are predicated on delicate grounds for which they would surprisingly be willing to die.

As the accounts of events in this book show, the desperate acts of Roman Emperors to stamp out Christianity in the first three hundred years that resulted in the persecutions and killings of innocent Christians did not stop the growth and advancement of the Christian faith.

In general, the world cannot stamp out religion because according to the World Population Review over eighty per cent of the population of the people in the world are affiliated to one religion or the other and just about twenty per cent are classified as non-religious or atheists. Human beings are by nature religious beings with innate desire to relate with the supernatural. It is therefore better to seek ways of understanding religions rather than to try to eliminate religions out of policy considerations in educational and social policies of national governments. The 2020 World Population Review shows that Christianity is the most populous religion with about 33% adherents, followed by Islam with about 24% adherents. The total numbers of people who are adherents of the Christian faith and Islamic faith put together amounts to a staggering over four billion people which is well over half of the population of the world.[666] Instead of religion being removed from the educational curriculum in schools as it is being done in State Schools in the Western nations of the world, it should be made a compulsory subject to avoid a repeat of the disasters the world had experienced because of religious rivalry and religious misunderstandings as discussed above.

21.2 Ethnic-Nationalism, Religious Nationalism and Respect for Human Rights

The twenty-first century has already seen ethnic-nationalism and religious nationalism that have created humanitarian catastrophes. Some examples are the Armenia-Azerbaijan wars in which Armenians were almost ethnically cleansed from Nagorno-Karabakh in the Republic of Azerbaijan, the on-going Israel-Hamas war which is effectively Israel-Palestinian war, mindful of the thousands of Palestinians that have been killed, not just in Gaza but also in the West Bank as well as the Burmese Buddhists army's crackdown that led to what amounted to the expulsion of about a million Royingya Muslims of Myanmar in August 2017.[667] And that is besides the several hundred thousand that were said to have been killed by the Burmese Army. In the same vein, in the nation of Burkina Faso in West Africa, Muslim extremists have been killing the

---

[666] See the World Population Review 2020: https://worldpopulationreview.com/country-rankings/religion-by-country

[667] BBC World News Asia See "Myanmar Royingya: What you need to know about the crisis" 23 January 2020: https://www.bbc.co.uk/news/world-asia-41566561

Christian population of Burkina Faso since 2016, as already discussed in a bid to Islamize that country[668]. The ones that have escaped death have fled to other neighbouring countries to live as refugees.

In Afghanistan, the Taliban want that nation to be a hundred per cent Islamic country so the non-Muslim religious minorities have been chased out of their ancestral homes because of the Taliban's religious nationalism stance. In Iran where the constitution allows for the existence of people of other faith, the dress code requires every woman there to appear as a Muslim woman without exception to their own religious attire as the case of Mahsa Amini shows.

These are examples of ethnic-nationalism and religious nationalism with disastrous effects which the world does not need, if peace and stability must prevail. A repeat of these sad episodes or retaliations can only be avoided by proper religious education of the peoples of the communities and countries affected. In addition to that States must take seriously their obligations to implement and enforce human rights, especially the right for individual citizens to exercise their rights to freedom of conscience, religion, belief and practice. The peace and security of the individual person is what will ensure the peace and security of the entire community of people in the society as whole.

21.3 Holding States Accountable for Human Rights Violations, Crimes against Humanity and Genocide

The state parties that are members of the international committee under the auspices of the United Nations Organization have demonstrated their willingness to ensure that every individual person, irrespective of the country they live in enjoy human rights protection. This can be inferred based on the number of states that have ratified the United Nations International Covenant on

---

[668] BBC World News Africa: "Burkina Faso Christians killed in attack on Church. 29 April 2019: https://www.bbc.co.uk/news/world-africa-48094789

Civil and Political Rights, ICCPR, (1966)[669]; and the United Nations International Covenant on Economic, Social and Cultural Rights, ICESCR, (1966)[670].

However, even with the best will to protect and guarantee human rights, some States do not have the security and economic stability to guarantee the enjoyment of such rights for those within their territories. As the famous economists Acemoglu and Robinson stated in their book, Why Nations Fail:

"Conflict over institutions and the distribution of resources has been pervasive throughout history."[671]

For a number of developing countries and economies, there are political conflicts over institutions and the distributions of resources that manifest in huge acts of corruptions and affect the peace and security of the masses in such countries. Some of the countries that have been discussed in this book such as Iraq and Libya prior to the US led invasions were no doubt suffering from such political conflicts and distribution of resources. But the dictators that led them would have been overthrown without the destruction of those countries just as the Arab Spring brought down dictators such as Zine el-Abidine Ben Ali of Tunisia who ruled Tunisia from 1987 to January 2011; Hosni Mubarak who had been president of Egypt from 1981 but was also removed in January 2011; and Ali Abdullah Saleh al-Ahmar, who had been president of Yemen from 1990 before he was eventually forced out in February 2012[672] without invasion by the US or NATO. There is therefore no doubt that organised internal opposition would have forced Saddam Hussein out of power in Iraq as well as Muammar Gaddafi in Libya. Just as Egypt and Tunisia are stable

---

[669] The United Nations International Covenant on Civil and Political Rights, ICCPR, as date has over 173 states parties that have ratified the Covenant. These countries are listed in the following link: https://treaties.un.org/Pages/ViewDetails.aspx?chapter=4&clang=_en&mtdsg_no=IV-4&src=IND

[670] The United Nations International Covenant on Economic, Social and Cultural Rights, ICESCR, has over 171 states parties that have ratified the Covenant. The countries that have ratified the Covenant can be seen by opening the following link: https://treaties.un.org/Pages/ViewDetails.aspx?src=IND&mtdsg_no=IV-3&chapter=4

[671] Acemoglu, Daron & Robinson, James A., Why Nations Fail The Origins of Power, Prosperity and Poverty © 2012, 2013 Profile Books Limited p.184

[672] See "What became of the Arab Springs" "Analysis" by Adam Taylor, The Washington Post, December 4, 2017: https://www.washingtonpost.com/news/worldviews/wp/2017/12/04/what-became-of-the-arab-springs-ousted-dictators/

countries after the overthrew of dictators such as Hosni Mubarak and Ali Abdullah Saleh, Iraq and Libya would have remained stable countries if internal oppositions were responsible for the ousting of dictators such as Hussein and Gaddafi.

Holding States accountable for human rights violations and crimes against humanity is a difficult task especially in countries with developing economics and ineffective security institutions. This is well captured in the book by Paul Collier, The Bottom Billion, where he stated that:

> ALL SOCIETIES HAVE CONFLICT; it is inherent to politics. The problem that is pretty distinctive to the bottom billion is not political conflict but its form. Some of them are stuck in a pattern of violent internal challenges to government. Sometimes the violence is prolonged, a civil war; sometimes it is all over swiftly, a coup d'état. These two forms of political conflict both are costly and can be repetitive. They can trap a country in poverty.[673]

A country that is trapped in poverty cannot protect and guarantee the human rights of the people within its territory be it civil rights or economic rights as enshrined in the ICCPR or ICESCR.

It becomes even more difficult when a superpower nation such as the United States chooses to perpetrate human rights violations in the guise of stopping the production of weapons of mass destruction and using other nations as allies to perpetrate destruction and gross human rights violations, as it happened in Iraq between 2003 and 2011. More dangerous to humanity is when a huge military organization such as the North Atlantic Treaty Organization (NATO), decides to do the bidding of the United States as NATO did during the presidency of Barack Obama and went into Libya to destroy the country and its people in the desperation to kill Muammar Gaddafi and then left without answering questions about the apparent human rights violations and crimes against humanity that have been committed there.

---

[673] Collier, Paul, THE BOTTOM BILLION Why the Poorest Countries Are Falling and What Can be Done About It © 2008 Oxford University Press p. 17.

No one can police the actions of NATO with intent to hold it to account for human rights violations. But it behoves its member states to restrain the organization from becoming a military giant that will be trampling and violating the human rights of citizens of non-member states while destabilising sovereign states, even members of the United Nations Organization such as Libya.

Added to the danger here is the fact that any mistake made by the United Nations Security Council and the United Nations General Assembly, such as the manner in which Resolution 1973 of 2011 was passed by the United Nations General Assembly to satisfy Barack Obama's intent to invade Libya by force cannot be admitted as a mistake, let alone be remedied.

There are now manifest acts of States policing each other in order to prevent gross violations of human rights and genocide. This is obvious from recent applications filed at the International Court of Justice by States parties to the Genocide Convention against other States parties alleging violations. The following are some examples. The Gambia took Myanmar to the World Court alleging breaches of its obligation under the Convention for the Prevention and Punishment of the Crime of Genocide (1948) by genocidal treatment meted out to the Rohingya Muslims of Myanmar.[674] Although, Myanmar objected to the claims of The Gambia's Application to the Court, on grounds that The Gambia was acting at the behest of the Organisation of Islamic Cooperation (OIC)[675], which is not a party to the Convention, and that The Gambia was not an injured party, it was interesting that the ICJ, pointed that The Gambia had instituted the proceedings in its name and that under the Convention it has:

> "a common interest to ensure the prevention, suppression and punishment of genocide, by committing themselves to fulfilling the obligation contained in the Convention."[676]

---

[674] The Gambia v. Myanmar, Application of the Convention on the Prevention and Punishment of the Crime of Genocide, International Court of Justice, Document Number 178 – 20220722 – Sum -01 – 00 – EN 22 July 2022: https://www.icj-cij.org/node/106180

[675] Ibid.

[676] Ibid.

Having addressed the objections of Myanmar and established that The Gambia's application was admissible in its summary judgment of 22 July 2022[677], it remains to be seen if in its final judgment the International Court of Justice will rule that Myanmar committed acts of genocide against the Rohingya people that it expelled from their ancestral homes in Myanmar.

With respect to the case of South Africa against Israel at the International Court of Justice, while it is a good example of a State policing another State in a conflict to prevent gross violations of human rights and genocide, it is also a bad example of the application of the Genocide Convention as it seeks to exempt a State from self-defence in the event of a terrorist act, such as the Hamas terrorists attack on Israel on 7

October 2023. On the other hand, it is apparent that the State of Israel is fighting more of a ghost as it seeks to destroy Hamas with weapons that are usually deployed for human destruction instead of a ghost. This becomes real in the light of the thousands of innocent Palestinian civilians including women, elderly and babies that have been so far killed. Whatever the decision of the ICJ will be on the South Africa v Israel case, the jurisprudence of how and when 'intent to commit genocide' is should be understood as per Article II of the Convention on the Prevention and Punishment of the Crime of Genocide may be crystallised.

In the meantime, it is interesting that in the ICJ Order of 26 January 2024, it ruled that:

> In the Court's view, at least some aspects of the acts and omissions alleged by South Africa to have been committed by Israel in Gaza appear to be capable of falling within the provisions of the Convention.[678]

The ICJ went on to say it has:

---

[677] Ibid.

[678] See International Court of Justice, Order 26 January 2024 on the Application of the Convention on the Prevention and Punishment of the Crime of Genocide in the Gaza Strip (South Africa v Israel) at para.31: https://www.icj-cij.org/sites/default/files/case-related/192/192-20240126-ord-01-00-en.pdf

"prima facie jurisdiction pursuant to Article IX of the Genocide Convention to entertain the case.[679]

Sadly, Hamas' failure to release the remaining people they took hostage on 7 October 2023 during their terrorist attacks on the State of Israel makes it inevitable for Israel to continue to do whatever they consider necessary to find and free these hostages though it means more bombs and missiles aimed at Hamas but often destroying mostly innocent Palestinians.

In the genocide case instituted by Ukraine against the Russian Federation in the application they filed on 26 February 2022 at the International Court of Justice, the International Court of Justice in its 'Summary Judgment' delivered on 2 February 2024, have asserted its jurisdiction to entertain the Ukrainian submissions against the Russian Federation, except:

the acts complained by Ukraine in submissions (c) and (d) of the Memorial" because the ICJ views those aspects of their submissions as "not capable of constituting violations of the Convention relied on by Ukraine.[680]

Depending on the final judgment of the case, there is the possibility that even in situations where two States are at war with each other, it is still possible to hold one State liable for acts of genocide as Ukraine is alleging against Russia. This may serve as a caution for State to be wary even in times of war not to indulge in flagrant human rights violations of non-combatants and innocent civilians.

21.4 Recommendations

In order to achieve better protection and enforcement of human rights, the United Nations Security Council and the United Nations General Assembly need to assert themselves more authoritatively, especially, in persuading superpower States such as the United States, China, and

---

[679] Ibid.

[680] See Allegations of Genocide under the Convention on the Prevention and Punishment of the Crime of Genocide (Ukraine v Russian Federation: 32 States intervening) see paras 131 – 148: https://www.icj-cij.org/sites/default/files/case-related/182/182-20240202-sum-01-00-en.pdf

Russia to abstain from invading other countries. Unless, in order to restore peace following a United Nations Security Council decision on enforcement of a United Nations General Assembly Resolution for the use of force to restore peace in a state of conflict.

The UN General Assembly and the UN Security Council, respectively, need to make it known to states that the concept of state sovereignty does not bestow power and authority on irresponsible political leaders or religious leaders as in the case of the Taliban in Afghanistan and heads of governments to subject their citizens to any systematic human rights abuses, crimes against humanity, and destruction, especially, where there is no viable political opposition as it is now the case in Afghanistan. Situations of this nature will require proper consideration by the UN Security Council and actual intervention to prevent systematic destruction of human lives and gross violations of human rights.

If the world would have the peace every human society craves for, then the United Nations Security Council need to look into situations that cogently call for the application of Chapter VII Articles 42-47 of the UN Charter on the use of armed force for the maintenance of international peace and security.

At the moment, whether one is looking at the case of the former president of Yugoslavia, Slobodan Milosevic, who presided over the genocide of Bosnians before standing trial; or the current case of Afghanistan, where the Taliban government are perpetrating crimes against humanity over more than 20 million women and children, which is over half the Afghan population; the case of the Russian Federation's invasion of Ukraine; or the Israel-Gaza war, the position of the United Nations towards preventing human rights abuses and crimes against humanity, is both ineffective and in fact unclear.

At the moment, the balance between the sanctity accorded to a sovereign state with a responsible head of government in peace time, and the external intervention necessary to protecting people from a tyrannical leader and head of government in times of internal conflict and anarchy precipitating gross violations of human rights is missing. There is no doubt about the fact that there will always be a challenge in finding the balance that will justify intervention. But the difficulty in finding the balance should not result in the need to abandon the effort to do so, in to protect and enforce the human rights of hapless citizens trapped in the hands of a tyrannical leaders or government.

The on-going war between Russia and Ukraine with the gross violations of human rights associated with it, and which appears to be beyond the United Nations Security Council to stop, shows how vulnerable humanity still is in the world of the twenty-first century. And this poses grave threat to international peace and security.

The Russia-Ukraine war is looking like the late sixteenth century war between the then powerful Habsburg Empire and The Netherlands (1549 – 1567). While it is not realistic for Russia to conclude that they will succeed in annexing Ukraine as a part of its territory, it is just as unrealistic for anyone to assume that Ukraine will win the war because of arms supply from the United States, European Union member-states, and members states of the North Atlantic Treaty Organization, NATO, countries at large. The gross violations of human rights will continue to escalate as the war goes on. In the final analysis, it is much more realistic that the war will end with a peace agreement between the Federation of Russia and Ukraine than by the continuous use of the force of arms. In fact, the prolongation of the use of arms in the war will possibly lead to a wider war. While Ukraine deserves protection, supplying arms to Ukraine to carry on the war is not exactly protection as it simply leads to more Ukrainians and Russians to dying in a preventable war. Only the United Nations Organization through its Secretary-General now has the neutrality to initiate peace talks to end the war as no NATO member state head of government can now initiate peace talks due to NATO States perceived biased against Russia and Russia's suspicion of NATO which was what led to the invasion of Ukraine. If the protection of human rights is taken seriously, and the need to secure international peace and security is paramount to every Member State of the United Nations Organization, then the States outside the NATO member states such as China, India, Brazil, Saudi Arabia and some of the influential African States needs to broker peace between Russia and Ukraine and reduce the increasing prospect of the Russia v Ukraine war degenerating into a wider war that would involve other nations, and equally escalate the violations of human rights to a global level, as it is daily manifesting itself by the development of events.

In cases of states such as Australia, it has to be said that the treatment of the indigenous (Aboriginal) and Torres Strait Islanders people by the government of Australia which deprives them of the dignity of the human person by virtue of their omission from the constitution as citizens, should be a matter that the United Nations need to continuously demand the Australian government to address with urgency. The Australian government should be requested to urgently amend their constitution, to include them as citizens. It is only when a person is accorded the dignity of a human being that he or she can have human rights and there is no reason why any living human being in the twenty-first century should not be accorded the dignity of a human being.

As for the prospect of peace between Armenia and Azerbaijan, it should be a matter of interest for the international community and not just for Armenians and Azerbaijanis, to work towards securing peace as it would end the decades of gross human rights violations in that region. One way of guaranteeing this is for Azerbaijan to implement the International Court of Justice's binding order of 17 November 2023, made against it, and this should be duly monitored.

On the more serious note concerning guaranteeing of human rights protection, the Israel-Palestine conflict over the past 75 years has been the most severe test of the United Nations' ability to maintain peace and security as it has proven that neither the United Nations General Assembly nor the United Nations Security Council have effectively exercised the powers of the UN Charter to achieve peace, where member states are biased either politically or religiously, and vote in resolutions according to their political interests or religious biases, instead of seeking peace for the common good of humanity and the protection of human rights in keeping with international human rights law.

Clearly, until states leaders and heads of governments learn to consciously make decisions and take actions that will enhance human rights protections and enforcements, which invariably will lead to peace and security in the world, no form of government in itself, whether religious nationalism as practiced in Iran, ethnic-nationalism and religious nationalism as practised in Israel or secular democratic governments as practised in the United States of America and in various other places in the world, can by itself prevent human rights violations and guarantee peace and security in the world.

It is becoming increasingly the trend that States contest the jurisdiction of the International Court of Justice to decide cases instituted against them at the Court. It is important that States take their obligations that are enshrined in international treaties that they have signed seriously so that in the first place, they would not be taken to the International Court of Justice for breaching such treaties as Human Rights Covenants and the Convention on the Prevention and Punishment of the Crime of Genocide. The closing remark in the Summary Judgment of Ukraine v Russian Federation of February 2024 is apt where the Court stated thus:

> The Court recalls, as it has on several occasions in the past that there is a fundamental distinction between the question of acceptance by States of the Court's jurisdiction and the conformity of their acts with international law. States are always required to fulfil their obligations under the Charter of the United Nations and other rules of international law. Whether or not they have consented to the jurisdiction of the Court, States remain responsible for acts attributable to them that are contrary to international law.[681]

The desire of our common humanity towards the pursuit of peaceful co-existence of states over the last 75 years is continuously challenged by the inability of the member-States of the United Nations Organisation, particularly the UN Security Council to maintain peace in the Middle East, especially, between the State of Israel and the Palestinian people in Palestine. The shock of the Hamas attack of 7 October, 2023, on Israel and the excessive and destructive military might with which Israel set out to destroy Hamas that has resulted into destruction of the entire city of Gaza and thousands of innocent Palestinian civilians now leaves both Israel and Palestinians trapped in a cycle of competitive victimisation that will make peace for both Israel and Palestine elusive as well as the realisation of the sovereign State of Palestine a more distant dream. The United Nations member-states needs to do more not only to achieve a ceasefire but also to offer emotional support and assistance to the

---

[681]   Ibid. paras 149-150.

hundreds of thousands of Palestinians that are affected to enable them indulge in cognitive reappraisal that will free them from the rumination with emotional overload that focuses them on violence revenges that will not serve them a profitable result and peace.

The evidence from the almost 80 years of the United Nations Organization's existence point to the singular fact that leaders of members-states must do more to enhance human rights protection and enforcement in order to have a world of peace and security for all humanity.

BIBLIOGRAPHY

Acemoglu, D. & Robinson, J.A, Why Nations Fail The Origins of Power, Prosperity and Poverty © 2012, 2013 Profile Books Ltd

Aquinas, Thomas, The Summa Theologica of St. Thomas Aquinas (Five Volumes) © 2023 Grapevine India

Aristotle's Nicomachean Ethics A New Translation by Robert C Barlett and Susan D Collins © 2012 University of Chicago Press

Asch, R., The Thirty Years War © 1997 MACMILLAN PRESS LTD

Bantekas, Ilias and Oette, Lutz, International Human Rights Law and Practice Second Edition © 2016 Cambridge University Press

Bhutto, Benazir, Daughter of the East, An Autography, © 1988, 2007 Simon & Schuster

Borchert, Thomas, Edited, Theravada Buddhism in Colonial Contexts © 2020 Routledge

Brownlie, Ian, Principles of Public International Law Sixth Edition © 2003 Oxford University Press

Brownlie, Ian, (Edited) Basic Documents in International Law Sixth Edition © 2009 Oxford University Press

Bunton, Martin, The Palestinian-Israeli Conflict A Very Short Introduction © 2013 Oxford University Press

Carson, D.A., R.T. France, J.A. Motyer & G.J. Wenham (Contributing Editors), New Bible Commentary, IVP Reference Collection © Universities and Colleges Christian Fellowship, Leicester, England, 1953, 1954, 1970, 1994.

Cialdini, Robert B., Influence, The Psychology of Persuasion © 1984, 1994, 2007 Collins Business An Imprint of HarperCollinsPublishers.

Clinton, Bill, My Life © William Jefferson Clinton 2005 Arrow Books

Collier, Paul, THE BOTTOM BILLION Why the Poorest Countries Are Falling and What Can Be Done About It © 2008 Oxford University Press

Collier, Paul, WARS, GUNS & VOTES, DEMOCRACY IN DANGEROUS PLACES © 2009 Published by Vintage 2010

Conte, Alex and Burchill, Richard, Defining Civil and Political Rights. The Jurisprudence of the United Nations Human Rights Committee Second Edition © 2009 Published 2016 by Routledge

Cross, F.L. and Livingstone, E.A., (Edited), The Oxford Dictionary of The Christian Church © 1974 Oxford University Press

Fenwick, Helen, Civil Liberties and Human Rights, 4th Edition Routledge –Cavendish 2008

Gerges, Fawaz A., The Rise and Fall of Al-Quaeda, © 2011 Oxford University Press

Galtung, Johan, PEACE BY PEACEFUL MEANS Peace and Conflict, Development and Civilization © SAGE Publications Ltd 1996.

Ghali, Mark and Oslen, Ted, Editors, 131 Christians Everyone Should Know © 2000 Christianity Today, Inc, B & H Publishing Group

Gothofredus, Dionysiue, Corpus Juris Civilis Romani

Guinn, Jeff, The Road To Jonestown Jim Jones And The Peoples Temple © 2017 by 24Words LLC

Herzog, Tamar, A Short History of European Law The Last Two And A Half Millennia © 2018 Harvard University Press

James, Lawrence, The Rise & Fall of the British Empire © 1994, 1998 Abacus.

Juergensmeyer, Mark, The New Cold War? Religious Nationalism Confronts the Secular State © 1993 University of California Press.

Lake, John G; His Life, His Sermons, His Boldness of Faith © 1994 Kenneth Copeland Publications.

Locke, John, The Second Treatise of Government and A Letter Concerning

Toleration, Dover Publications, Inc, Mineola, New York, (c) 2002.

Khalidi, Rashid, The Hundred years' War on PALESTINE A History of Settler Colonialism and Resistance, 1917 – 2017. Picador Metropolitan Books © 2004, 2005.

Luther, Martin, 95 Theses, Translated by Adolph Spaeth, First Rate Publishers.

Magna Carta with a new commentary by David Carpenter © 2015 Penguin Classics

Maitland, Frederic William and Montague, Francis C., A Sketch of English Legal History Edited with Notes and Appendices by James E. Colby, © The Lawbook Exchange Edition 1998, 2010

Masalha, Nur, Palestine A Four Thousand Year History © 2018 Reprinted by I.B. Tauris in 2022.

McGoldrick, Dominic, The Human Rights Committee. Its Role in the Development of the International Covenant on Civil and Political Rights © 1994 Clarendon Paperbacks, Oxford University Press

Mills, David Charles, Unholy Bible © 2010 by David Charles Mills

Mopho, MacDonald I.J., LAW, CHRISTIANITY AND RELIGIOUS FREEDOM © 2021 New Generation Publishing.

Moyn, Samuel, Christian Human Rights © 2015 University of Pennsylvania Press

Padoa-Schioppa, Antonio, A History of Law in Europe. From the Early Middle Ages to the Twentieth Century. Translated by Caterina Fitzgerald. First published in a revised and updated English version by Cambridge University Press 2017.

Pawson, David, Unlocking The Bible, Omnibus © 2003 HarperCollinsPublishers

Plato, The Republic, With an Introduction by Melissa Lane, Penguin Classics; 3rd Edition 2007.

Popkin, Jeremy D., You Are All Free. The Haitan Revolution And The Abolition of Slavery © 2010 Cambridge University Press

Reavis, Dick J., The Ashes of WACO, An Investigation © 1995 First Syracuse University Press Edition 1998.

Robertson, A.H., and Merrills, J.G., Human Rights in the World, An Introduction to the study of the international protection of human rights, Fourth Edition, Manchester University Press © 1996

Sheikh, Bilquis, I DARED TO CALL HIM FATHER © 2003 Chosen Books, 25th Anniversary Edition.

Sieghart, Paul, The Lawful Rights of Mankind. An Introduction to the International Code of Human Rights. Oxford University Press 1986.

Sirleaf, Ellen Johnson, This Child Will Be Great, © 2010 Harper Perennial Edition

Stephenson, Paul, Constantine Unconquered Emperor, Christian Victor © 2009 Quercus

Sorenson, M., (Ed.), Manual of Public International Law © 1968 Macmillan London.

Tabor, James D., and Gallagher, Eugene V., Why Waco?, Cults and the Battle for Religious Freedom in America © 1995 by The Regents University of California

Tate, Joshua C., Reinaldo de Lima Lopes, J., and Botero-Bernal, A., Global Legal History, Routledge © 2019

Thomas, Hugh, The Slave Trade The History of The Atlantic Slave Trade 1440-1870 © 1997 Picador an imprint of Macmillan Publishers Ltd.

Witte, John & Christian Green, M., Religion & Human Rights. An Introduction. Oxford University Press 2012.

Journal Article:

Frank Cranmer and Russell Sandberg, Chaplin v Royal Devon and Exeter Hospital NHS Trust: Exeter Employment Tribunal, April 2010 Religious Symbol – uniform policy – Employment Equality, Ecclesiastical Law Journal, Cambridge University Press Volume 13 Issue 2 – May 2011.

INDEX

Printed in the United States
by Baker & Taylor Publisher Services